CW00339313

The *BEST* PUBS *for* FAMILIES

The BEST PUBS for FAMILIES

David Perrott

CAMRA

BOOKS

Author: David Perrott

Published by CAMRA Books, Campaign for Real Ale,
230 Hatfield Road, St Albans AL1 4LW
Tel: 01727 867201 Fax: 01727 867670
Managing Editor: Mark Webb

ISBN 1-85249-141-8

First Edition, September 1998

Great effort has gone into researching the contents of
this book, but no responsibility can be taken for errors.

CONTENTS

Special thanks are extended to all
the publicans who kindly supplied information,
to CAMRA Regional Directors
for their help with checking the text,
and to Morag for her patience.

INTRODUCTION

A lifetime of visiting pubs prompts the recollection of earliest memories. These involve sitting on the doorstep of the Baker's Arms in Leyton, East London, with a glass of Tizer and a bag of crisps while my parents enjoyed the forbidden delights inside. In those days (and I'm not prepared to say when that was) the thought of children being taken inside, and presumably either being corrupted or wrecking the place, was unthinkable.

The gradual realisation of personal independence meant that it was soon not *de rigueur* to be seen out with Mum and Dad, so I would have the occasional brown ale shandy at home, with pubs not featuring at all, until a bicycle and a couple of mates made lunchtime visits to pubs in Hertfordshire seem a good idea. I vaguely remember 'Benskins Colne Spring Ale' rendering me very sleepy in a pub garden one hot summer day (and I also vaguely recall riding home!).

The next instalment came with work in London, and 5.30 socials, participating, until I learnt better, in Watney's 'Red Revolution'. Hand pumps had become items of decorative nostalgia, while the 'beer' now squirted from an illuminated tap on the bar. It was at that time that other, *wiser*, souls also realised something was going badly wrong with beer, our great British institution, and decided to act, forming CAMRA.

An introduction to 'White Shield Worthington' whilst still in my teens – including decoding the label to ascertain exactly when it was brewed, and careful pouring to avoid disturbing the sediment – then confirmed me as a real ale devotee.

INTRODUCTION

Now we can usually get a pint of something decent when we visit a pub, but it has taken a further good few years for the trade to realise that families might want to socialise as a group, with any children who happen to be included not being treated as outcasts, banished to the garden or doorstep. Thank goodness we are now beginning to see the light, realising that pubs are social places, where people, including families, can relax and enjoy a beer and a meal.

Of course children who visit pubs must behave in a civilised manner, but so must adults, and especially young adults. It seems to me that if there are problems, they are not usually caused by young children. Feeling welcome in a pub is not just a question of law, it is to do with the whole ambience of those running it, and the other customers.

All of the pubs in this book make children very welcome, but this does not mean that they are necessarily organised along the lines of a tea party or funfair. Quieter establishments which simply extend a friendly welcome are just as valid as the pubs which make special efforts to attract families with amusements and entertainment.

We have tried not to include those pubs which *only* allow children in if you are having a full meal. Hopefully, you can visit any of the pubs in this book with your family for just a beer and some crisps, or a ploughman's, if you want to.

The assumption has been made that virtually all pubs have darts, and that these are dangerous in the wrong (that is, too young) hands. So we don't mention darts as a feature, but we do mention pool, bar billiards, skittles, cribbage and so on, realising that their use depends *solely* on the landlord's view of things. Often pool tables are used for tournaments, and mistreatment does not go down well. But a young-ish child MAY be allowed to play with Mum or Dad, who keep things under control, but may NOT be allowed to play with their younger brother or sister, when things can easily get out of hand! So please remember – the use of games in pubs is a matter between you and the publican, and our mentioning them *does not convey any automatic entitlement*!

Place names in addresses are usually as given in popular road atlases, with any further directions in the entry. Like us, map publishers are not perfect, and in a few cases what appear on the ground to be significant places are not mentioned at all on a popular road atlas. In these few cases we have put the pub under the place name, and given what we hope are clear directions so you can find it. The telephone number of each pub is *always* given – so if you are having trouble locating your chosen venue, or you are concerned about the facilities, ring the pub in question and find out!

It was unfortunately impossible to personally visit all the pubs, so a good deal of information, supplied by the various managers, is taken on trust. Every pub included *has* been contacted, but if you experience something different from that which is implied by the description, please let us know. Your personal help would be invaluable for future editions. All the real ales listed are subject to change, although they were thoroughly checked while this edition was being prepared.

INTRODUCTION

Entertainment is mentioned where we think it may apply to children. This can be regular, such as music on a Friday evening, or occasional, such as visits from the Mikron Theatre Company or Punch & Judy shows.

Within the entries here you will find pubs which: have rugby and cricket on the beach; have a resident magician; give free kids meals (along with adult meals); have a birds quiz; have a climbing wall in the bar; and hold a Sunday School on the premises! Lots of pubs have garden toys, but you must appreciate that many of these will be put away during the winter months.

The pub, and real ale, are both very admirable institutions. If our young generation learn to both enjoy and appreciate them now, their respective futures will hopefully be assured.

Symbols used within the pub descriptions

⊠	Children restricted to certain areas	↽	Children's menu
⛄	Family room	⚡	No smoking area
♣	Bar games	⛻	Accommodation
❀	Garden	▽	Nappy changing area
⊞	Garden toys		
◖	Lunchtime meals	⚲	Entertainment
◗	Evening meals	⏰	Children's time limit
◑	Food lunchtime and evenings	▶	Attraction nearby

ENGLAND

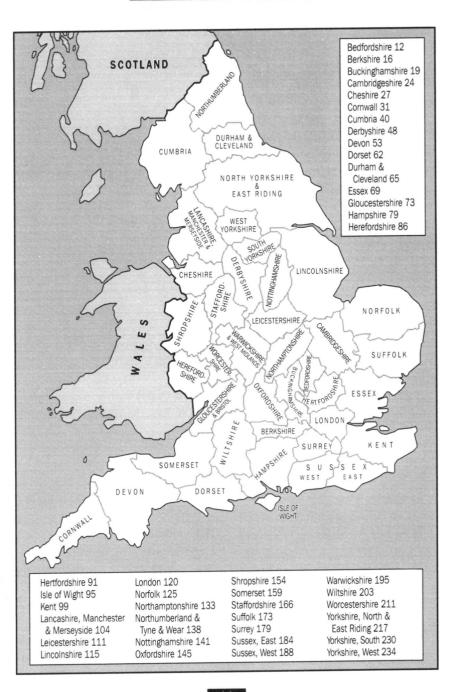

SCOTLAND

NORTHUMBERLAND

CUMBRIA

DURHAM & CLEVELAND

NORTH YORKSHIRE & EAST RIDING

LANCASHIRE, MANCHESTER & MERSEYSIDE

WEST YORKSHIRE

SOUTH YORKSHIRE

CHESHIRE

DERBYSHIRE

NOTTINGHAMSHIRE

LINCOLNSHIRE

WALES

SHROPSHIRE

STAFFORD-SHIRE

LEICESTERSHIRE

NORFOLK

WARWICKSHIRE & WEST MIDLANDS

WORCESTER-SHIRE

HEREFORD-SHIRE

NORTHAMPTONSHIRE

CAMBRIDGESHIRE

SUFFOLK

OXFORDSHIRE

BUCKINGHAMSHIRE

BEDFORDSHIRE

HERTFORDSHIRE

ESSEX

GLOUCESTERSHIRE & BRISTOL

LONDON

WILTSHIRE

BERKSHIRE

SURREY

KENT

SOMERSET

HAMPSHIRE

SUSSEX WEST

SUSSEX EAST

DEVON

DORSET

ISLE OF WIGHT

CORNWALL

Bedfordshire 12
Berkshire 16
Buckinghamshire 19
Cambridgeshire 24
Cheshire 27
Cornwall 31
Cumbria 40
Derbyshire 48
Devon 53
Dorset 62
Durham & Cleveland 65
Essex 69
Gloucestershire 73
Hampshire 79
Herefordshire 86

Hertfordshire 91
Isle of Wight 95
Kent 99
Lancashire, Manchester & Merseyside 104
Leicestershire 111
Lincolnshire 115

London 120
Norfolk 125
Northamptonshire 133
Northumberland & Tyne & Wear 138
Nottinghamshire 141
Oxfordshire 145

Shropshire 154
Somerset 159
Staffordshire 166
Suffolk 173
Surrey 179
Sussex, East 184
Sussex, West 188

Warwickshire 195
Wiltshire 203
Worcestershire 211
Yorkshire, North & East Riding 217
Yorkshire, South 230
Yorkshire, West 234

Bolnhurst

Ye Olde Plough

Kimbolton Road, Bolnhurst Top End (01234 376274). *On the B660 between Bedford and Kimbolton.* This fine old building was originally built as a farmhouse around 1480, and probably housed a troop of Henry VIII's soldiers when his wife, Catherine of Aragon, was imprisoned in Kimbolton Castle. It survived the great plague of 1665, when the rest of the village, apart from the church, was burnt down. It became a pub soon after 1813. Special evenings are now held, including country dancing and visits from a clairvoyant.
Ruddles and Courage, with typical guests including Nethergate, and John Smith's.

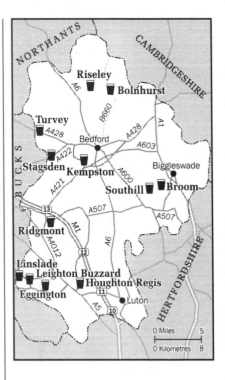

Broom

The Cock

23 High Street (01767 314411). *Just off the A1 at the Biggleswade turn-off.* A This is a gem of a pub with no bar, the beer being dispensed from casks in the cellar. There are many rooms off a central corridor, and the fine building has a Grade II listing. Skittles are played, and children are wel-

comed in the family room. The garden has a slide and a climbing frame.
Greene King.

Eggington

Horseshoes

High Street (01525 210282). This is a very pretty 'picture-postcard' village pub with an upstairs gallery, serving good food and a wide range of wines. Dominoes and cribbage are played here, and children are welcome away from

the bars.
Theakston and Wadworth, with bottles from the Vale Brewery.
❀ ◐ *no food Mon*

Houghton Regis

The Chequers Inn
East End (01582 865970).
Described as 'a family pub with
something for everyone', it seems
that children are especially well
catered for here, and if they are
amused, you will be able to enjoy
a beer and a chat in peace. Pool,
fruit machines and video
machines can be played, and
there is indoor play equipment.
In the garden you will find climbing frames and slides. During the
school holidays entertainments
are organised, with such things as
discos, clowns and face painting.
Nappy changing facilities 'similar
to MacDonald's'.
Boddingtons, Flowers and Fuller's, with Morland as a guest.
🐎 ♣ ❀ 🏠 ◐ ↩ ✂ ▽ ♟

Kempston

King William IV
56 High Street (01234 854533).
There are tales of a ghost lurking
in this handsome timber-framed
building which dates from circa

1560, when it was built as a farmhouse. Today it is justly popular,
with a large garden, climbing and
adventure equipment and good
disabled access to the bars.
Adnams and Morland.
🏃 ♣ ❀ 🏠 ◐ *not Sun or Mon eves* ↩ ◷ *21.00*▶ The Cecil
Higgins Art Gallery, Bedford
Museum, Bunyan Meeting House
and the Bunyan Museum (to see
copies of The Pilgrim's Progress).

Leighton Buzzard

The Claypipe
Appenine Way (01525 384387).
The Ouse runs through this town
which was, until 1966, still offi-
cially known as Leighton Buzzard
on one side of the river, and
Linslade on the other. There is
not a great deal of history: the
market was founded in the 11thC,
and a Benedictine cell once exist-
ed here, but this has long since
disappeared. You should, however, take a look at the splendid
church of All Saints, built of iron-
stone and with a fine steeple.
Almshouses were founded by
Edward Wilkes in 1603 in North
Street, on condition that the
bounds be beaten every Rogation
Sunday. This tradition is maintained, and on 23 May each year
a choir boy stands on his head in

front of the almshouses, while extracts from Wilkes will are read out. Refreshment is available in this welcoming two-bar local, adjacent to the Narrow Gauge Railway. Pool and dominoes are played, and there are swings and a Wendy house in the garden. Food is only served by prior arrangement.

Bass, Tetley and Worthington, with Adnams and Flowers as guests.

🐎 ♣ ♣ 🏠 ▶ Narrow Gauge Railway, Grand Union Canal nearby

Linslade

Hunt Hotel

19 Church Road (01525 374692). Calm and relaxing, this hotel has an ochre-coloured bar, which has recently been refurbished. There are 15 bedrooms, if you fancy a stay in the area.

Bass, Fuller's and Tetley.
♣ ◑ 🍺 🛏

Ridgmont

Rose & Crown

89 High Street (01525 280245). *On the A507 midway between Ampthill and Woburn.* A 300-year-old village pub which has been in every edition of the Good Beer Guide. Children can use the Goose Bar and games room.

Charles Wells and Adnams, with Mansfield as a typical guest.

🐎 ♣ ♣ 🏠 ◑ 🍺 🕐 20.00
▶ Woburn Safari Park and Woburn Abbey

Riseley

Fox & Hounds

High Street (01234 708240). You will certainly get a friendly welcome at this pub, which specialises in offering very fine steak meals. There is an enormous garden.

Charles Wells plus a guest, which might, for example, be Caledonian.
♣ ◑ 🍺

Southill

The White Horse

High Street (01462 813364). *2 miles from the main A1 exit at the Caldecote roundabout.* Established around 1770, this handsome brick-built pub was once owned by Samuel Whitbread of Southill Park. The extensive gardens contain a miniature railway. It has an à la carte restaurant, and an extensive bar menu which includes spicy

Lincolnshire sausages.
Fuller's and Marston's. Typical guests include Flowers and Chadwicks.
♣ ✿ ◑ ☞

Stagsden

Royal George
57 High Street (01234 822801). Friendly and welcoming, and with a family room, this pub has a fine garden, so it is a nice place to come on fine days. You can sit outside and enjoy your pint while your children rush around on the slide, swings and climbing frames. Skittles, cribbage and dominoes are played inside. All the food is home-made here, and that includes the chips!

Charles Wells, with Greene King, Everards and Fuller's as guests.
🎠 ♣ ✿ ⊞ ◑ ☞ ▶ Stagsden Bird Gardens

Turvey

The Three Cranes
High Street Loop (01234 881305). *On the A428 midway between Bedford and Northampton.* This is a handsome 17thC ivy-covered stone inn, with a timber porch. Children are welcome in the dining areas.
Courage, Fuller's and Theakston, with Bass and Adnams being typical guests.
🔪 ✿ ◑ ☞ ⏱ 21.30

BERKSHIRE

Aldermaston

The Butt Inn
Aldermaston Wharf (0118 971 2129). *100 yards from the canal bridge.* On the Kennet & Avon Canal, with a couple of locks close by.
Butts, Boddingtons and Wadworth, with Hook Norton and Gale's being typical guests.
♣ ❀ 📻 ◑ ⌣ ⏱ *21.00*▶ Kennet & Avon Canal

Crazies Hill

The Horns
(01189 401414). Straightforward and totally charming, this pretty little pub has open fires, plenty of beams and wooden furniture. One of the rooms has been opened to the roof, making it spacious and barn-like. The garden has a climbing frame and a play area.
Brakspear, with guests such as Adnams.
❀ 📻 ◑ ⌣

Crookham

Fox & Hounds
(01252 615980). Boaters will find a landing stage at this fine friendly canalside local. Skittle nights are held by arrangement.

Courage, with frequently changing guests such as Gale's, Fuller's and Wadworth, plus a variety of changing real ciders.
🐕 ❀ ◑ ⌣ ⊱ 🚐▶ Basingstoke Canal, boat rallies

Eton

The Watermans Arms
Brocas Street (01753 861001). Popular with both locals and tourists, this pub is well situated near the Eton College Boat House and has a fine conservatory.
Courage, Marston's, John Smith's and Theakston, with Brakspear as a typical guest.
♣ ◑ *not Sun evening* ⊱ ▶ River Thames

Hare Hatch

The Queen Victoria
The Holt (01189 402477). *Just off the A4, midway between Reading and Maidenhead.* A popular local pub with three-dimensional noughts and crosses, and an adventurous value-for-money menu.
Brakspear.
♣ ❀ ◑ ⌣ ⊱

BERKSHIRE

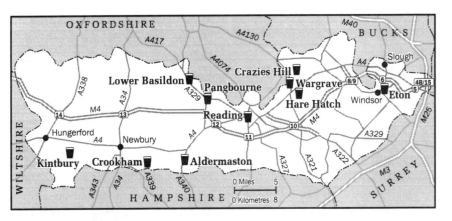

Kintbury

The Dundas Arms
53 Station Road (01488 658263).
*1 mile south of the A4 between
Newbury and Hungerford.* The
pub takes its name from Lord
Dundas, who opened the Kennet
& Avon Canal in 1810. Indeed the
canal runs to one side of the pub,
with the River Kennet on the
other – there's a patio and jetty by
the water.
*Arkell's and Morland, with
guests such as Ringwood,
Wadworth and Wells.*
❀ ◑ ☙ 🖼️▶ Kintbury Lock and
canal

Lower Basildon

The Crown
Reading Road (01491 671262).
Very handy for lunch if you are
visiting Beale Park, which adjoins
the River Thames and has a collection of birds, including pea-
cocks, and some fine statuary, or
perhaps Basildon Park, a splendid Georgian Mansion built by
John Carr of York in 1776 for Sir
Francis Sykes. Amazingly this
stately pile was facing virtual
dereliction in 1952, but was res-
cued by Lord and Lady Iliffe. Lots
to see inside, and majestic gardens. Absorbing all that culture is
thirsty work, so a retreat to the
quiet lounge of The Crown will
bring some welcome relief, and
your children can expend their
energy on all the play equipment
in the garden, which includes a
slide and 'walk in' play house in
a secure play area, while you
enjoy a game of bar billiards. The
toilet has a nappy changing unit.
Morland and Ruddles.
🛏️ ♣ ❀ 🖼️ ◑ ☙ ✂▶ Beale Park,
Basildon Park

Pangbourne

The Swan

Shooters Hill (0118 984 4494).
This is a beautifully situated
riverside pub & restaurant, overlooking Pangbourne Weir. It is
where Jerome K Jerome, two col-
legues and a 'shamed-looking
dog' gave up their 'Three Men In
a Boat' journey, on the way back,
and caught the train to London.
Children are welcome in the no-
smoking areas, and can play
Connect-4 and Jenga. Fine riverside patio.
*Morland, with guests such as
Marston's and Ruddles.*
🏃 ♣ ✿ ◗ ➰ ⚞ ▶ River Thames

Reading

Fisherman's Cottage

224 Kennet Side, off Canal Way
(0118 957 1553). *East of the town
centre along the canal.* Just to the
west of Blake's Lock, this is a
pretty 18thC pub. It has a small
children's room, and a marquee,
which is heated in winter.

*Fuller's, with guests including
Gale's, Marston's and Morland.
Bottle conditioned Fuller's 1845.*
✿ ◗ ➰ ▶ Blake's Lock Museum,
the Kennet & Avon Canal and
River Thames.

Pipers Island

Caversham Bridge (0118 948
1088). An interestingly positioned pub – half-way across the
bridge, in the middle of the River
Thames, with a sheltered terrace.
Carpet bowls are played.
*Brakspear, Flowers and
Marston's, with Wadworth as a
typical guest.*
♣ ✿ ◗ ➰ ⏱ *21.00*▶ River
Thames

Wargrave

St George & Dragon

2 High Street (01189 403852).
This fine riverside restaurant and
pub was once visited by Jerome
K. Jerome. The original old hotel
sign is displayed inside.
Hancock's.
✿ ◗ ⚞ ▽ ▶ River Thames

BUCKINGHAMSHIRE

Amersham

Queens Head

Wheilden Gate (01494 725240). *Take the Winchmore Hill turning off the A404 Amersham to High Wycombe road, then turn immediately left.* A traditional country pub with a slide, swings and a Wendy house in its large garden. Great choice of pizzas.

Adnams, Flowers and Rebellion, with Morrells as a typical guest.

🐎 ♣ ✿ ⊞ ◑ *not Sun evening* ✄

Aylesbury

Bell Hotel

Market Square (01296 489835). A fine traditional country town hotel, not far from the terminus of the Aylesbury Arm of the Grand Union Canal. The town centre is still quite attractive, being made up of a number of squares, and the 13thC church, standing quietly in a secluded churchyard, is worth seeking out.

Flowers, John Smith's, Tetley and Worthington.

◑ *not Fri, Sat or Sun evenings* ◔ ✄ 🛏

Clifton Reynes

Robin Hood

(01234 711574). Families can use the conservatory in this 16thC pub, which has a fine 3 acre garden containing a football pitch. Bar billiards are played here.

Greene King.

✿ ◑ *not Sun evening or Mon* ◔

Fingest

Chequers

(01491 638335). Charmingly old-fashioned, the bar is warmed by a log fire when the weather is chilly. On sunny days you can enjoy the large garden.

Brakspear.

🐎 ✿ ◑ *not Sun or Mon evening* ✄

Great Linford

Black Horse

Wolverton Road (01908 605939). *Canalside at Black Horse Bridge.* What you see now is an amalgamation of several separate buildings, some of which predate the canal, that have been combined to create this renowned waterways pub. Inside you will find three separate bars, open fires, wooden settles and plenty of atmosphere. Dominoes and cards are played, and during the summer there is often a bouncy castle in the garden.

ABC, Marston's and Tetley,

along with Addlestone's real cider.

♣ ❀ 🏢 ◑ ☕ ⊁ 🕙 *21.00* ▶ Grand Union Canal

Iver

Fox & Pheasant

22 Thorney Lane (01753 653175). Lively and bustling, this friendly country pub has entertainment in some form or another every evening. It is just a short walk away from the Slough Arm of the Grand Union Canal. The garden has a ball pond and a bouncy castle, and entertainments include parties, face painting and a play bus.
Burton, Marston's, Theakston and Wadworth, with guests such as Courage and Fuller's.
❀ 🏢 ◑ ☕ ⊁ ♠ ▶ Grand Union Canal

The Swan Inn

2 The High Street (01753 655776). *Opposite the church at the end of the village.* This handsome and heavily beamed coaching inn/restaurant serves fine food and a good choice of ales.
Courage, Brakspear and Adnams, with guests such as Black Sheep, Hopback, Rebellion and Scanlons. Bottle-conditioned ales include Fullers 1845, Gibbs Mew Bishops's

Tipple and Marston's Pedigree.
♣ ❀ ◑ ☕ ⊁

Little Woolstone

Barge

Newport Road (01908 208891). Situated between Willen Lake, which covers an area of 170 acres and is used for water-sports, and the peaceful Grand Union Canal, this food orientated pub is a handy stop if you are in the area. Log fires warm the bars when the weather is chilly. Children are welcome as long as they stay away from the bars.
Bass and Hancock's.
❀ ◑ ☕ ⊁ ▽

Marsworth

The Red Lion

Vicarage Road (01296 6689366). Do not be put off by the ominous-looking stocks outside – this is a friendly village pub with an open fire and bars on two levels. Bar billiards, dominoes, and a skittle alley on certain nights.
Fuller's, Hancock's and Red Lion, with Greene King, Shepherd Neame and Theakston as typical guests. Also Westons real cider.
♣ ❀ ◑ *not Sun eve* ☕ ▶ Grand Union Canal

BUCKINGHAMSHIRE

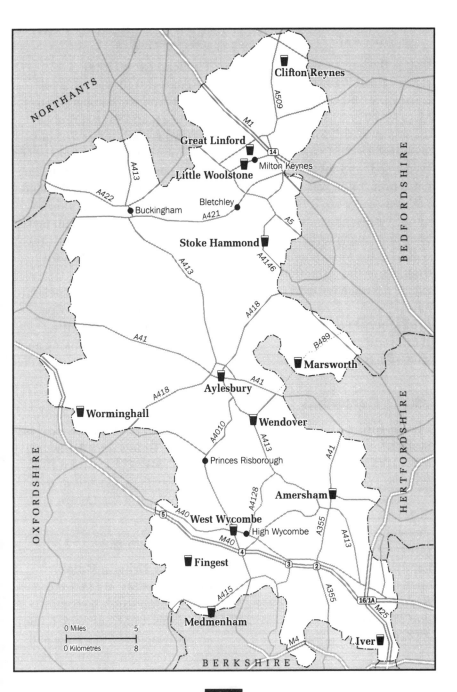

NORTHANTS

Clifton Reynes

A509

M1

Great Linford

14

Little Woolstone

Milton Keynes

A413

A422

Buckingham

Bletchley

A421

A5

Stoke Hammond

A4146

A413

A418

B489

BEDFORDSHIRE

A41

Marsworth

A41

Aylesbury

A418

Worminghall

A4010

Wendover

A413

A41

Princes Risborough

A4128

Amersham

A40

West Wycombe

5

High Wycombe

A355

A413

HERTFORDSHIRE

M40

4

Fingest

3

2

A415

A355

16/1A

M25

Medmenham

M4

Iver

OXFORDSHIRE

| 0 Miles | 5 |
| 0 Kilometres | 8 |

BERKSHIRE

BUCKINGHAMSHIRE

Medmenham

Dog & Badger
Henley Road (01491 571362).
During the 18thC the nearby St
Mary's Abbey was the home of
the orgiastic Hell Fire Club,
organised by Sir Francis
Dashwood, and this pub, which
dates from 1390, was associated
with this carry on. It is, today,
totally respectable, and a fine
place to bring your family, who
will be made welcome in the
front bar or the restaurant. There
is also a terrace for warm summer
days.
*Brakspear, Fuller's and
Whitbread.*
⚹ ❀ ◑ *not Sun evening* ⌣

Stoke Hammond

The Dolphin
Stoke Road (01525 270263). *On
the A4146 north of Leighton
Buzzard.* You will find plenty of
toys, including a climbing frame,
tikes cars and play tunnels – and
sometimes a bouncy castle in the
garden of this pleasant village
family pub. Inside there is an
open fire and a piano.
*Boddingtons, Flowers, Tetley
and Wadworth.*
♣ ❀ ▦ ◑ ⌣ *not Mon* ☕ *21.00*

Wendover

The Red Lion Hotel
9 High Street (01296 622266).
Oliver Cromwell, Robert Louis
Stevenson and Rupert Brooke
have all stayed in this fine old
inn, and they too could have been
accompanied by children as long
as the 'sprogs' had stayed seated
with their adult companions.
Built in the 16thC, this inn makes
a handy base for exploring the
Chiltern Hills and Ridgeway
Path, as well as visits to
Waddesdon Manor and the fasci-
nating Buckinghamshire Goat
Centre at Stoke Mandeville.
There is an outside drinking area,
and a nappy changing unit in the
ladies' toilet.
*Bass, Brakspear, Courage,
Hancock's and Young's, with
guests such as Adnams, Badger,
Fuller's, Gale's and Wadworth.*
❀ ◑ ⌣ 🛏 ⌇ ▶ Chiltern Hills,
Ridgeway Path, Waddesdon
Manor, Bucks Goat Centre

West Wycombe

George & Dragon Hotel
(01494 464414). *On the A40, 3
miles west of High Wycombe.* A
handsome 15thC inn with a fine
archway opening to a large and
pleasant garden. There is a family

room, and the secure garden has a climbing frame and swings. *Courage, with guests including Gale's, Marston's, Rebellion and Wadworth.* West Wycombe Park

Worminghall

Clifden Arms

75 Clifden Road (01844 339273). This is a thatched, cottagey 16thC

pub with swings, a slide, aunt sally and a 'boot' in the garden. The cosy bar has beams festooned with interesting objects, and there is a fine fire on cold days. *Adnams, Boddingtons, Fuller's, Hook Norton, with guests such as Bass, Vale and Young's.* Waterperry Gardens

Cambridge

The Cambridge Blue

85-87 Gwydir Street (01223 361382). *Off Mill Road.* A late 19thC terraced pub, which allows children in the conservatory and large garden, where there is a Wendy house and push-alongs. *Nethergate, and a choice of guests (they've had over 1000!). There is always a mild.*
🏇 ❀ 🎱 ◑ ☕ ⚲

Etton

The Golden Pheasant

1 Main Road (01733 252387). *Just off Helpston Road.* This charming and friendly country pub has an (almost) one acre garden with seats for 150 people, floodlit when dark. There are also swings, bars, football net and a petanque area.
Adnams, Bass, IPA and Woodforde's, with Fuller's, Shepherd Neame and Wadworth as typical guests.
🏇 ♣ ❀ 🎱 ◑ ☕ ⚲ 🛏

Godmanchester

Black Bull Inn

Post Street (01480 453310). A fine traditional 17thC inn, with a large, cosy inglenook, plenty of brass and a family room. The attractive garden has a climbing frame and 'horse and ride' on a spring.
Black Bull, Boddingtons, Flowers and Wadworth.
🏇 ❀ 🎱 ◑ ☕ ⚲ 🛏

Hildersham

Pear Tree

(01223 891680). *Just off the A1307, between Linton and Little Abington.* An unusual timbered bar. The hanging tables and ancient bric-a-brac are a feature in this traditional village pub. The garden has an aviary.
Greene King.
❀ 🎱 ◑ ☕

Holywell

The Old Ferry Boat Inn

(01480 463227). *From the A14 follow signs towards St Ives, then take the Earith–Ely road to Needingworth. Turn right to Holywell.* This is a very ancient inn, pre-dating 960 and once a ferry house for the monastery, situated in a very peaceful riverside hamlet. Damaged by fire early in 1997, the pub has been completely restored. If you visit on 17 March you *may* see their resident ghost! The garden, river and ani-

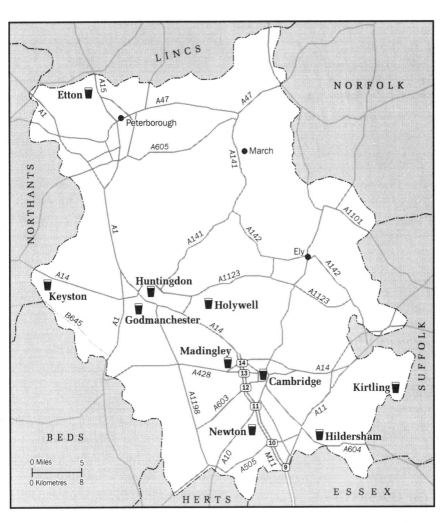

mal farm (pigs, goats, chickens and rabbits) are extremely popular.

Bass, Nethergate and Wadworth, together with guests such as Adnams, Fuller's and Jennings.

❀ 🏛 ◑ ☂ ⚒ 🛏

Huntingdon

The Old Bridge Hotel

1 High Street (01480 452681). At one time a private bank, this is now a handsome ivy-covered red-brick 18thC inn. Excellent food and a fine wine list. Note the

murals in The Terrace, painted by Julia Rushbury.

Adnams, Everards, plus guests, such as Fenland.

❀ ◑ ❤ ✂ 🖼▶ Great Ouse, Oliver Cromwell's birthplace

Keyston

The Pheasant Inn

Village Loop Road (01832 710241). *Just south of the A14 between Kettering and Huntingdon.* There is an outstanding small restaurant in this picturesque thatched inn which stands behind a pretty shaded garden, with beamy bars.

Adnams, with guests such as Hobsons, Fuller's and Morrells. A bottled beer, Orval, the only ale produced by the Abbaye d'Orval in Belgium, is also kept.

❀ ◑ ❤ ✂

Kirtling

The Queens Head

The Street (01638 731737). Warmed by two open fires, and furnished with two chesterfields, old pine tables and plenty of antiques, this fine, beamy old pub dates from 1558. Excellent range of inventive food and good wine.

Tolly Cobbold.

❀ ◑ *not Sun evening* ❤

Madingley

The Three Horseshoes

High Street (01954 210221). *One-and-a-half miles west of junction 13 on the M11.* A very pretty thatched pub with a conservatory-restaurant and a large garden extending towards the village cricket pitch. The excellent food has an Italian bias, and tends to draw folk from Cambridge. There is a good choice of Italian wines.

Adnams, Everards, Hook Norton, Marston's and Theakston, with guests such as Shepherd Neame, Smiles, Ridleys and Woodforde's.

❀ ◑ ❤

Newton

The Queen's Head

(01223 870436). *South of junction 11 on the M11.* You will find a log fire and high-backed settles in this very fine, old-fashioned, beamy country pub. Children are welcome in the games room. Table skittles, darts and dominoes are all played here.

Adnams, and real cider.

🐎 ♣ ❀ ◑ ❤ ⏱ *20.30*

CHESHIRE

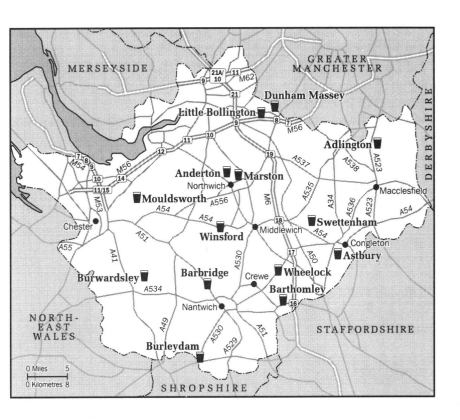

Adlington

Miners Arms
Wood Lane North (01625 872731). A large, lively, thriving country pub close to the Macclesfield Canal. The garden has an adventure play area. *Boddingtons, Flowers and Theakston, with guests such as Adnams, Caledonian and Exmoor*.
🎠 ♣ 🎴 🀫 ◑ ☕ ⚑ ▽ ▶
Macclesfield Canal

Anderton

The Stanley Arms
Old Road (01606 75059). This is a friendly canal-side pub opposite the splendid (but currently inoperable) Anderton Boat Lift, which linked the Trent & Mersey Canal with the River Weaver, some 50 ft below. The garden has a slide, swings and climbing frame. *Greenalls and Tetley*.
🎴 🀫 ◑ ☕

Astbury

The Egerton Arms

(01260 273946). *Right by the church, with its conspicuous steeple.* Standing opposite St Mary's church, which is a remarkable building with an airy interior, conspicuous battlements and a tower standing separately from the main body of the church, this is a handsome village pub and restaurant. Its garden has a play centre, with swings and a slide.
Robinson's and Frederics.
🐎 ❀ 🏠 ◑ 👝 ✄ ▶ St Mary's Church

Barbridge

The Barbridge Inn

Old Chester Road (01270 528443). *Off the A51 between Tarporley and Nantwich.* A friendly and welcoming canalside pub, very well disposed towards families. There are bar games and jazz every Thur eve, a children's play area, Halloween and Christmas parties, and visiting attractions include Morris dancing and Punch & Judy. Boats moor at the bottom of the garden. They also have a disabled toilet, with a baby changing fixture.
Boddingtons and Cains, with
Elgood's, Jennings, Maclay's and Tisbury as guests.
♣ ❀ 🏠 ◑ 👝 ✄ ▽ 👤
▶ Shropshire Union Canal

Barthomley

The White Lion Inn

(01270 882242). *Take junction 16 on the M6 for Alsager, then first left.* Black and white timber and thatch 'no frills' pub, dating from 1614.
Burtonwood.
🏠 ❀ ◖ *not Thur* 👝 🛏 *(hostel)*
🕐 *20.30*

Burleydam

Combermere Arms

(01948 871223). This 16thC pub is warmed by coal fires in winter. For children there is an indoor play area, called Monty's Adventureland, plus pin-ball, pool and a quiz machine.
Bass and Worthington, with Everards, Fuller's, Hardys & Hansons, Jennings and Charles Wells as typical guests
♣ ❀ ◑ 👝

Burwardsley

The Pheasant Inn

(01829 770434). *From the A41, follow visitor sign 'Cheshire*

Workshops'. Set halfway along the 'Sandstone Trail', this 300 year old half-timbered and sandstone inn occupies a splendidly elevated position overlooking the Cheshire Plain. The landlord keeps pedigree Highland cows in the surrounding fields. The beef served here is home grown!
Bass and Whitbread, with guests such as Fuller's and Weetwood.
🏂 ❀ 🏛 ◗ ☕ ✄ ⏱ *20.00*

Dunham Massey

Axe & Cleaver
School Lane (0161 928 3391). This cosy village pub offers a warm relaxing atmosphere, with crackling log fires. Good food is served at candlelit tables.
Courage, Ruddles, Theakston and Webster's, plus guests.
❀ ◗ ☕

Higher Sutton

The Hanging Gate Inn
(01260 252238). *North of the A54 between Congleton and Buxton.* A fine 16thC inn enjoying panoramic views of the Cheshire Plain and Pennines. Real fires.
Courage, Ruddles and Theakston, with guests such as Moorhouse's.
🐎 ❀ ◗ ☕ ✄

Little Bollington

The Swan With Two Nicks
Park Lane (0161 928 2914). *Take junction 7 on the M56 towards Lymm. Turn first left into Park Lane.* The unusual name recalls a time when swans were taken as food – birds marked with nicks on their beaks belonged to the Vintners Company, which was founded by royal gift in 1357. It is very similar to 'Swan Upping' on the River Thames. This pub is cosy and traditional, with walls full of pictures and brass. Good food.
Boddingtons, Flowers, Marston's and Whitbread, with guests such as Coach House.
❀ ◗ ☕ ⏱ *20.00* ▶ Bridgewater Canal, Dunham Massy Hall

Marston

The Salt Barge
Ollershaw Lane (01606 63043). *Opposite the Lion Salt Works.* The modest exterior of this fine, friendly pub belies the space inside! It is divided into cosy areas, and has a family room and an indoor play area.
Burtonwood, with Church End and Morland as guests.
🐎 ♣ ❀ 🏛 ◗ ☕ ✄ ▶ The Lion Salt Works – well worth a visit.

Mouldsworth

The Goshawk

Station Road (01928 740302).
Very much a country pub, set in
its own nine-acre site by the
Delamere Forest Country Park,
this is an excellent place for a
family meal if you have been
enjoying a walk, or perhaps visiting the nearby Windsurfing
Centre. The fine garden contains
an extensive adventure play area,
with a wooden fort, rope pulleys
and other equipment, with special facilities for the younger set.
Pool and dominoes are played,
plus a bowling green.
***Bass and Greenalls, with guests
including Exmoor & Rebellion.***
♣ ❀ 🏠 ◑ *not Mon* ☙ ▶
Delamere Forest Country Park

Swettenham

The Swettenham Arms

(01477 571284). *From Holmes
Chapel take the A535 towards
Jodrell Bank. Turn right into
Forty Acre Lane and follow signs
for Swettenham Village.* Old and
heavily timbered, this inn may
have originally been a nunnery
built at the same time as the
13thC parish church, and once

used as a resting place by funeral
parties. It is thought that the nunnery and church were once
linked by an underground passage. It became an inn during the
17thC, nestling in a lovely spot in
the Dane Valley. Good food.
Greenalls and Tetley.
❀ ◑ ☙ ✂

Wheelock

The Nags Head Hotel

504 Crewe Road (01270 762457).
*Take junction 17 on the M6 to
Sandbach, then turn left to
Wheelock.* A small but lively
black and white canalside pub.
***Boddingtons, Flowers and
Whitbread (Chester's).***
♣ ❀ ◖ ☙

Winsford

Golden Lion

164 High Street (01606 592750).
This is a friendly town-centre
pub. The well equipped play area
in the garden has a bouncy castle
at weekends. There is also a five-
a-side football pitch.
Boddingtons and Greenalls.
♣ ❀ 🏠 ◖ ☙

CORNWALL

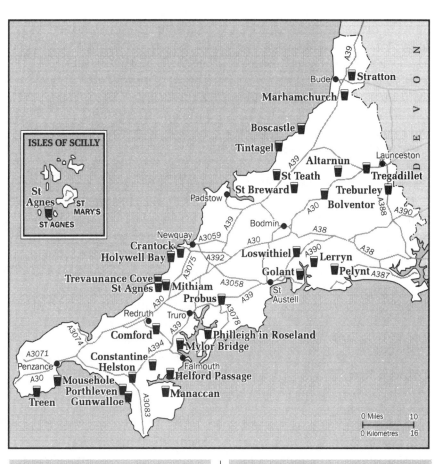

ISLES OF SCILLY

St Agnes

ST MARY'S

ST AGNES

Bude • ● Stratton

Marhamchurch

Boscastle

Tintagel

Altarnun

Launceston

St Teath

Tregadillet

St Breward

Treburley

Padstow

Bolventor

Bodmin

Newquay

A3059

Crantock

Loswithiel

Lerryn

Holywell Bay

A392

Golant

Pelynt

A387

Trevaunance Cove

St Agnes

Mithiam

A3058

St Austell

Probus

Redruth

Truro

Comford

Philleigh in Roseland

Penzance

Constantine

Mylor Bridge

A3071

Helston

Falmouth

A30

Mousehole

Helford Passage

Porthleven

Treen

Gunwalloe

Manaccan

0 Miles 10

0 Kilometres 16

Altarnun

Rising Sun Inn
Near Launceston (01566 86332).
Just a mile outside the village, on the way to Camelford. This is a fine rambling 16thC moorland inn, with an open fire.
Six regularly changing ales, such as Flowers, Fuller's, Sharp's and Wadworth.
❀ 🏛 ◑ ⌣ 🛏

Bolventor

Jamaica Inn
Near Launceston (01566 86250).
On the A30 between Bodmin and Launceston. A handsome and historic 400-year-old inn which now incorporates the intriguing Museum of Curiosity (charge) and the Daphne Du Maurier room, to honour the novelist who stayed here in 1930 and wrote the fine

novel of the same name. Open fires, stone walls and beams, and Percy, the resident parrot, who is over 40 years old. Children are welcome, except in the bars. Play area in the garden.

Bass and Flowers, with guests such as Marston's, Theakston and Wadworth.
🐎♣❀🏠◖☕✁🛏▽▶ Mr Potter's Museum of Curiosity (which opened at Bramber in Sussex in 1861 and moved here in 1988), the Daphne Du Maurier room, Dozmary Pool (where Arthur is said to have thrown the sword Excalibur) and the moor

Boscastle

Cobweb Inn

(01840 250278). *At the bottom of the village, near the harbour.* Pleasantly old-fashioned, this pub has beams bedecked with bottles, an open fire and wooden settles. Dominoes and cards can be played here.

Bass, Greene King and St Austell, with a variety of guests such as Exmoor, Fuller's, Sharp's, and Shepherd Neame.
🐎♣❀◖☕▶ The harbour

Napoleon Inn

High Street (01840 250204). *At the top of the village.* A solid 16thC stone-built pub of great

character. Its name derives from its use as a recruiting station during the Napoleonic wars. Children are welcome in the lounge.

Bass and St Austell.
🏹❀◖☕✁▶ Close to the sea

Comford

The Fox & Hounds

(01209 820251). *On the A393 Redruth to Falmouth road, just 2 miles south-east of Redruth, at the junction with the B3298 near Gwennap.* Unspoiled, this is a genuine 18thC pub, with traditional pub games and a pool room. Pleasant garden.

St Austell, with Bass as a guest.
♣❀◖☕✁🕐 *21.00*

Constantine

Trengilly Wartha Inn

Nancenoy (01326 340332). *One mile from Constantine, off the Gweek to Porth Navas road.* Trengilly Wartha means 'the settlement above the trees', and the hotel does indeed nestle invitingly in the wooded valley of Polpenwith Creek, surrounded by six acres of gardens and meadows, including a cricket pitch. Inside it is warm, friendly and inviting, with a cosy wood-burning stove and high-backed settles. The lounge is comfortable and beamy, with old-style sofas, armchairs, books and magazines and, of course, an open fire. The restaurant is designed to mirror the atmosphere of a French family hotel, and fresh local produce is used. Pool and video games can be played. There is a changing mat and cleaning things in the toilets.

Sharp's, with guests such as St Austell and Exmoor, and Sheppy's and Porthallow Vineyards' cider.
🐎♣❀◐🍺✂🛏▽

Crantock

Old Albion Inn
Langurroc Road (01637 830243). *In the middle of the village, next to the church.* A friendly and traditional thatched village pub, where children are welcome in the family dining room. There are baby changing facilities in the ladies' toilet.

Courage, John Smith's and Skinner's, with Sharp's as a typical guest.
🚶♣❀◐🍺▽

Golant

The Fishermans Arms
Fore Street (01726 832453). Beware – one of the roads to this fine riverside pub is submerged at high tide! Take heed of the warning notices. It's cosy, haphazard and friendly, and splendidly situated.

Ushers.
🐎♣❀◐🍺

Gunwalloe

Hazlephron Inn
(01326 240406). A traditional small coastal pub, where children are welcome in the family room.

St Austell and Sharp's.
🐎❀◐🍺✂🛏 *(but no accommodation for children!)*

Helford Passage

Ferryboat Inn
(01326 250625). *2 miles on through the village of Mawnan Smith.* Just a few yards from a sandy beach, so it is popular during the summer. The ferry to Helford is nearby. Children are welcome in the main bar area. Pool and Cornish snooker are played, and there is music three or four evenings each week during the summer.

St Austell

🏃 🌸 ◑ ☕ 🔧 ▶ The beach

Helston

Blue Anchor Inn

50 Coinagehall Street (01326 562821). Rambling and pleasingly unspoilt, this 15thC inn has a thatched roof, and its own long-established brewery at the rear. There is also a skittle alley. *Spingo ales, brewed on the premises*.

🐎 🌸 ◑ ☕ 🔧

Holywell Bay

Treguth Inn

Near Newquay (01637 830248). This fine 13thC thatched pub is popular with surfing folk. The lounge has open fires in cold weather. *Courage and John Smith's, with Sharp's and Skinner's as guests*.

🐎 🌸 ◑ ☕ ▶ Beach and surfing

Lerryn

Ship Inn

(01208 872374). *3 miles south of the A390 at Loswithiel*. Pictures of the annual small craft race, held here each year, are displayed in this friendly riverside country pub.

Fuller's, Greene King, Morland and Wadworth.

♣ 🌸 🏨 ◑ ☕ 🔧 🛏

Lostwithiel

Royal Oak Inn

Duke Street (01208 872552). An attractive 13thC pub not far from Restormel Castle, where children are welcome in the family room. *Bass, Fuller's, Marston and Sharp's, with Cotleigh, Summerskills and Cottage as typical guests*.

🐎 ♣ 🌸 ◑ ☕ ▶ Restormel Castle

Manaccan

The New Inn

Near Helston (01326 231323). A splendid old thatched village pub with an open fire in the inglenook, and another at the other end of the bar. There is a swing in the garden. In summer they occasionally have barbecues, troll hunts and face painting. *Flowers, Marston's and Wadworth, with guests such as Boddingtons*.

♣ 🌸 🏨 ◑ ☕ ⏱ 21.00

Marhamchurch

The Bullers Arms

Near Bude (01288 361277). Large

and popular, this pub has traditional bars, and log fires when the weather is chilly. It is licensed for civil marriages! Darts, dominoes, pool and cards are played here, and there are singers and comedians each Saturday evening. *Bass, Marston's, Sharp's and Theakston, with guests such as Adnams, Badger, Fuller's and Greene King.*
🐂♣❀◑👓⚲🛏▽🎤

Mithian

The Miners Arms
Nr St Agnes (01872 552375). There are intimate rooms and warm fires in winter in this historic 16thC Cornish pub. *Boddingtons, plus guests such as Bass, Marston's and Wadworth.*
🐂❀◑👓⚲▶ The beach

Mousehole

Ship Inn
(01736 731234). Right by the harbour in an attractive village, which is very popular with holiday-makers, so it can be busy during the summer. Just before Christmas, on Tom Bawcock's eve, you can enjoy Starry Gazy pie, baked to commemorate his brave expedition during a gale. The cosy bar has an open fire

during chilly weather.
St Austell.
🐂❀◑👓🛏🛏▶ Seaside, and harbour lights at Christmas time.

Mylor Bridge

The Pandora Inn
Restronguet Creek (01326 372678). *Follow the brown signs from the A390 Truro to Falmouth road.* Parts of this fine and historic thatched waterside inn date from the 13thC. Its name commemorates the ship sent to Tahiti to capture the mutineers of Captain Bligh's Bounty. The Pandora unfortunately sank when it struck a reef in 1791. Inside the pub you will find cosy traditional bars, warm stoves and an interesting collection of bric-a-brac. Excellent food, and showers if you arrive by yacht! Children are welcomed away from the bars. *Bass and St Austell, together with scrumpy from Callestick Cider Farm.*
◑👓⚲▽▶ Restronguet Creek, boats

Pelynt

Jubilee Inn
(01503 220312). *Between Looe and Polperro on the B3359.* Once a 16thC farmhouse, it was origi-

nally the Axe Inn, changed in 1887 to celebrate Queen Victoria's reign. It is now a very comfortable inn with Windsor chairs and a log fire in winter. The bar has a Delabole slate floor, and is decorated with Queen Victoria memorabilia. Excellent seafood is served, alongside other dishes. There is a children's play room, and a slide and swings in the garden.
Bass and St Austell.
🐎♣❀🖼️◐↩️🏨▶ It is not far to Looe

Philleigh in Roseland

Roseland Inn
(01872 580254). *Off the A3078, or take the King Harry ferry from Feock to Philleigh*. Rugby and rowing pictures decorate the beamy bar of this very pretty 15thC country inn. Children are welcomed in the Middle Bar and dining room, and the garden has buggies and bowls.
Bass, Marston's, Sharp's and Wadworth. Guests might include Whitbread Castle Eden. West Country Scrumpy, from Cheddar, is also available.
🏃❀🖼️◐↩️▽

Porthleven

The Ship Inn
(01326 572841). *On the west side of the harbour*. An old smugglers' pub, with fine views over the harbour (which is floodlit during the evening). The atmospheric bars have large open fireplaces, where logs burn when the weather is cool. Children are welcome in the family room.
Fuller's, Greene King and Sharp's.
🐎♣❀◐↩️▽▶ Harbour

Portmellon

Rising Sun Inn
Portmellon Cove (01726 843235). In an excellent setting, this is a fine family pub, with a balcony overlooking the cove. There is a viewing panel over the old well in the passageway at the back.
Boddingtons, Marston's and Wadworth.
🐎❀◐↩️🍴🏨▶ The seaside!

Probus

Hawkins Arms
Fore Street (01726 882208). Have a look at the church tower in the village – it is reputedly the highest in Cornwall – before visiting this sociable pub, which has a

very fine assault course in the beautiful gardens.
St Austell.
♣ ❀ ❀ ◑ ⅄ 🛏 ⏰ *21.00*

St Agnes (Isles of Scilly)

Turks Head

(01720 422434). *Reached by ferry from St Mary's.* The most south-westerly pub in Britain, in a superb island situation, with fine sea views. The welcoming bar has a maritime theme, as you would expect. Winter opening times may be irregular.
St Austell and Ind Coope, with guests such as Flowers and Whitbread.
❀ ◑ ⌣ ⅄ 🛏

St Breward

The Old Inn

(01208 850711). Standing next to the highest (above sea level) church in Cornwall, this is a tra-ditional moorland inn with slate floors, granite walls and cosy log fires. Children are welcome in the family room, which has some amusements, and restaurant.
Bass, Ruddles and Sharp's.
🐎 ♣ ❀ ◑ ⌣ ⅄

St Teath

White Hart Hotel

Near Bodmin (01208 850281). A 400-year-old pub quite close to three golf courses, standing by a mid-14thC church, and warmed by a cosy stove. There is a fine brass diving helmet on display.
Ruddles and Ushers.
🐎 ♣ ❀ ▦ ◑ ⌣ ⅄ 🛏

Stratton

Tree Inn

Fore Street (01288 352038). Situated in the ancient market town of Stratton, it is close to some of Cornwall's most beauti-ful beaches and scenery. The Tree Inn is scheduled as a Historic Monument, and parts of the building date from the 13thC. It was formerly the manor house of the Grenville family, and in 1643 was Sir Beville Grenville's head-quarters before he led the Royalists to victory against the Earl of Stamford on the 16th May at the Battle of Stamford Hill. Antony Payne, one of the last of the Cornish giants, was born here in 1610 – he grew to be 7 feet 4 inches tall and weighed a mighty 38 stones. When Sir John Grenville became Earl of Bath he appointed Antony Payne hal-

berdier (guardian) of the guns. He died at the inn in 1691. The bars are warm and welcoming, with flagstone floors and log fires, and the restaurant is built with timbers from local shipwrecks. Skittle and pool are played here. *Bass and St Austell, along with various guests*.
🐎 ♣ ❀ ◑ ♒ 🛏

Tintagel

The Mill House Inn
Trebarwith Strand (01840 770200). *South of Tintagel*. This handsome 16thC mill stands beside a trout stream, set in 7 acres of grounds. Children are welcome in the family room and pool room.
Sharp's, with guests such as Bass, St Austell, Princetown and Exmoor.
🐎 ♣ ❀ ◑ ♒ ✁ 🛏 ▶ It is a short walk to Trebarwith Strand, a surf beach

Treburley

The Springer Spaniel
(01579 370424). *On the A388 between Launceston and Callington*. Children are made very welcome here – to quote the owner 'they are tomorrow's customers'. There is a very friendly

and comfortable bar, with a high-backed settle and a log-burning stove. Backgammon and bagatelle can be played.
St Austell, with Sharp's as a guest, and Wilkins Farmhouse cider from Wedmore in Somerset.
🐎 ♣ ❀ ◑ ♒

Treen

Logan Rock Inn
Nr St Levan (01736 810495). *On the coast road*. An unspoiled village inn, with low ceilings and warm coal fires on cold days. There are bar games during the winter.
St Austell.
🐎 ♣ *winter only* ❀ 🏥 ◑ *until 18.30 in winter* ▶ *Logan Rock, Minack Theatre*

Tregadillet

Eliot Arms, The Square and Compass
(01566 772051). *Off the A30 west of Launceston*. Established in 1625 and modernised in 1840, this fine old village pub is festooned with antique clocks, and warmed with open fires. Children are welcome in the family room. And yes, apparently it does have two names!

CORNWALL

Flowers, Wadworth and Whitbread, with guests such as Marston's.
🐕 ❀ ◑ 🍴

Trevaunance Cove

Driftwood Spars Hotel

St Agnes (01872 552428/553323). Trevaunance is a popular Cornish Cove, with a fine surf beach which looks out towards the Bawden Rocks. It is naturally lively during the summer, when surfers cruise down the hill on skate-boards, with their surf-boards carried on their heads, and visitors sun-bathe and eat ice cream. The sands are splendid, and the shell of an engine house overlooks all from the top of the cliffs. Walkers will enjoy the sections of the Coastal Path which pass here. The Driftwood Spars is a fine old inn, built with enormous beams and warmed by log fires. When you have enjoyed their real ales, you might like to dip into the selection of single malt whiskies. Pool is played here.

Bass, Burton, St Austell, Sharp's and Tetley, with guests such as Fuller's, Morland, Robinson's and Skinner's, and Stonehouse real cider.

🐕 ♣ ❀ ◑ ᵔ 🍴 ▶ The seaside, surfing, coastal walks

CUMBRIA

Alston

Angel Inn
Front Street (01434 381363). The bar in this friendly 17thC pub and hotel gleams with brass, and is warmed by an open fire during cool weather.
Boddingtons and Flowers.
♣ ❀ ◑ *not Tue evenings* ↩ ⋈
⏰ *21.00*

Ambleside

Golden Rule
Smithy Brow (01539 432257). Basically a beer house, but it's warm and friendly, and children are made welcome in the two small side rooms. Sandwiches are available at lunchtime.
Robinson's.
⚡ ❀

Appleby-in-Westmorland

The Royal Oak Inn
Bongate (017683 51463). A fine traditional medieval coaching inn in the oldest part of Appleby-in-Westmorland. Children are welcomed everywhere except The Taproom. There is a terrace in front of the inn.
Black Sheep, Bongate, Tetley and Yates, with guests such as Caledonian, Hexhamshire and

Marston's.
⚡ ◑ ↩ ✗ ⋈ ▽

Bassenthwaite Village

The Sun Inn
(01768 776439). *On the A591, 6 miles north-west of Keswick.* It is preferred that children use the side rooms whenever possible in this friendly 17thC village pub.
Jennings.
⚡ ❀ ◑ *not Sun evenings, or Mon & Wed lunchtime in winter* ↩

Boot

Burnmoor Inn
01946 723224). *Off the Eskdale to Hardknott road.* A beautifully situated Lakeland inn, parts of which date from 1578. It has been tastefully modernised, but if you want to *see* something 400 years old, have a look at the beams in the dining room! Co-owner Heidi lends an Austrian touch to the meals. There is a pool table, and a slide and swings in the pleasant garden.
Jennings.
♣ ❀ ◑ ↩ ⋈ ▶ 'Lal Ratty' miniature steam trains to the coast, walks

CUMBRIA

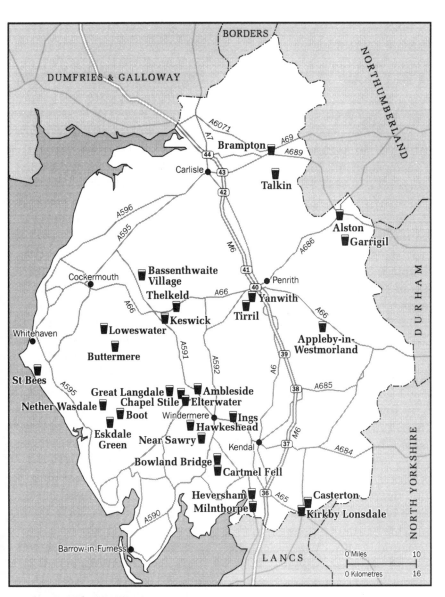

BORDERS

NORTHUMBERLAND

DUMFRIES & GALLOWAY

A6071

A7

Brampton

A69

A689

Carlisle

44

43

Talkin

42

A596

Alston

A595

Garrigil

A686

M6

Bassenthwaite
Village

41

Penrith

Cockermouth

Thelkeld

40

Yanwith

A66

A66

Tirril

Keswick

Loweswater

Appleby-in-
Westmorland

Whitehaven

A591

Buttermere

39

A6

St Bees

A595

A592

A685

Great Langdale

Ambleside

38

Nether Wasdale

Chapel Stile

Elterwater

Windermere

Ings

Boot

M6

Eskdale
Green

Near Sawry

Hawkeshead

37

A684

Kendal

Bowland Bridge

Cartmel Fell

DURHAM

NORTH YORKSHIRE

Heversham

36

A65

Casterton

Milnthorpe

Kirkby Lonsdale

A590

Barrow-in-Furness

LANCS

0 Miles 10

0 Kilometres 16

Bowland Bridge

Hare & Hounds
(01539 568333). *West of the*

A5074. Ex-footballer Peter
Thompson and his wife Debbie
run this handsome 17thC inn in
the Winster Valley. It has com-

fortable and spacious bars and a garden, with swings and a slide.
Tetley, with Cartmel as a guest.
❀ ⊞ ◑ ➳ 🛏

Brampton

Abbey Bridge Inn
Lanercost (01697 72224). *1½ miles off the A69 at Brampton, following signs for Lanercost Priory and Hadrian's Wall.* This handsome 17thC riverside inn was voted Best Real Ale Pub in Cumbria in 1992.
Up to 25 guest real ales each week!
❀ ◑ ➳ 🍴 🛏 ▶ Lanercost Priory, Hadrian's Wall

Buttermere

The Bridge Hotel
(01768 770252). *Take the A66 from junction 40 on the M6, and follow the Newlands Pass west of Keswick.* First licensed in 1735, this smart hotel stands beside a pack-horse bridge. There are comfortable bars and an elegant restaurant. Alfred Wainwright, creator of the splendid walks guides, once stayed here.
Black Sheep, Marston's, Tetley and Theakston.
❀ ◑ ➳ 🛏 ▶ Wainwright memorial in Buttermere church, walks

Cartmel Fell

Masons Arms
Strawberry Bank (01539 568486). *Strawberry Bank is about a mile north of Cartmel Fell, on minor roads north-east of Newby Bridge, which is on the A590.* Friendly and welcoming, it is well worth seeking out this pub which, when you find it, will reward you with splendid views of Whitbarrow Scar, Witherslack Woods and the Winster Valley. It has plenty of 'olde worlde' charm, with small rooms, slate floors and beamy ceilings, and offers an absolutely splendid range of beers from the UK and around the world. For £1 you can buy their 'Beer List' which details the delights available, with notes on each beer's taste and origins. From Germany to Australia, via Europe, America and Africa, the selection is awesome. Not satisfied with this, they also brew house ales in a micro brewery. Excellent selection of food, choice wines, their own spring water, and apartments and cottages to let (so you won't have to worry about driving!).
A choice of excellent real ales, plus their own brews, are available from five handpumps. There is also a vast selection of

bottled beers from around the
world.
🐕 🏵 ◑ ↩ ⅍ 🛏 *self-catering* ⏱
21.30 ▶ Walking (perhaps!)

Casterton

Pheasant Inn
(01524 271230). *From M6 exit 36,
on the A683 Kirkby Lonsdale to
Sedbergh road.* An old and welcoming inn, where the host offers
'a natural welcome for children,
not some carnival atmosphere' –
and that sounds just fine.
*Marston's, Theakston and Wells,
with guests such as John
Smith's.*
🐕 🏵 ◑ ↩ ⅍ 🛏

Elterwater

The Britannia Inn
Near Ambleside (01539 437210).
An old and traditional pub, with
open fires, which extends a
friendly welcome to walkers and
other visitors. A personalised
activity sheet with crayons is
given with each child's meal.
*Coniston and Jennings, with
Dent's, Orkney and Kelham
Island as guests.*
🏵 ◑ ↩ ⅍ 🛏 ▽

Garrigil

George & Dragon Inn
(01434 381293). *Leave the M6 at
junction 40 and head east on the
A686. Shortly before reaching
Alston, turn right to Garrigil.* This
17th century inn was once associated with the lead and zinc min-
ing community, and is now a
popular stop on the Pennine
Way, the Coast to Coast cycle
route and the Ravenglass to Holy
Island Walk. The bar, warmed by
a log fire and with a flagged floor,
fears no booted foot! Pool.
*Boddingtons, Marston's and
Whitbread Castle Eden, with
guests such as Flowers,
Theakston and Wadworth.*
♣ 🏵 ◑ ↩ ⅍ 🛏 ▶ Walking, skiing in a cold winter!

Chapel Stile

Wainwright Inn
Nr Ambleside (01539 438088). A
well situated Lakeland pub, with
slate floors, settles and a range.
There is a patio for fine days.
Jennings, with various guests.
🐕 🏵 ◑ ↩ ⅍ ⏱ 21.30

Eskdale Green

King George IV Inn
(01946 723262). *About 400 yards*

east of Eskdale Green railway station. Fine and old-fashioned, this inn has open fires and a stone-flagged floor. Baby changing facilities are excellent – they have won 'Cumbria Pub Loo of the Year' 1994–97!
Cumberland and Theakston.
♣ ❀ ◐ ⌣ ⅍ 🛏 ▽

Great Langdale

Old Dungeon Ghyll Hotel
Nr Ambleside (01539 437272). *On the B5343, north of the A593 from Ambleside.* A fine stone inn surrounded by dramatic scenery.
Black Sheep, Coniston and Greene King, with Old Rosie as a guest.
❀ ◐ ⌣ 🛏

Hawkshead

The King's Arms Hotel
The Square (01539 436372). Set right at the heart of a pretty Lakeland village, this is a warm and comfortable family run inn, with oak beams and open fires. If you need to change baby's nappy, you can use a bathroom.
Greenalls, Tetley and Theakston, with guest beers from local micros.
❀ ◐ ⌣ ⅍ 🛏 ▽ ▶ Beatrix Potter Museum, Wordsworth Museum

Heversham

Blue Bell Hotel
Princes Way (01539 562018). *7 miles south of Kendal on the A6.* What is now a very pretty and traditional village inn was at one time the local vicarage, dating from 1460. The comfortable bar has an open fire, and there is a period restaurant.
Samuel Smith.
🐴 ♣ ❀ ◐ ⌣ ⅍ 🛏

Ings

The Watermill Inn
School Lane (01539 821309). *On the A591 east of Windermere.* Frequently a winner of the 'CAMRA Westmorland Pub of the Year', this is a quiet family-run pub with some unusual bottled beers. Children are welcome in the lounge. Table skittles, Jenga, cards and darts are played, and Taffy Thomas & Co tell stories on the first Tue of each month.
Black Sheep, Coniston, Lees and Theakston, with guests such as Adnams, Caledonian, Jennings, Ridleys and so on. Weston's Old Rosie draught cider, and some excellent bottled beers, such as Chimay, Liefmans and Timmermans.
🖼 ❀ ◐ ⌣ ⅍ 🛏 ♟

Keswick

George Hotel
3 St John Street (01768 772076).
A plaque set in the outside wall
tells the building's story: 'This
hotel is the oldest inn in
Keswick. It was originally the
George and Dragon but the name
Dragon was dropped on the
Accession of George I. Here
German miners of lead and silver,
whose smelting house was at the
forge, paid their dues to the offi-
cers of Queen Elizabeth I, and
here also many unscrupulous
traders bought the plumbago ore
stolen from the mines in
Borrowdale'. The Earl of
Derwentwater called in the last
time he was in Keswick, to quaff
a tankard of ale from the saddle,
after which he rode off to join in
the 1715 rebellion, which ended
in his death on the scaffold on
Tower Hill, London. Today there
is often music in the cosy picture-
hung bar, and a comfortable
lounge with a roaring log fire on
chilly days. Its claim to be one of
England's oldest coaching inns
seems quite justified. Good food.
Jennings.
◑ ↶ 🛏️⏲ *21.00* ▶ The Lakes,
walking, boating, pony-trekking,
fishing are among the delights

Kirkby Lonsdale

The Sun at Kirkby Lonsdale
Market Street (01524 271965). An
inn was recorded on this site in
the 11thC, when St Mary's
church and Devil's Bridge were
being built. Renovated during the
17thC, it was visited by the artist
Turner in 1818, at a time when
the proprietor would stand at the
door and read aloud the London
Newspaper. It took two weeks to
come by horse from London, and
cost 2 pence.
Black Sheep, Boddingtons,
Dent's and Selby.
◑ ↶ 🛏️

Loweswater

Kirkstile Inn
(01900 85219). *On a minor road*
south of Cockermouth.
Comfortable and friendly, this
inn dates from the 16thC, and lies
in the shadow of Melbreak,
between Loweswater and
Crummock Water.
Jennings.
🐎♣◑↶🛏️

Milnthorpe

Kings Arms Hotel

Hale (01535 963203). *Leave the M6 at junction 35 and head north on the A6. You will reach Hale, 2 miles south of Milnthorpe.* While you are enjoying a pint in the lounge, you can have a look at their large collection of plates, prints and photographs and ignore the traffic whizzing by outside. It is a haven of peace in a busy world. The family room is upstairs, and there is a nice garden for sunny days. Pool and dominoes are played here. *Mitchell's.*

🐕 ❀ 🎱 ◑ 👓 ✗ 🛏

Near Sawry

The Tower Bank Arms

(01539 436334). *Half-way between Lake Windermere and Hawkshead.* Situated right next door to Beatrix Potter's house, and featured in her 'Tale of Jemima Puddleduck', this pub, along with the house and nearby Hill Top Farm, are all owned by the National Trust. The pub remains virtually as it would have been in Beatrix Potter's time so you will not need to be told that this whole area can be very busy during the tourist season.

Children are welcome in the bar and dining room at lunchtime, but are restricted to the dining room only during the evening. *Theakston, with Coniston, Jennings and Mitchell's as guests. Also Young's Double Chocolate Stout is kept.*

🖼 ❀ ◑ 👓 ▶ Beatrix Potter's House, Hill Top Farm

Nether Wasdale

The Screes Hotel

Seascale (01946 726262). *½ mile from Wastwater, 4 miles from Gosforth and the A595.* Superbly situated, giving fine views of the Wasdale Valley.

Black Sheep, Jennings, Theakston and Yates, with guests such as Butterknowle and Holts. Also bottle conditioned Black Sheep and Jennings.

🐕 ♣ ❀ ◑ 👓 ✗ 🛏

St Bees

Manor House Hotel

11-12 Main Street (01946 822425). At the heart of a seaside village, this historic former coaching inn is handy for the western Dales. Pool, darts and dominoes are played here. *Theakston and Younger.*

❀ ◑ 👓 🛏 ▶ The seaside

CUMBRIA

Talkin

Hare & Hounds

(0169 773456). This excellent country inn, not far from Carlisle, is set in the heart of the Cumbrian Fells. It was once used as a stop-over by monks on their way from Armathwaite to Lanercost Priory, and it still retains a traditionally warm atmosphere, with antique furniture, plenty of beams and cosy log fires. It is set in splendid countryside, and specialises in walking holidays. Talkin Tarn is just half a mile away.
Jennings, with Black Sheep, Mansfield and Morland as guests.
♣ ❀ ◐ *Mon-Fri only outside school holidays* ↶ ▶ Talkin Tarn, walking

Threlkeld

Salutation Inn

(01768 779614). This nice village local has a good family room upstairs, and swings in the garden. Pool, darts and dominoes are played.
Courage, Marston's and Theakston.
🐎 ♣ ❀ 🏠 ◐ ↶ 🛏

Tirril

Queen's Head Inn

(01768 863219). *On the B5320 between Penrith and Pooley Bridge.* Built in 1719, this is a very fine, beamy inn, owned between 1817 and 1837 by William Wordsworth and his brother. It has four open fires and plenty of brasses and cosy places to sit – the original wooden and flagstone floors have been recent-ly exposed. A fine selection of single malts is kept, including several from Islay, and a 28-year-old Glengoyne. Their 'Cumbrian' beer and sausage festival is held here over a weekend in mid-August. Excellent food, and coun-try fruit wines by the glass.
Black Sheep, Coniston, Hesket Newmarket, Wadworth and many other regulars and guests. Also bottle conditioned Black Sheep and Jennings.
♣ ◐ ↶ ✂ 🛏

Yanwath

The Yanwath Gate Inn

(01768 862386). *Off the B5320 between Ullswater and Eamont Bridge.* Friendly and welcoming 17thC inn with an inglenook.
Creaking Gate and Theakston.
❀ ◐ ↶ ✂

DERBYSHIRE

Brailsford

Rose & Crown Inn

Main Road (01335 360242). *On the A52 between Ashbourne and Derby.* Dating from the 18thC, this was originally a Temperance House, but times change, and the successful change with them. Children are welcome in the lounge and the restaurant. Pub games, such as pool and skittles, are played here. The attractive garden often has a bouncy castle. ***Burtonwood, with Gale's as a guest***

⚷ ♣ ❀ ◑ *not Mon evening* ⌖ ✄
🛏️🕐 *21.30*

Buxton

Bull i'th' Thorn

Ashbourne Road, Hurdlow (01298 83348). Built in 1472, this is a fascinating medieval hall packed with fine statuary set amongst sturdy beams, comfy settles and, naturally, a large open fire. Pool can be played, and toys are thoughtfully provided for children. The garden has a pirate fort, a bouncy castle and swings. The menu contains a selection of 40 main courses, and there is a separate choice for children. ***Robinson's.***

♣ ❀ 🔳 ◑ ⌖ ✄ 🛏️

Buxworth (High Peak)

Navigation

Brookside Road (01663 732072). This very fine and hospitable old pub looks out over the fascinating canal basins at Buxworth. It is definitely worth taking a walk around this complex, to see where limestone was once tran-shipped from the Peak Forest Tramway, built in 1799. This little line, just six-and-a half miles long, only ever used horse-power, apart from a 500-yard section at Chapel-en-le-Frith, which climbed an inclined plane using the weight of the full wagons coming down to pull the empty ones up. The tramway closed in 1926, and the sidings and basins became overgrown, but now, thankfully, enthusiasts and British Waterways are working towards their eventual restoration. So enjoy your exploration, then retire to the pub for a pint. Pool and dominoes are played here. The garden has swings, a slide and a pets corner. ***Marston's and Timothy Taylor, plus various guests. In summer there is usually a real cider available.***

♣ ❀ 🔳 ◑ ⌖ 🛏️ ▽ 🕐 *21.00* ▶
Buxworth Canal Basins

DERBYSHIRE

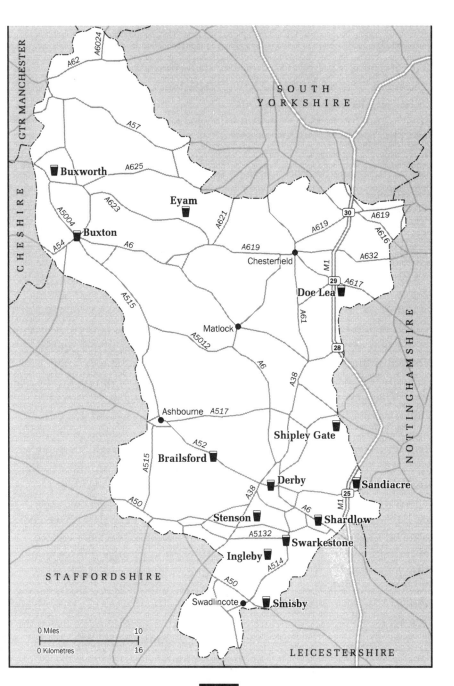

GTR MANCHESTER

SOUTH YORKSHIRE

CHESHIRE

A62
A6024
A57
Buxworth
A625
A623
Eyam
A621
A619
A5004
Buxton
A6
A619
A54
A515
Chesterfield
A619
A616
A632
M1
Doe Lea
29 A617
A61
28
Matlock
A5012
A6
A38
NOTTINGHAMSHIRE
Ashbourne A517
Shipley Gate
A52
A515
Brailsford
A38
Derby
Sandiacre
25
A50
Stenson
A6
M1
Shardlow
A5132
Swarkestone
Ingleby
A514
STAFFORDSHIRE
A50
Swadlincote
Smisby

LEICESTERSHIRE

| 0 Miles | 10 |
| 0 Kilometres | 16 |

Derby

The Brunswick Inn

1 Railway Terrace (01332 290677). *Two minutes walk from the station, towards the city centre.* This traditional railwayman's pub offers a vast selection of beers, including its own brews. *17 beers from handpumps and 2 or 3 from casks in the cellar.*
🐎 🎋 ◖ ◗ *by prior arrangement* 🍴

Maypole Inn

42 Brook Street (01332 344560). *Between Kedleston Road and Ashbourne Road, at the west end.* Bustling and traditional back-street pub, with a friendly and sociable atmosphere, which extends to the games room at the rear. This is equipped with a pool table, a few toys and plenty of space. Other games include pinball, video games and a video quiz. Lunchtime food is substantial and basic, such as burgers and chips, so most offspring will be kept happy. Beer prices here are very reasonable, and there is entertainment on Thur, Fri, Sat & Sun evenings. *Theakston, with Marston's as a guest.*
🐎 ♣ ◖

Doe Lea

Hardwick Inn

Hardwick Park (01246 850245). *Turn off the M1 at junction 29 and head west towards Clay Cross. After ¼ mile turn left to Hardwick Hall and Stanley. Continue for 2 miles, going under the motorway. The inn is on the left at a staggered cross-roads.* This very handsome stone building dates from 1607, and is set in beautiful grounds adjacent to Hardwick Hall, a fine stately house built by the redoubtable Bess of Hardwick in 1597, who was recorded as being a 'grasping and intriguing, if undeniably able, woman'. She had four husbands, all of whom died. The last, George Talbot, sixth Earl of Shrewsbury, passed away in 1590, seven years after separating from this redoubtable lady, who had instigated a rumour of a liaison between him and Mary Queen of Scots. Her later husbands were very rich, so as a consequence Bess became wealthy enough to indulge her passions, one of which was building. Unfortunately the gardens which surrounded the house have disappeared. The inn has no less than three family rooms. Extensive bar menu.

Theakston and Younger's, with Courage & Morland as guests. ☙ ❀ ◑ ▶ Hardwick Hall

Eyam

Miners Arms
Hope Valley (01433 630853). Families are made welcome in this hospitable pub, which has several pleasantly beamy rooms, with open fires. It is worth noting that this pub doesn't open Sunday evening or Monday lunchtime, except on Bank Holidays.
Stones and Tetley.
❀ ◑ *bar meals lunchtime Tue-Sat, restaurant meals Tue-Sat, & Sun lunchtime* ➷ *lunchtimes*

Ingleby

John Thompson Inn
(01332 862469). Opened in 1969, when John Thompson converted his 15thC farmhouse into a pub. There are plenty of oak furnishings, paintings and antiques. Brewing began on the premises in 1977 with a brew to celebrate the Queen's Silver Jubilee.
John Thompson's own beers, with Bass as a typical guest.
☙ ♣ ❀ ◑ ➷ ✄

Sandiacre

The Plough
Town Street (0115 949 9190). This smart brewery pub has a very pleasant canalside garden, so on a sunny summer day you can watch the boats cruise by while your children amuse themselves on the climbing frame. Families are made welcome in the lounge, and pool and skittles can be played.
Bass, along with a guest beer.
🏃 ♣ ❀ 🏠 ◑ *not Sun evening* ➷ ✄ ⏰ *21.00* ▶ Erewash Canal

Shardlow

The Malt Shovel
The Wharf (01332 799763). Shardlow is a rare surviving example of a canal village, built to serve the waterway during the 19thC. South-west of the pub you will find the splendid Trent Mill, which has a large central arch where boats once entered to unload. There is a Heritage Centre close by, where the history of this fascinating port is explained. The Malt Shovel is an intrinsic part of the port, being built in 1779, and its dark and interesting bar looks out over the waterway. Seating outside on the wharf. Good food.

Marston's, along with various guests (maybe Oyster Stout!).
�✿ ◖ *not Sun* ◔ ◕ *Young children should leave by 21.00* ▶ Shardlow

Shipley Gate

Shipley Boat Inn

(01773 530313). *South-west of Eastwood, to the west of Shipley Lock on the Erewash Canal.* This very handsome old pub has been in the same family for some 400 years. Children are welcome in the function room and restaurant, and there is an adventure playground. Pool is played.
Mansfield.
⚐ ♣ ✿ ⌗ ◑ ◡ ✄ ▶ Canal

Smisby

Mother Hubbards

Annswell (01530 413 604). *On the A511, about 1½ miles north-west of Ashby, towards Burton upon Trent.* This pub takes its name from a former landlady, and has nothing at all to do with the nursery rhyme. It has a large comfortable bar, and there is a slide and a toddler's swing in the garden. Nappy changing in a cubicle in the ladies toilet. *Closed Mon, except Bank Holidays.*
Marston's and Tetley, with Shardlow as a guest, and

Addlestone's real cider.
✿ ⌗ ◑ *not Sun evening or Mon* ◡ ✄ ▽ ▶ Castle

Stenson

The Bubble Inn

(01283 702205). *3 miles south of Derby city centre.* A fine modern pub in a converted barn, right by the Trent & Mersey Canal.
Marston's and Theakston.
✿ ◖ ◡ ▶ Trent & Mersey Canal

Swarkestone

Crewe & Harpur

(01332 700641). *On the A514 south of Derby.* The name of this pub recalls the Harpur family, who built the extraordinary Summer House, a lonely building just east of the village, which overlooks a square enclosure called 'The Cuttle', where bull-baiting may have taken place, although it seems more likely it was used as a 'bowle alley'. It was also in this village that Bonnie Prince Charlie gave up his attempt on the throne of England during the rising of 1745. The pub has indoor and outdoor play areas: also face-painting sessions.
Marston's.
⛝ ✿ ◑ ◡ ✄ ▶ Summer House, River Trent,Trent & Mersey Canal

DEVON

Bampton

Exeter Inn
Tiverton Road (01398 331345). Dating from 1495, this fine old inn has in the past served both the lime kiln and quarrying trades. Horse riding, shooting and fishing can be arranged.
Cotleigh, Exmoor and Worthington, with guests from local breweries. Also bottle conditioned Exmoor Gold and Old Speckled Hen.
🐎♣❀◑❤️🛏

Bideford

Kings Arms
(01237 475196). Right on the quayside, this open-plan pub manages to retain some cosy corners. Pool, cards, videos and quizzes.
Bass, Flowers and Jollyboat, with numerous guests, averaging about 100 each year. Also Marston's in bottles.
❀◑❤️✂🛏▶ The seaside

Bideford East-the-Water

Ship on Launch
(01237 472426). A 400-year-old pub, where a ship's mast has been used as a beam in The Old Bar, which has remained virtual-ly unchanged since the late 1800s. Children are welcomed everywhere except in The Old Bar. Bicycles can be hired here, and baby-changing facilities *are planned.*
Butcombe's and Wilmots. Also Taunton and Thatcher's real cider.
🚶🐎♣❀◑❤️

Berrynarbor

Ye Olde Globe
(01271 882465) *Half a mile off the coast road between Ilfracombe and Combe Martin.* Originally a row of three cottages dating from circa 1280, converted into a pub in 1675. The original buildings reputedly housed the masons who worked on Berrynarbor church. Today it's a cosy welcoming place, with an open fire in winter. Children are welcomed in the children's room, kitchen bar and function room, and there is ball play and a climbing frame indoors, and a play-house and slide in the garden.
Courage and Ushers, with Thatcher's cider.
🚶🐎♣❀▦◑❤️✂▽

53

Bovey Tracey

The Old Thatched Inn
Station Road (01626 833421). A thatched 17thC coaching house, where children are welcome in the family room and restaurant. *Furgusons, Tetley and Wadworth.*

Broadclyst

Red Lion Inn
(01392 461271). This country inn has oak beams and a log fire, and stands in the centre of the village, next to the church. Skittles can be played. *Bass, Eldridge Pope, Wadworth and Worthington, with guests such as Fuller's and Greene King.*

Buckfastleigh

The Tradesmans Arms
Scorriton (01364 631206). An atmospheric, 300-year-old pub built to serve the local tin mines. Chess and board games. Children are welcome in the family room. *Bass and Princetown, with bottle conditioned Flowne's Neck and Luscombe's.*
no food Mon

Buckland Brewer

Coach & Horses Inn
(01237 451395). *South of Bideford, west of the A388.* This 13thC building was once used as the village court-house, and at one time used to be the last stop-over for the London to Barnstaple horse-drawn coach. There is a skittle and pool room, together with draughts, dominoes and chess. The garden has slides, ropes and a swing. *Fuller's and Flowers, with guests such as Marston's, Theakston and Wadworth.*
(accommodation not suitable for children)

Clayhidon

The Merry Harriers
Forches Corner (01823 421270). A fine country watering-hole in the Blackdown Hills. Built in 1492, it has beamy ceilings, a cosy inglenook and a friendly bar. Skittle alley, bar billiards, and a large garden with plenty of swings, a slide and Wendy house. Forches Corner was a favourite site for ambushes during the 17thC Monmouth Rebellion. *Badger, Cotleigh, Exmoor and Wadworth.*
20.00

Cockington

The Drum Inn

(01803 605143). *A mile along Cockington Lane from Torquay.* Both large and handsome, this thatched pub was designed by Sir Edwin Lutyens, who also designed the Cenotaph in Whitehall, London, and the Roman Catholic Cathedral in Liverpool. It has extensive gardens, and stands in a picturesque village. Children are welcome in the family area, skittle alley and restaurant. There is a games room, and a climbing frame and slide in the garden.

Furgusons and Marston's.

🐎 ♣ ❀ ▦ ◑ ➹ ⚒ ▶ Torquay is just a mile away!

Dousland

The Burrator Inn

Near Yelverton (01822 853121).
*On the B3212 Yelverton to
Princetown Road.* A friendly and
welcoming Victorian country inn,
close to Burrator Reservoir. The
garden has slides, swings, nets
and a roundabout.
*Bass, Princetown, St Austell,
Theakston and Wadworth, with
Boddingtons and Flowers as typical guests.*
🎠 ♣ ❀ 🏥 ◑ 👓 🛏

Exeter

Double Locks Hotel

Canal Bank (01392 256947).
*Follow signs for Marsh Barton,
then to the incinerator.* This is a
relaxed and slightly eccentric
canalside pub, with a fine old bar
and two family rooms. It has an
immense garden, with an extensive assault course and volleyball, and a wheelchair toilet.
*Adnams, Greene King, Heritage,
Smiles and Wadworth, with
guests such as Branscombe Vale
and Hop Back. Also Gray's Farm
cider.*
🎠 ♣ ❀ ◑ 👓 ▶ Exeter Ship
Canal

Exmouth

The Grove

The Esplanade (01395 272101).
Large, warm and friendly, this
seafront pub is not far from the
docks. It welcomes families, and
has a large enclosed garden, with
a bouncy castle. Beer festivals are
staged in winter. Wheelchair toilet.
*Brakspear, Greene King, Otter,
Branscombe Vale and
Theakston, with guests such as
Adnams and Fullers.*
🎠 ❀ 🏥 ◑ 👓 ▽ ▶ The seaside!

Galmpton

The Manor Inn

2 Stoke Gabriel Road (01803
842346). *There are, confusingly,
two Galmptons in this part of
Devon. This one is on the A3022
between Brixham and Paignton.*
Close to the beautiful Galmpton
Creek on the River Dart estuary,
this is a charming family-run inn
set in a pleasant 'old world' village. A nearby passenger ferry
crosses the river to Dittisham,
passing Greenway House, the former home of Agatha Christie. A
preserved steam railway links the
village to the ferry, and continues
on to Kingswear, so there is plenty to do and see here. And you

DEVON

could always walk about a mile to the beach. Skittles are played at the pub.
Marston's and Tetley.
🐴♣❀◑☞✄🛏▶ Steam railway, nearby beach

Haytor Vale

The Rock Inn
(01364 661305). *On the B3387.* The 14thC settlement of Haytor Vale developed around an ancient iron ore mine. The line of cottages beside the Rock Inn were built for the miners and quarry-men who worked the old granite quarries on the moor behind Haytor Rock. The rock was moved by the horse-operated Haytor Granite Railway, which opened in 1820 and was the earli-est railway in Devon. You can still see parts of the trackway. The bulk of the inn was built around 1750, although parts are much older. It operated as a coaching inn at one time, as the stone trough and stables in the yard indicate. Children are wel-come away from the bars.
Hardy, Eldridge Pope and St Austell, with Bass as a guest.
❀◑☞✄🛏

Kingston

The Dolphin Inn
Nr Bigbury (01548 810314). *From the A379 take the B3392 at Harraton and follow signs to Kingston.* A very pretty, historic beamed inn with a friendly wel-come, and blazing log fires in the inglenook when the weather is cool. There are three gardens – one with a swing.
Courage and Ushers.
🐴❀▥◑☞✄🛏▶ Wonwell Beach

Lundy

The Tavern
(01237 431831). *By boat from Bideford. You can stay on Lundy by booking your accommodation with The Landmark Trust on 01628 825925.* Lundy is a splen-did island in the approaches to the Bristol Channel, with tall cliffs, three lighthouses, a castle, a church, an active farm and a variety of fine buildings, many of which have been converted to accommodate visitors. Henry III built the castle around 1250, and paid for it by selling rabbits. It replaced an earlier castle built by the Mariscos, which stood behind the farm. During the Civil War Thomas Bushell held Lundy for

57

the Royalists. It is thought he may have minted coins here. The resident population is around 15, but this swells during the summer. The Tavern is the island's social meeting place, and the door is never locked.

Butcombe, sold as Lundy Island Old Light Bitter

♣ ✿ ◑ *the availability of food is naturally restricted during the winter months* ☻ ✄ ⬭ ▽ *near The Tavern* ⊘ *21.30* ▶ *Lundy Island*

Lustleigh

The Cleave

(01647 277223). *Just west of the A382 between Moretonhampstead and Bovey Tracey.* Standing at the heart of a pretty Devon village, this is a suitably attractive 15thC thatched inn. The family room has toys and books, and there is a swing in the garden.

Bass and Flowers, with Whitbread as a guest.

🐎 ✿ ▦ ◑ ☻ ✄ ▽

Lutton

The Mountain Inn

Cornwood, Ivybridge (01752 837247). Voted 'Plymouth District CAMRA Pub of the Year 1997', this is a traditional country *pub*, with cob walls, settles and a large

fireplace. Children are welcome in the family room and lounge. ***Sutton and Darkside of the Mountain, with two guests, which change on a weekly basis.***

🐎 ✿ ◑ ☻

Lydford

The Castle Inn

Near Okehampton (01822 820241). *One mile off the A386 between Okehampton and Tavistock.* Beautifully situated beside Lydford Castle, a stannary (tin-miners') prison built in 1195, this very attractive inn has splendid dark bars with stone walls, open fires and well seasoned timbers. Look for the seven Lydford Pennies produced by the Saxon mint at the time of Ethelred the Unready. Children are welcome in the Snug restaurant. The garden has a pets' corner.

Blackawton and Fuller's, with guests such as Sutton and Wadworth.

▦ ♣ ✿ ◑ ☻ ✄ ▶ Lydford Castle, Lydford Gorge

The Mucky Duck Inn

Lydford Gorge, near Okehampton (01822 820208). A warm and friendly country pub with slate floors and stone walls. Large family room. Skittles, pool and bar

billiards may be played here.
Sharp's, with various guests.
🐎♣️❀️🈱️◑🍴▶ Lydford
Castle, Lydford Gorge

Mary Tavy

Elephants Nest Inn
Horndon (01822 810273). *1½ miles off the A386 between Tavistock and Okehampton.* Set in the Dartmoor National Park, this is a traditional old inn with an open fire, and cushioned window seats. The large garden contains dogs, cats, horses, rabbits, ducks and chickens amongst others!
Boddingtons, Palmers and St Austell, with two guests – one changed each cask, one changed every three weeks. Also Inch's Harvest real cider.
🐎❀️◑🍴▶ Dartmoor

The Mary Tavy Inn
Nr Tavistock (01822 810326). *On the A386 between Tavistock and Okehampton.* You may stable your horse (or take riding lessons) at this fine 16thC roadside inn on the western edge of Dartmoor. Bar skittles, shove ha'penny and dominoes can be played here.
Bass, St Austell and Hydes Anvil mild, with guests such as Princetown amongst others.
🐎♣️❀️◑🍴✂️🛏️▶ Dartmoor

Mortehoe

Ship Aground
The Square (01271 870856). Converted from two cottages, this is now a very fine village pub, with a beamed ceiling and a log fire. Skittles and pool can be played here.
Cotleigh, Flowers and Wadworth, with guests such as Morland. Hancock's Devon Cider is available during the summer.
🐎♣️❀️◑🍴▽▶ The seaside

Moretonhampstead

White Hart Hotel
The Square (01647 440406). A welcoming hotel in a listed Georgian Post House of great architectural and historic interest. Oak pews and armchairs furnish the lounge, which is warmed by log fires. There is also a patio.
Bass, Butcombe's and Whitbread, with Princetown beers as typical guests.
❀️◑🍴✂️🛏️▶ Dartmoor

Noss Mayo

The Old Ship Inn
01752 872387). An old-fashioned river-side inn.
Bass, St Austell and Sutton, with

guests such as Badger, Vaux and Wadworth.
🐎❀◖♺⚓

Okehampton

The Plymouth Inn

26 West Street (01837 53633). An old coaching inn with a cosy bar, which brings a country atmosphere into the town. Cards, dominoes and children's board games can be played.
Sharp's, with a continually changing range of guests from small south-western breweries.
🐎❀◖♺⚓

Plymouth

The Millbridge Inn

23 Molesworth Road, Stoke (01752 563056). Situated in the city, this traditional pub, popular with locals and students, has wooden floors and plenty of beams. It stages two major beer festivals: at Easter and early November, with smaller events at the end of each month. Pool and pin-ball can be played here. Children are welcomed into the Back Room Bar.
Bass, Courage, Theakston and Wadworth, with numerous guests such as Brains, Fuller's, Smiles and others. Bottle condi-

tioned Old Rosie is also kept.
🐎♣❀◖♺

Princetown

The Plume of Feathers Inn

The Square (01822 890240). Right in the centre of this moorland settlement, this pub dates from 1785, which makes it the oldest building in the village. It retains plenty of original features, including granite walls, oak beams and cosy open fires. Family run, it caters well for visitors to this National Park, and incorporates a camp-site and an 'Alpine Bunkhouse', which sleeps 20 people. The family room has games, and there is a large and pleasant garden, with a slide, see-saw, cable ride, Wendy house and swivels. The imposing nearby jail was originally built to house French and American prisoners of war.
Bass, Feathers and St Austell, plus Countryman real cider.
🐎♣❀▦◖♺⛺▽▶ Moorland walks, plus sailing, riding, canoeing and climbing nearby

Shebbear

Devil's Stone Inn

(01409 281210). This 14thC inn, supposedly haunted, has a cosy

bar with an open fire when the weather is cool. There is a slide, swings and climbing frame in the garden.
Brakspear and Flowers, with a different guest each week.
🐎♣❀🏠 ◐ ➳ 🍴 🛏 ⏱ *21.00*
▶ Devil's Stone

Stoke Fleming

Green Dragon
Church Road (01803 770238). There are strong nautical associations in this friendly pub, which is not surprising as it is run by Peter Crowther, a noted yachtsman. Books and toys are kept inside, and there is a climbing frame in the garden.
Bass, Flowers, Hardy and Wadworth, with guests such as Boddingtons and Marston's.
❀🏠◐➳▶ The seaside

Torcross

Start Bay Inn
Nr Kingsbridge (01548 580553). *On the A379 between Kingsbridge and Dartmouth.* A thatched, 14thC sea-front inn with cosy bars, decorated in a suitably nautical theme. Pool table.
Bass and Flowers, with Heron

Valley Farmhouse cider.
🐎♣❀◐➳🍴▽▶ The beach!

Two Bridges

Two Bridges Hotel
Nr Princetown, Dartmoor (01822 890581). *On the junction of the B3212 and B3357, at the heart of Dartmoor.* An 18thC former coaching inn in a beautiful riverside situation.
Princetown.
❀◐➳🍴🛏

Welcombe

The Olde Smithy Inn
(01288 331305). *Off the A39 – follow signs to Welcombe Mouth and Pottery.* Close to the northwestern tip of Devon, this is a charming old 13thC pub, complete with thatched roof and beamy ceilings, set in an area of outstanding, if a little windswept, natural beauty. It has a fine large garden, with some farmyard animals. You will find a nappy changing table in the ladies toilet.
Butcombe's, Flowers and Wadworth, with Morland as a guest.
❀◐➳▽

DORSET

Bridport

George Hotel
4 South Street (0138 423187). A friendly, well established pub for discerning locals and visitors. The landlord has been here for over 21 years, and the bar manager for over 20 years, so you are assured of a warm reception, with good beer and fresh food. Children are welcomed in the side room, affectionately known as 'Whipsnade'!
Palmers.
🏃 ◗ *not Sun lunch* 🛏 ▽ *in the upstairs bathroom* ▶ Seaside

Charminster

The Inn for All Seasons
16 North Street (01305 264694). One of the great attractions of this pub is its setting in beautiful countryside, not far from the Cerne Abbas giant, a fellow who makes no secret of his major asset. Skittles are played in the pub, and there is a riverside garden (take care with very young children) and an extensive play area. Children are welcome in the lounge and restaurant.
Butcombe's, Fuller's, Otter and Ringwood, with Eldridge Pope as a guest.
🏃 ♣ ❀ 🏠 ◗ 🛏 ✄ 🛏 ▽

Lyme Regis

Pilot Boat Inn
Bridge Street (01297 443157). A bright and airy seaside pub, nicely situated. Children are welcome in the large family bar, and the menu includes local seafood specialities. Skittles and cribbage are played here.
Palmers.
♣ ❀ ◗ 🛏 ✄ ▶ The seaside

Marshwood Vale

Shave Cross Inn
Nr Bridport (01308 868358). This is a pretty 14thC thatched inn, with timber and flagstone bars. Children are welcome in the lounge, and the garden is pleasant.
Badger, Bass and Hardy, with a selection of guests.
🏃 ❀ ◗ 🛏 ✄

Osmington Mills

The Smugglers Inn
(01305 833125). *A mile south of the A353, 4 miles east of Weymouth.* Built in the 13thC, this is an inn of great character, tucked away in a valley. Associated in the past with smuggling, it was once the refuge of Pierre Latour, the most notorious

DORSET

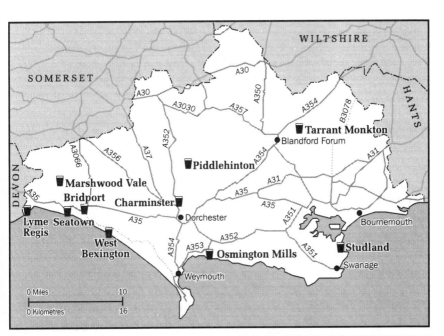

smuggler of them all. The Dorset
Coastal Path passes close by, and
there are fine cliff-top views. The
garden has swings, a slide and an
aerial slide.
*Courage and Theakston, with
guests such as Ringwood.*

Piddlehinton

The Thimble Inn
(01300 348270). A pretty
thatched pub by the River Piddle.
A separate room is available for
baby-changing.
*Badger and Ringwood, with
Thatcher's real cider.*
🌼 ◑ ◡ ▽

Seatown

The Anchor Inn
Nr Bridport (01297 489215). *2
miles west of Bridport on the
A35: turn south at Chideock.*
Superbly situated right on the
coast, this pub is close to Golden
Cap, the highest point on the
south coast of England (626 ft). It
has a large patio and cliff garden,
with a sand pit, play speed-boat
and free electric ride. Camping
and caravan park not far away.
Adnams and Palmers.
♣ 🌼 🏮 ◑ *no food Sun, or winter
eves* ◡ ⚒ 🛏 ▽

DORSET

Studland

The Bankes Arms Hotel
Watery Lane (01929 450225).
Well tucked away in Studland
Bay, this 15thC coaching inn was
at one time the haunt of smugglers. It is leased from the
National Trust, and stands in ¾ of
an acre of fine grounds, offering
excellent views. Close to the
beach, it is also handy for walks
along the South West Coast Path.
Pool, bar billiards and various
board games are played here.
Poole, with a variety of guests.
🐎🍀❀◑☞✆🛏

▶ Attractions include water
sports, horse riding, nature trails
and the nearby Swanage Steam
Railway

Tarrant Monkton

The Langton Arms
Nr Blandford Forum (01258
830225). *Off the A354, to the
north-east of Blandford Forum.* A
very handsome red-brick and
thatch 17thC pub situated in a
pretty village in 'Hardy' country.
Children are welcomed in the
family room. Skittles and pool
can be played, and there is often
a bouncy castle in the garden.

*Ringwood, with guests such as
Orkney. Bottle conditioned
Wychwood is also kept.*
🐎🍀❀🏥◑☞✆🛏

West Bexington

The Manor Hotel
(01308 897616). *Off the B3157
east of Bridport.* Built in the
11thC and mentioned in the
Domesday Book, this is a welcoming place, with panelled
walls, flagstone floors, beamy
ceilings and an atmospheric
Cellar Bar.
*Tetley, Palmers and Wadworth,
with St Austell as a typical
guest.*
❀🏥◑☞✆🛏▶ Chesil Beach

Barnard Castle

The Charles Dickens
14 Market Place (01833 690333).
Centrally situated, this old coaching inn was visited by Charles
Dickens while researching
'Nicholas Nickleby' in 1838. It
has large, oak-panelled, lounge
bars.
*Courage, with guest beers
changing each month.*
❀◑☞✆🕐 20.30

DURHAM & CLEVELAND

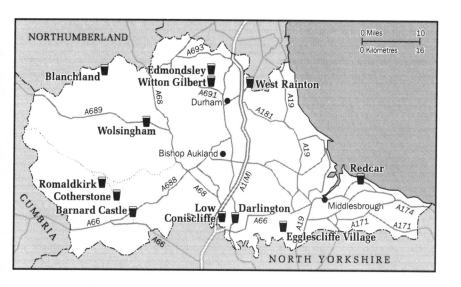

Blanchland

Lord Crewe Arms Hotel

Nr Consett (01434 675251). A very fine old inn, in a remarkably attractive village. If you are fortunate enough to be able to stay here, you could choose the Bamburgh Room, haunted by Dorothy Forster, heroine of the 1715 Jacobite uprising. Another room has an 'air bath'. Atmospheric bars, and splendid grounds.
Vaux.
❀ ◑ ☕ 🛏 ▶ Derwent Reservoir

Cotherstone

The Fox & Hounds

Nr Barnard Castle (01833 650241). *On the B6277.* In Upper Teesdale and overlooking the village green, this cosy and traditional coaching inn has plenty of old oak beams, and a real fire. *Black Sheep, with guests such as Village Brewer (Hambleton).* ❀ ◑ ☕ 🍴 🛏 ▽ ▶ Percymire Rock, a viewpoint 900 ft above sea level

Darlington

The Arts Centre Foyer Bar

Vane Terrace (01325 462313). There is regularly a splendid array of stimulating events at the Arts Centre, from films and children's theatre to jazz and comedy, with lots in-between. It is all contained within a beautiful and rambling old building. There is a bistro here and, of course, a bar. **Courage, John Smith's and Theakston, with Morland as a guest.**

🐎 ♣ ✿ ◖ ☜ ✄ 🛏 ▶ Lots of events in the Centre

Edmondsley

The Charlaw Inn

29 Wheatley Green, Blackhouse (01207 232085). Soccer memorabilia is featured in this large and lively pub. There is a fine view from the garden, which has a climbing frame, and plenty of seating. Children are welcomed in the Green Room, restaurant and patio. Every Saturday, 17.00-19.00, the Kids Club meets for face painting, games, a magician, and a meal and a drink, all for a modest charge.

Black Sheep, Theakston and Worthington, with guests such as Butterknowle and Hull.

🏃 ♣ ✿ 🏠 ◖ ☜ ✄

Egglescliffe Village

Pot and Glass

Church Road (01642 651009). *Turn into Butts lane, off Yarm Road.* A charming small country pub, where the ornate bar fronts were carved by a former licensee.

A ghost contributes to this pub's long history. Children are welcomed in the side-room, and there are swings and a baby-slide in the garden.

Bass.

🏃 ✿ 🏠 ◖ ☜ ⏰ *20.30*

Forest-in-Teesdale

High Force Hotel

(01833 622222). *Right opposite the waterfall.* This compact, stone-built hotel is one of the highest in Britain, well situated close to High Force, a spectacular 70-foot waterfall, where it drops over the Great Whin Sill escarpment.

High Force, with guests such as Theakston, and bottle conditioned Cauldron Snout.

✿ ◖ ☜ 🛏 ⏰ *21.00* ▶ High Force falls, with Cauldron Snout, the highest waterfall in England, 4 miles to the west

Low Coniscliffe

Baydale Beck

Coniscliffe Road (01325 469637). *On the A67 west of Darlington, by the motorway.* It takes its name from the beck which flows by the pub, which is on a particularly scenic reach of the Tees. Indeed the historic Tees Cottage

DURHAM & CLEVELAND

Pumping Station, now a working museum, is nearby. This is a busy and friendly local pub, where families are welcome in the conservatory. The garden has a play area, with swings, a slide, ropes and a climbing frame. Various entertainments are organised during the summer months.
Arkell's, Marston's, Morland, Ridleys and Wadworth, with guests such as Boddingtons and Thwaites.
⚐ ❀ ♨ ☾ ◑ ⏰ 21.00

Redcar

Pig & Whistle
47 West Dyke Road (01642 482697). This traditional 100-year-old town centre pub has an astonishing collection of 2500 ornamental pigs! Children are welcome in the games room.
Courage, Marston's, John Smith's and Theakston, with North Yorkshire as a typical guest.
⚐ ♣ ⏰ 19.00

Turners Mill
Greenstones Road (01642 496021). This is a friendly family pub, which happily serves the local community. Children are welcome in the lounge.
Bass and Worthington, with guests such as Fuller's, Highgate

and Ushers.
⚐ ❀ ♨ ◑ ☞ ✂ ▽ ⏰ 21.00

Romaldkirk

Rose & Crown Hotel
Nr Barnard Castle (01833 650213). *On the B6277 between Barnard Castle and Middleton-in-Teesdale.* A sturdy and handsome coaching inn, built in 1733, with a cosy bar with a shuttered window, a log fire and plenty of glinting copper and brass. Outside are the stocks and water pump. The church next door, St Romald's, is known as 'The Cathedral of the Dale', and the village is very pretty, with no less than three greens.
Marston's and Theakston.
◑ ☞ 🛏 ⏰ 21.00 ▶ Village stocks, Egglestone Abbey

West Rainton

The Three Horseshoes
Pithouse Lane, Leamside (01915 842394). *Between the A1(M) and the A690.* This cheery country pub has a large bar and an outside play area for children.
Boddingtons and Theakston, with guests such as Black Sheep, John Smith's and Ruddles. Bottle conditioned seasonal ales are kept.

67

🐴 ❀ ♨ ◑ *not Mon, Tue or Wed lunchtimes* ➳

Witton Gilbert

Travellers Rest
Durham Road (01913 710458). *Off the A691 Durham to Consett road.* Friendly and popular, this village pub/restaurant is attractively decorated. Children are welcome in the conservatory and no-smoking room. Boules can be played here. Folk and blues on Sunday eves.
Courage, John Smith's and Theakston, with guests such as Butterknowle, Cropton's, Rooster's, Timothy Taylor and many others.
🏃 ❀ ◑ ➳ ⚔ ▽ 🎤

Wolsingham

The Bay Horse Hotel
59 Uppertown (01388 527220). A 19thC country hotel, in a pleasantly rural setting on the edge of Wolsingham, with views along Weardale.
Ruddles and Tetley.
♣ ❀ ◑ ➳ 🛏 ▽ ⏱ *20.00* ▶
Fishing at Tunstall Reservoir and River Wear

Castle Hedingham

The Bell Inn
St James Street (01787 460350). Well timbered and with plenty of rooms, this friendly 15thC pub stands in the middle of the village. Large garden with a play area. Music on Friday evenings.
Greene King and Shepherd Neame, with Morland as a typical guest.
🐴 ❀ ♨ ◑ *not Mon eve or Sun eve Oct-Mar* ⚔ ▽

ESSEX

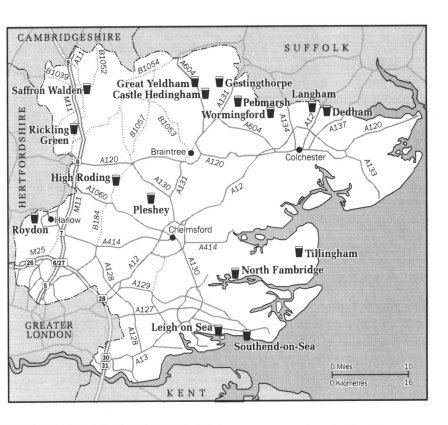

Dedham

The Sun Hotel

High Street (01206 323351). *Some 7 miles south of Ipswich, east of the A12.* A fine 15thC hotel in the village which was home to the artist John Constable (1776-1837). ***Adnams, Courage, Theakston and others, with guests such as Fuller's and Shepherd Neame.*** 🐎🌸▦◐⅄🛏▶ Church, as painted by Constable, which contains a pew with a medallion commemorating the first moon landing in 1966

Gestingthorpe

The Pheasant

Audley End (01787 461196). *East of the B1058, south-west of Sudbury.* This is a 15thC coaching inn with log fires and oak settles. High chairs are provided. ***Adnams, Greene King and Nethergate, plus guests.*** 🌸◐ *not Mon eve* ☂

ESSEX

Great Yeldham

The White Hart

Poole Street (01787 237250). This handsomely timbered Tudor pub was built on the edge of the village in 1505. It has comfortable bars, and serves a range of good food.

Adnams and Nethergate, with guests such as Fuller's and Shepherd Neame.
❀ ◑ ⇔ ✄

High Roding

The Black Lion

(01371 872847). *On the B1084 between Ongar and Dunmow.* Elizabethan and thus timber-framed, this pub serves a selection of good food.

Ridleys.
🐎 ❀ ◑ ⇔

Langham

The Shepherd & Dog

Moor Road (01206 272711). *Take the first exit from the A12 north of Colchester.* When the weather is cold you will find welcoming log fires in this friendly village pub, where the food has an excellent reputation, and a reasonable price! Food theme nights, such as Indian, English (with jellied eels)

and French.

Green King and Nethergate, with Ridleys as a typical guest.
❀ ◑ ⇔

Leigh-on-Sea

The Broker

213-217 Leigh Road (01702 471932). A family pub with a warm friendly atmosphere, 'in London's seaside'.

Crouch Vale, Fuller's and Shepherd Neame, with Eldridge Pope and other guests. Black Sheep and Ridleys are amongst the bottled ales kept.
❀ ◑ ⇔ ▽ ⊙ *19.30* ▶ Seaside

North Fambridge

The Ferry Boat Inn

Near South Woodham Ferrers (01621 740208). *Pass Fambridge railway station and stop before you reach the River Crouch.* Set in 3 acres of grounds, this fine 500-year-old weather-board pub has a family room and a children's room. Open fires in winter in the comfortable, homely bars.

Flowers, Theakston and Wadworth, with guests such as Boddingtons.
🐎 ❀ ◑ ⇔ ▶ Duck pond

70

ESSEX

Pebmarsh

The Kings Head
The Street (01787 269306). *East of the A131 between Halstead and Sudbury.* The beamy oak interior of this pub dates from 1470, and there is a skittle alley in the barn, as well as pool and table football.
Always four constantly changing real ales, with Timothy Taylor as a typical guest.

Pleshey

The White Horse
The Street (01245 237281). An attractive and beamy village pub, with a fine large garden.
Crouch Vale, Nethergate, Ridleys and Tolly Cobbold, with Everards & Jennings as guests.

Rickling Green

Cricketers Arms
(01799 543210). *Just off the B1383 at Quendon.* In a splendid setting, overlooking the cricket green, where Essex play each year. Cricketing memorabilia permeates this fine family-run pub. Children are welcome, except in the main bars.

Flowers, plus a selection of a strong and a best bitter, and a mild, which change each month. Cricket matches

Roydon

The New Inn
90 High Street (01279 792225). *West of Harlow, Roydon is on the B181.* There is a large garden and an adventure play area for the children by this cosy and beamy village pub. Bank holiday barbecues, with a bouncy castle.
Ansells and Tetley, with guests such as Bass.
not Sun & Mon eves 21.00 ▶ River Stort

Saffron Walden

Eight Bells
18 Bridge Street (01799 522790). A fine old timbered inn with a warming open fire.
Adnams, Ind Coope and Tetley, with guests such as Greene King, Marston's and Theakston. Audley End

Southend-on-Sea

Liberty Belle
10-12 Marine Parade (01702 466936). Fine and friendly, this is a sea-front pub, almost opposite

71

the famous mile-long pier. *Courage, with a constantly changing range of guests, plus real draught ciders such as Weston's.*
🏹🐎♣🕸️🎱◐⌣🛏️▶ The Pier, amusements and beach

Tillingham

The Cap & Feathers Inn
South Street (01621 779212). *10 miles east of Latchingdon, between Bradwell and South-minster.* A very fine example of a traditional Essex weatherboard building, dating from the 15thC. The inside is cosy and beamy, with polished wood floors, open fires and a log burner in the restaurant. The resident ghost is known as Captain Cook, and only appears at breakfast time, dressed in sailor's clothing. Excellent food, including Scotch beef and trout smoked over hardwood shavings in their own smoke-house. Bar billiards and skittles are played here, and Morris dancers entertain occasionally during the summer. Children are welcomed in the family room. *Crouch Vale, with guests such as Archers, Hook Norton, Smiles and Ushers. Thatcher's real cider is also kept.*
🐎♣🕸️◐⌣🍴🛏️🍷⏰ 20.30
▶ Excellent walking

Wormingford

The Crown Inn
(01787 227405). *On the B1508 between Bures and West Bergholt.* Constable has featured the village church in his paintings, and some of his family lie buried in the graveyard. The Crown is just uphill from the church, and it is a typically quiet and welcoming country pub, with open fires. Pleasant large garden. *Greene King.*
♣🕸️◐⌣🍴🛏️

GLOUCESTERSHIRE

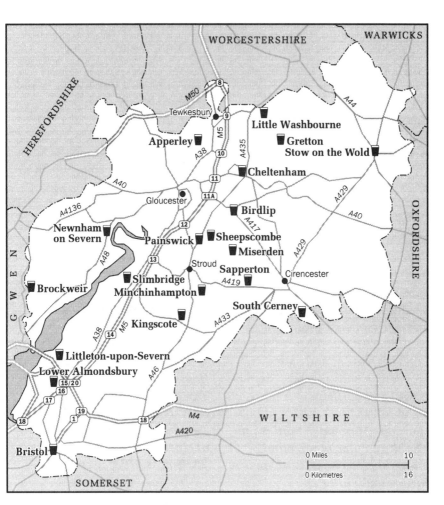

Apperley

The Farmers Arms

Lower Apperley (01452 780307). *On the B4123, west of the A38 between Gloucester and Tewkesbury.* An attractive and welcoming pub, selling its own brewery beer.

Their own brew, together with Wadworth and a guest.

Birdlip

Golden Heart

Nettleton Bottom (01242 870261). *On the A417 Gloucester to*

Cirencester Road. You will find a splendid inglenook and wooden settles in this traditional warm and cosy pub. Children are welcome, except in the bar area.
Bass, Hook Norton and Marston's, with guests such as Archers and Uley.
🖾 🐎 ❀ ◑ ⌣ ⽹ 🛏

Bristol

The Annexe Inn
Seymour Road, Bishopston (0117 949 3931). *500 yards from the county cricket ground.*
Traditional pub with a pleasant and safe garden. Children are welcomed in the conservatory. Pool, bar skittles and shove ha'penny can be played. There is access for wheelchairs, and disabled toilets.
Courage, Marston's, Smiles and Theakston plus others, and guests such as Bass, Brakspear, Brains and Fuller's.
🐎 ♣ ❀ ◑ *not Sun eve or Mon* ⌣ ⽹ ▽ ⏲ *20.30*

Brockweir

Brockweir Country Inn
(01291 689548) *Just off the A466.*
You can sit on one of the old church pews dotted around the place, or admire the sturdy beams

taken from a sailing barge while you enjoy a pint, or a meal. Indeed barges used to trade to the quay here, and these were towed by gangs of men as far as Hereford, and sometimes Hay-on-Wye. The guns on display are real, and at one time such weapons may have been used to sort out the village's 'ungodly' inhabitants, although the Protestant Bristol Moravians, who set up a church near the pub in 1831 would have used more peaceful methods. The pub now enjoys custom from locals, visitors, and walkers making their way along Offa's Dyke Path. There is a pleasant river-side garden, and a covered terrace.
Hook Norton, Morland and Thwaites, with guests such as Bass, Fuller's, Greene King and Tanglefoot. Bulmer's Traditional cider is also available.
🐎 ♣ ❀ ◑ 🛏 ▶ River Wye

Cheltenham

Beaufort Arms
184 London Road (01242 526038). An excellent friendly local, with pictures of Cheltenham Race-course decorating the bar. Skittles and pool are played here.
Badger and Wadworth, with

guests such as Adnams,
Bateman's, Cains and Shepherd
Neame.

John Smith's, Theakston and
Uley, with guests such as
Archers, Goff's and Wickwar.
♣ ❀ ▦ ◐ ☕ ✁

Ebrington

The Ebrington Arms
Nr Chipping Campden (01386
593223). *East of Chipping*
Campden, north of the B4035.
Friendly and unspoilt, this
Cotswold village pub has a fine
inglenook in the dining room.
Cribbage and shove ha'penny can
be played here.
Donnington and Hook Norton,
with guest beers changing each
week. Also Bulmer's Traditional
draught cider.
❀ ◐ *not Sun eve* ☕ 🛏

Gretton

Royal Oak
(01242 602477). *About 1½ miles*
from Winchcombe, going towards
Gotherington. A handsome
Cotswold pub where GWR steam
trains run at the bottom of the
garden. Inside it is all very cosy,
with flagstones, beams and log
fires in winter. Panoramic views
from the restaurant and the garden, where they have swings and
a see-saw, and a tennis court for
hire. Live music *Weds.*

Kingscote

Hunters Hall
(01453 860393). *On the A4135*
between Tetbury and Dursley.
This ivy-covered 16thC pub
caters well for families. There is a
good choice for children on the
menu, while the garden contains
an exiting adventure play area,
along with a slide and swings.
Bass, Courage, Theakston and
Uley.
♣ ❀ ▦ ◐ ☕ ✁ 🛏 ⏰ 21.30

Littleton-upon-Severn

Whitehart Inn
(01454 412275). When it's cold
outside you will find warm fires
in this atmospheric converted
17thC farmhouse, which has
wooden settles and tiled floors.
Smiles, with at least three
guests, such as Greene King and
Scottish Courage. Also bottle
conditioned Smiles.
🐎 ♣ ❀ ◐ ☕ ✁ 🛏

Little Washbourne

Ye Olde Hobnails Inn

(01242 620237). *On the B4077 about 6 miles east of Tewkesbury, close to Alderton.* This pub dates from 1474, and has been run by the same family since Lady Day 1743. It is a place of great character, and offers a warm welcome to families, who may use the room set aside. Shove ha'penny is played here, and the good food includes a children's menu. *Boddingtons, Flowers and Wadworth, with Hook Norton as a guest.*

🐎 ♣ ⚘ 🏠 ◑ ⌣ ⚲

Lower Almondsbury

The Bowl Inn

16 Church Road (01454 612757). *Off the A38 west of junction 16 on the M5.* Deriving its name from the edge of the flatlands surrounding the Severn estuary, this inn has stood since the 16thC, although buildings once on the site dated from 1146. It stands next door to the church, to which it is connected by tunnels, built as a means of escape from invaders. The Grey Lady is the resident ghost, seen around the place since the 19thC. A large and cosy stove warms the bar.

Courage and Theakston, with Otter as a typical guest, and Naish's cider.

⚘ ◑ ⌣ 🛏

Minchinhampton

The Old Lodge Inn

Minchinhampton Common (01453 832047). Originally built in the 16thC as a hunting lodge for Henry VIII, it later became, in 1889, the home of Minchinhampton Golf Club. It is not therefore a surprise to learn that the golf course is right alongside, in the midst of 600 acres of National Trust land. The area is known as the Royal Triangle, and is popular with kite and model aircraft fliers, as well as balloonists, and much of this activity can be seen from the pub garden, providing a useful diversion for the children. One of the bars in the pub is known as 'Tom Long's' – he was highwayman, ultimately hanged from a post not far from here. There is a skittle alley. *Fuller's and Vaux.*

♣ ⚘ ◖ *Tue-Thur & Sun* ▶ *Tue-Sun* ⌣ *ends 20.00* ⚲

Miserden

The Carpenters Arms

(01285 821283). *Signposted from*

the B4070, Birdlip to Stroud road. A fine traditional pub, dating from the 18thC, in the heart of Miserden, a conservation village at the centre of the Miserden Farming Estate. *Boddingtons, Brakspear and Wadworth*.
❀ ◑ ➷ ⅚ ⏰ *21.00*

Newnham on Severn

The Greyhound Inn
Popes Hill (01452 760344). *On the A4151 towards Littledean*. This friendly pub contains decorative montages made out of clock and watch parts in the bar. Swings and a climbing frame in the garden.
Freeminer, with guests from Adnams and small local breweries.
🐴 ♣ ❀ ▦ ◑ ➷

Painswick

The Falcon Inn
(01452 814222). *On the A46 Cheltenham to Bath road*. This historic and handsome inn was built in 1554, and served as a courthouse until the 17thC. Cockfights were once common, and the first Masonic ceremony was staged here. From the 19thC it became a regular coaching stop. It

has recently been restored, and has a warm and friendly bar, with wood panelling and a log fire. This is a popular walking area, and The Falcon has a drying room for wet anoraks. The Church of St Mary's nearby has 99 yew trees – legend has it that the 100th will not grow.
Boddingtons, Brakspear, Greene King and Wadworth, with Bulmer's Traditional Cider on draught.
❀ ◑ ➷ ⅚ 🛏

Sapperton

The Daneway Inn
(01285 760297). *1½ miles north of the A419 Cirencester to Stroud road*. An idyllic 19thC country pub in a fine position near the western end of the disused Sapperton Tunnel, on the Thames & Severn Canal. Fine Dutch-carved fireplace in the lounge. This is wonderful walking country. Ring the horn and quoits can be played here.
Adnams, Greene King and Wadworth, with guest seasonal ales and Weston's real cider.
🐴 ♣ ❀ ◑ ➷ ⅚

Sheepscombe

The Butchers Arms

(01452 812113). *Off the A46, near Painswick.* The very fine and famous sign, showing a butcher sipping a pint of beer, and with a pig tied to his leg, marks this 17thC stone-built pub. The name is thought to have originated during the reign of Henry VIII, when he hunted deer in the area. Views from the garden are splendid.
Archers, Hook Norton and Uley, with Bulmer's Traditional Cider on draught.
✿ ◑ ☕ ✗ ⏱ *21.00 in the bar*

Slimbridge

Tudor Arms

Shepherds Patch (01453 890306). *Follow the brown Slimbridge wildfowl duck signs.* This country pub, built during the 1800s, was once a market garden. It then became a beer house for the navvies digging the Gloucester & Sharpness Canal. There are toys in the family room.
Hook Norton, Uley and Wadworth, with Crown Buckley as a typical guest.
🐎 ♣ ✿ ◑ ☕ ✗ 🛏 ▶ Gloucester & Sharpness Canal, Slimbridge Wildfowl Trust

South Cerney

The Eliot Arms Hotel

Clarks Hay (01285 860215). *Clearly signposted off the A419, 1 mile from Cirencester.* Racing-car pictures are amongst the decorations in this cosy 16thC riverside inn, with a log fire. Skittles, shove ha'penny and dominoes can be played here. Assistance will be given if you need to change baby's nappy – just ask.
Boddingtons, Flowers and Wadworth, with a variety of guests.
✿ 🏨 ◑ ☕ ✗ 🛏

Stow on the Wold

Horse & Groom Inn

Upper Oddington (01451 830584). *Just off the A436, 2 miles east of Stow on the Wold.* A beamy bar, plenty of brass and an open fire make this a warm and enticing place, with a fine large garden, climbing frame, swings and a slide. Children are welcome in the restaurant and dining area. Aunt Sally can be played.
Hook Norton, with guests such as Mitchell's, Thwaites, Wadworth and Wychwood. Also Bulmer's Traditional draught cider.
🧍 ♣ ✿ 🏨 ◑ ☕ 🛏 ⏱ *21.00*

HAMPSHIRE

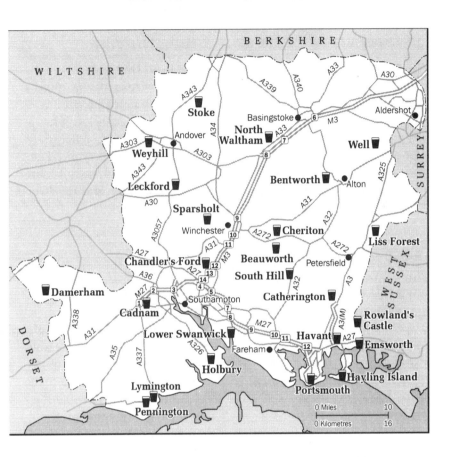

Beauworth

The Milburys

(01962 771248). *South of the A272.* This fine inn was known as The Hare & Hounds in the 18thC and The Fox & Hounds from the 1850s until quite recently. The Mill-*barrow*, from which the pub takes its present name, lies 150 yards to the east, and is a substantial Bronze Age monument. A 600-year-old well sinks 300 feet into the chalk: it is marked by a massive 250-year-old tread-wheel. The cosy, beamy bars are warmed by log fires when the weather is cool. Skittles can be played here.
Boddingtons, with other real ales from local breweries.
🐎 ✿ ▦ ◑ ➹ 🚐 ▶ Bronze Age barrow

Bentworth

The Sun Inn

Nr Alton (01420 562338). *Off the A339 Alton to Basingstoke road.* A charming 17thC pub retaining much character.
Cheriton, Courage and Ringwood amongst others, with guests such as Timothy Taylor.
🐎 ✿ ◑ 👌

Cadnam

The White Hart

Old Romsey Road (01703 812277). *Half a mile east of junction 1 on the M27.* A comfortable and welcoming pub.
Courage, Flowers and Wadworth, with Theakston as a typical guest.
✿ ◑ 👌

Catherington

The Farmer Inn

300 Catherington Lane (01705 592402). Friendly and hospitable country pub, with a spacious garden containing a slide, a climbing frame and a tree house. There is also an aviary and two friendly donkeys, Barney and Pedro. Pool is played.
Gales.
♣ ✿ ▦ ◖ *with a roast on Sun* 👌

Chandlers Ford

Cleveland Bay

1 Pilgrims Close (01703 269814). A relatively new pub which caters well for families. It has a welcoming bar with a flagstone floor and bare brick walls. The garden has a children's play area.
Adnams, Badger and Wadworth, with various guests.
✿ ▦ ◑ 👌 ✗

Cheriton

The Flower Pots Inn

(01962 771318). Dating from 1840, its unusual name was given by the head gardener of nearby Avington Park. It is a sociable place, with its own micro-brewery. Children are welcomed in the small sitting room off the lounge bar.
Cheriton.
✿ ◑

Damerham

The Compasses Inn

(01725 518231). *From the centre of Fordingbridge, follow signs to Sandleheath and Damerham.* Standing virtually on the village green, this traditional country inn is very well placed for visits to the New Forest. And if you are in the area in winter, call in for a pint and warm yourself by their cosy open fires. Pool and dominoes are played here, and the garden contains a swing and a see-saw. Nappy changing facilities are available in the disabled toilet.

Hop Back, Ringwood and Wadworth, with guest ales 'too many to mention'.

🐎 ♣ ❀ 🏫 ◑ ❤ ✂ 🛏 ▽ ▶ New Forest

Emsworth

The Coal Exchange

21 South Street (01243 375866). Emsworth was a prosperous port at the head of Chichester Harbour during the 18thC, but its commercial importance has declined since then, and it has now become a rather chic yachting centre. This pub is handy for the quayside, and is not far from the tide mill.

Gale's, with guests such as Adnams, Fuller's and Shepherd Neame.

❀ ◑ ❤ ⏰ *21.00*

The Lord Raglan

35 Queen Street (01243 372 589). Cast an architectural eye over some of the buildings in this street: number 23 is attractive, while on the north side

Newnham House is worth a look: then retreat here for a well earned pint.

Gale's, plus Fuller's, Marston's and Timothy Taylor as guests, along with Bulmer's Traditional draught cider.

❀ ◑

Havant

The Royal Oak

19 Langstone High Street (01705 483125). *Take the Hayling Island turn-off from the A27. It's the fourth turning on the left.* This beautiful and traditional brick pub is superbly situated right on the edge of Chichester Harbour. Inside you will find oak beams, stone-flag floors and roaring log fires on cool days. Fruit wines and home made food, with fish a speciality. Children welcomed, except at the bar, and there are colouring books and jig-saws, together with draughts, chess and cribbage.

Boddingtons, Flowers and Whitbread, with guests such as Gale's and Theakston, and Bulmer's Traditional draught cider.

❀ and sea wall patio ◑ ❤ ✂ ▶ Chichester Harbour

Hayling Island

Kittiwake

1 Sandy Point Road (01705 463489). There was once a small priory on Hayling Island, but this was lost to the first of several inundations by the tide, leaving the island much smaller now than it once was. A bridge to Hayling Island from Havant was opened in 1824, but development stuttered and didn't really start until the 1930s. Today it is a pleasant south coast resort, worthy of a visit, and you can bring your family here for refreshment. There are Punch & Judy shows from time to time.

Gale's, with Fuller's, Hook Norton and Wadworth as guests, along with bottles of Gale's Prize Old and Anniversary Ales.
🐴 ❀ ◐ ↩ ⚲

The Rose in June

2 Selsmore Road (01705 463208). Often warm and sunny during the summer, Hayling Island separates Langstone Harbour from Chichester Harbour at the heart of this yachtsman's paradise. The Rose in June, a very pleasant old four-bar pub, makes an excellent stop if you are visiting, as it is quite close the beach. Pool, cribbage and dominoes are played, and there are swings a slide and a climbing frame in the garden.

Bass and Courage.
🐴 ♣ ❀ 🏠 ◐ ↩ ⏱ *21.00* ▶ The seaside

Holbury

The Old Mill Inn

Lime Kiln Lane (01703 891137). *Holbury is on the A326 south of Southampton. Turn right at the Hardley Industrial Estate roundabout: the pub is ¼ mile down on the right-hand side.* The original buildings, a barn and adjoining thatched cottage dating from the 14thC have been sympathetically converted into a rambling pub, with a large family room close to the bar. There is a big-screen TV, plus pin-ball and pool indoors, and a large play area with a climbing frame and other play equipment in the garden. Every Tue & Sun live music is played.

Courage and Ringwood.
🐴 ♣ ❀ 🏠 ◐ ↩ ✂ ⚲

Leckford

The Leckford Hutt Inn

London Road (01264 810738). *North of the A30 between Sutton Scotney and Stockbridge.* There is a 250-foot-deep well at this traditional 18thC drovers' pub. The brass handpumps are reputed to have been installed when the pub was built. Pool and shuffle board can be played here. Camping and caravanning in the field next-door.

Archers, with guests such as Hop Back.
🐎♣❀◑⚘

Liss Forest

The Temple Inn
82 Forest Road (01730 892134). This pub has a Wendy house in the garden, and a petanque terrain.

Gale's.
❀▣◑not *Sun evening or Mon*⚘🕐 *21.00*

Lower Swanwick

The Old Ship
261 Bridge Road (01489 575646). *On the A27 near Bursledon.* A fine 16thC inn which is very handy for the yacht marinas. Children are welcome in the top bar, away from the bar area.

Gale's.
♣❀◑⚘

Lymington

The Chequers Inn
Lower Woodside (01590 673415). *At the end of Ridgeway Lane off the roundabout on the A337 west of Lymington.* This picturesque 16thC inn on the edge of the salt marshes welcomes family groups who 'sit together and *stay* together on a family outing'.

Bass, Fuller's and Wadworth, with Greene King, Marston's, Ringwood and Worthington as guests.
❀◑⚘

North Waltham

The Sun Inn
Winchester Road (01256 397234). *On the A30, 4 miles south-west of Basingstoke.* This popular old-world road-house stands back from the A30, in surroundings which appear quite rural. Table football is played here, and in the garden you will find the delights of a trampoline, swings, a see-saw and other equipment. Good range of food, and a children's menu.

Courage and Fuller's, with Brakspear as a guest.
🐎♣❀▣◑⚘✂

HAMPSHIRE

Pennington

The Musketeer
26 North Street (01590 676527).
A friendly, traditional, pub with
an interesting sign.
*Brakspear and Ringwood, with
guests such as Fuller's and
Gale's, with bottles of Gale's
Prize Old Ale.*
🐎 ❀ ◖ *not Sun* ⏰ *21.00*

Portsmouth

Ye Olde Oyster House
291 Locksway Road, Milton
(01705 727456). *Off Eastern
Road: follow the seafront and
turn left at St James's Hospital.*
This is a large, friendly and
authentic pub, with pool and
video games in the family room.
*Brains and Brewery on Sea,
with a range of guests and a
draught cider.*
🐎 ♣ ❀ ◖ ⌣ ⋡ ▶ The Docks
and the Mary Rose

Rowland's Castle

The Castle Inn
1 Finchdean Road (01705
412494). *Close to the railway
bridge.* This friendly village pub
has earned a good reputation for
its food. The garden has swings
and slides, and there is a large

family toilet.
*Gale's, with Fuller's as a guest.
Also bottle conditioned Gale's
Prize Old Ale.*
🐎 *in summer* ❀ ▦ ◖ *not Sun
evenings* ⌣ 🛏 ▽ ⏰ *21.00*

South Hill

White Horse Inn
Droxford (01489 877490). *On the
A32 between Alton and Fareham.*
An attractive 16thC inn with
pool, table football and a range of
other fun games.
*Flowers, Greene King,
Theakston and Vaux.*
🐎 ♣ ❀ ◖ ⌣ ⋡ 🛏

Sparsholt

The Plough Inn
(01962 776353). *Just south of the
A272 between Winchester and
Stockbridge.* The garden of this
fine country pub has a play fort
and a donkey paddock. Inside
you will find log fires and freshly
cooked food.
*Wadworth, with Adnams,
Bateman's, Smiles and Wells as
typical guests.*
❀ ▦ ◖ ⌣ ⋡

Stoke

The White Hart
Near Andover (01264 738355). A fine, old fashioned, village pub with a conservatory. Pool, snooker and bar billiards played here. ***Brakspear, Fuller's and Hampshire.***
🐶 ♣ ❀ ◑ *not Sun evening, Monday, or Tues evening* 👅

Well

The Chequers Inn
Long Sutton (01256 862605). *Leave the A31 at Bentley, and follow signs to Well.* This picturesque 16thC country pub has a vine-covered seating area at the front and a beer garden to the rear.
Badger.
❀ ◑ 👅

Weyhill

Weyhill Fair
(01264 773631). *West of Andover on the A342.* Children are welcome in the no-smoking area of this friendly family-run free house, which has been in the Good Beer Guide since 1985. They stage an annual beer festival, and occasionally there is music. Set in three acres of grounds, with goats and a camping and caravanning area. ***Morrells, with guests such as Adnams, Fuller's, Shepherd Neame and Woodforde's.***
❀ ◑ *not Sun eve* 👅 ⚥ ⏰ *20.30*

HEREFORDSHIRE

Brimfield

Roebuck Inn

(01584 711230). Charming and comfortable, with a large inglenook fireplace and wood panelling, this friendly old pub is noted for its good food. Bar billiards, shove ha'penny and other bar games are played. *Morland and Tetley, plus a variety of guests. Dunkertons real cider is also served.*
♣ ◑ ✆ ⚒ 🛏 ▽ ⏱ 20.00

Dorstone

The Pandy

(01981 550273). *On the B4348, 6 miles from Hay-on-Wye, 15 miles from Hereford.* It has stood for over 800 years, and is the oldest pub in Herefordshire. It is situated in a very pretty village. Inside there are flag floors, plenty of beams and a log fire. You can play quoits, and there are swings in the garden. The food is good. *Bass and Wye Valley, with guest ales.*
♣ ❀ ⌸ ◑ ✆ ⚒

Fownhope

The Green Man Inn

01432 860243). *On the B4224 mid-way between Hereford and Ross-on-Wye.* A black-and-white coaching inn, with open fires, close to the River Wye and wooded hills. It dates from 1485, and was occupied in 1645 by a troop of Roundhead soldiers on their way to occupy Hereford. During the 18th and 19thC the Petty Sessional Court was held here: the cell, iron bars and special lock can still be seen. Tom Spring, bare-fist fighter and heavyweight champion of England, was once the landlord. Have a look for the fine sign over the entrance to the coaching yard. *Courage, Hook Norton and Marston's.*
🐴 ❀ ⌸ ◑ ✆ ⚒ 🛏

Hereford

Three Elms

1 Canon Pyon Road (01432 273338). This is a refurbished one-bar pub with a friendly and enthusiastic landlord serving a good range of real ales. The garden has a climbing frame, a slide and rocking animals. *Boddingtons, Flowers and Marston's, with three constantly changing guest beers from independent brewers.*
🐴 ❀ ⌸ ◑ ✆ ▽

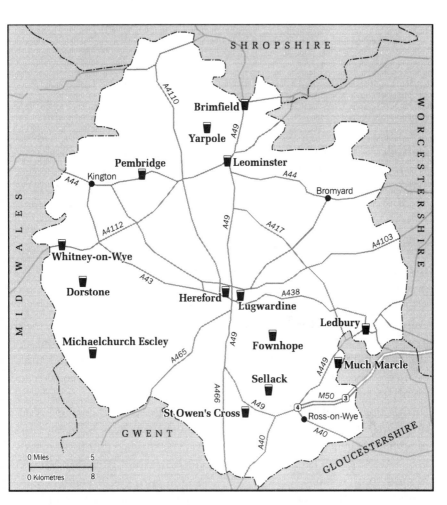

SHROPSHIRE

Brimfield

Yarpole

Pembridge

Kington

Leominster

Bromyard

Whitney-on-Wye

Dorstone

Hereford

Lugwardine

Ledbury

Michaelchurch Escley

Fownhope

Much Marcle

Sellack

St Owen's Cross

Ross-on-Wye

GWENT

GLOUCESTERSHIRE

MID WALES

WORCESTERSHIRE

0 Miles 5
0 Kilometres 8

Ledbury

The Feathers

High Street (01531 635266). This 16thC inn is one of the most attractive buildings in Ledbury, a town described by the poet John Masefield, who was born here, as 'pleasant to the sight, fair and half-timbered houses black-and-white'. Narrow streets lead up the church, which has a 'golden vane surveying half the shire'. The bars are very comfortable, and a log fire provides a warm welcome. *Real ales changing too often to name (they assure us).*
❀ ◑ 🛏 ▽

Lugwardine

Crown & Anchor
Cotts Lane (01432 851303). This is a well kept and welcoming black-and-white Herefordshire inn, just to the east of Hereford. *Hobsons, Wadworth and Worthington, along with Westons real cider.*
✿ ◑ ☞ ⚭

Michaelchurch Escley

Bridge Inn
(01981 510646). Easy to find in a tiny village, this friendly pub enjoys a pleasant situation down by the river, with a small camp-site next door. The bar is warmed by a woodburner, and there are plenty of table games available. During the summer you can use the camp-site showers if you need to change a nappy – just ask for a key. The pub is closed Monday lunchtime. *Ruddles and Wye Valley, along with guests such as Rooster's, Shepherd Neame, Smiles, Charles Wells and Woodhampton.*
♣ ✿ ◑ *no food Mon* ☞ ⚭ ▽ *use the camp-site showers during the summer* ⏰ *21.00*

Much Marcle

The Slip Tavern
Watery Lane (01531 660246). Fine gardens here contain a variety of fascinating plants, and there are also swings and a see-saw. Inside it is a very pleasant country pub. *Hook Norton and Wadworth, along with Westons real cider.*
✿ ▦ ◑ ☞

Leominster

The Royal Oak Hotel
South Street (01568 612610). *At the junction of the A44 and A49.* Leominster is a fine old wool town, set amidst splendid countryside rich with cider apples and hop fields. Indeed fine wool was first produced here in the 13thC, and was known as 'Lemster Ore'. Your children might be persuaded to visit the 11thC Priory Church with you if you tell them they will see a ducking stool, used to quieten nagging women until 1809. A meal and a pint here will round off the day nicely. No garden, but there is a patio. *Brains and Wood.*
✿ ◑ ☞ 🛏

Pembridge

The New Inn

Market Square (01544 388427). Pembridge is a lovely small border village, full of black-and-white half-timbered buildings and overlooked by the belfry of the 600-year-old church, which was used as a refuge for the villagers when border raiding was common practice in these parts. The cobbled square in front of the inn is also overlooked by the Wool Market. The 16thC black-and-white New Inn was once a court house, with the cellar used as a lock-up. It is said that the Treaty for England's Crown was signed in the inn's Court Room, as it is just 6 miles from Mortimer's Cross, where one of the decisive battle of the Wars of the Roses, 1455-85, was fought (this one was a Yorkist victory). Children are welcome in the lounge and restaurant, and nappies can be changed in a bathroom upstairs.

Ruddles and Three Tuns, with Adnams and Wood as guests. Westons real cider is also served.

⊠ ❀ ◑ ✿ 🛏 ▽ ⏱ 21.00

St Owen's Cross

The New Inn

(01989 730274). A warm and friendly 16thC coaching inn, with lots of cosy corners, and warm inglenook fires.

Bass, Fuller's, Smiles and Tetley are amongst the range of real ales kept here.

❀ ◑ ✿ 🛏

Sellack

Lough Pool Inn

(01989 730236). Pretty black-and-white timbered pub with beamy bars, flag floors and log fires. Children are welcome, as long as they stay away from the bars.

Bass, John Smith's and Wye Valley.

❀ ◑ ✿ ✕

Whitney-on-Wye

Rhydspence Inn

(01497 831262). *On the A438 one mile west of Whitney-on-Wye.* Straddling the Welsh border in 'Kilvert' country, you will find this smart and refined 14thC black-and-white inn – indeed the inn is mentioned several times by the Rev Francis Kilvert (1840-79), vicar of Bredwardine and famous diarist. Lots of original features, heavy beams, log fires, and a fine public bar.

Bass, Brains and Robinson's, with Dunkerton's real cider.

🐎 🏵 ◑ ☕ ✄ 🛏

Yarpole

The Bell Inn

Green Lane (01568 780359). *It is 5 miles north-west of Leominster, and 8 miles south-west of Ludlow.* This is a very picturesque 16thC black-and-white pub near Croft castle. It has three specialities: live music, Oriental food and real ale. Live music is featured three or four evenings each week; 80% of their customers order from the Oriental menu (one of the pub partners is a Japanese lady), but they of course serve other food, including a noted Sunday lunch. Lollipops are provided for children, and your dog may even get a treat! Morris dancers perform here on the major Bank Holidays. Pool and quoits are played, and there are swings and climbing frames in the garden.

Fuller's and Marston's, with Wood as a guest. Bulmer's real cider is available Spring and Summer.

♣ 🏵 🔳 ◑ ☕ ✄ 🎤

HERTFORDSHIRE

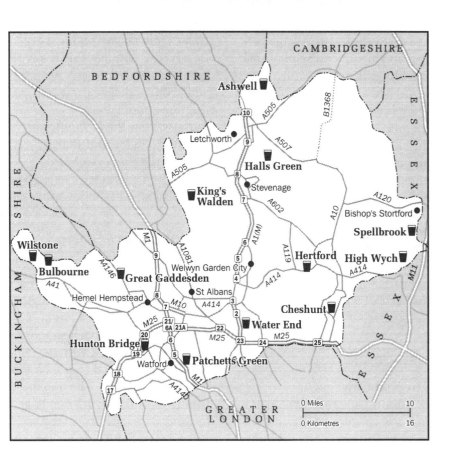

Ashwell

The Bushel and Strike

Baldock (01462 742394). *Turn off the A1(M) at junction 10 and follow signs to Baldock, and then to Ashwell.* Friendly and down-to-earth, this is a 'value-for-money' pub with a well-stocked bar. Table tennis can be played. **Charles Wells, with guests such as Brakspear and Morland, and Westons real cider.**

❀ ◐ *not Sun eves in winter* ⌂
⚚ 🛏

Bulbourne

The Grand Junction Arms

Bulbourne Road (01442 890677). *On the B488 Tring to Dunstable Road.* A friendly and traditional canal-side pub with a large garden and an adventure play area. Bar billiards, table skittles and board games can be played, and there is a barbecue and spit roast each weekend during the summer, with a children's karaoke and mini-disco each Sunday at 16.00.

Adnams, Caledonian, Greenalls, Jennings and Ridleys plus a weekly guest ale.

♣ ✿ ⌘ ◑ *not Mon eve* ♥

▶ Grand Union Canal, with lots of boats, and Marsworth Locks just a short walk away. Tring Reservoirs for walks

Cheshunt

The Red Cow

Windmill Lane (01992 632701). *Just 100 yards from Cheshunt railway station.* You will find a mature clientele in this friendly and well-appointed pub. Children are welcome in part of the lounge.

Bass and Greene King.

⌧ ✿ ◑ *no food at weekends*

▶ River Lee and the Lee Valley Regional Park close by

Great Gaddesden

Cock & Bottle

(01442 255381). *3 miles north of*

Hemel Hempstead on the A4146. Deservedly popular, this is a typical village pub with an open fire and good food. The games room has three pool tables.

Fuller's, Hop Back, Ringwood, Timothy Taylor and Ward.

♣ ✿ ◑ *not Sun eve or Mon*

▶ Children's farm with over 500 animals just half-a-mile away

Halls Green

Rising Sun

(01462 790487). Come here on a fine day and you can enjoy their 10-acre garden, which has a petanque pitch, a five-a-side football pitch, swings, a Wendy house and a special area set aside for the under fives. The pub itself is quite beautiful, with one large bar and a splendid conservatory. It is all very family orientated, so you are sure of a warm welcome. When you have enjoyed their real ales, you might wish to sample the range of six or seven Polish flavoured vodkas. Extensive and interesting menu. Bar billiards.

Bass, Courage and McMullen.

♣ ✿ ⌘ ◑ ♥

Hertford

The White Horse

33 Castle Street (01992 501950).

*In the cul-de-sac leading to
Hertford Castle.* The brewery tap
for the Dark Horse Brewery, with
a friendly atmosphere and no
canned music. Children are welcome in the upstairs lounge.
***Dark Horse, Fuller's and Hook
Norton, with at least four or five
guests from micros, and Inch's
real cider.***
🖼️ 🕸 ⊃ *not Sun* ♡ ⋈ ▶ Hertford
Castle

High Wych

Rising Sun
(01279 724099). A friendly local,
known as 'Sid's'.
***Courage, with varying guests,
such as Oakham, Woodforde's
and local micros.***
 🕸

Hunton Bridge

Kings Head
Bridge Road (01923 262307).
*Leave the M25 at junction 19,
turn left, then left again.* A friendly village pub of great character,
standing beside the Grand Union
Canal and with a 2½ acre garden
which contains some imaginative
and exciting play equipment,
including a rope slide. Children
are welcome in the family room
during the summer, and up in the

gallery during the winter.
Backgammon, cribbage and dominoes are played here, and they
have a skittle alley. Langleybury
Church is right opposite, with its
twin-roofed Norman tower.
***There is always a choice of four
real ales, which include
Benskins and Marston's, with
guests such as Brierley Court.***
♣ 🕸 🖼️ ◑ *not Sun evening* ♡

King's Walden

Plough
(01438 871394). *South-west of
Hitchen, between the A505 and
the B651.* Sociable country pub
with a large 3-acre garden, containing a football pitch, swings, a
golf course, and woods to play in.
The family room has bar games
and toys, and there is also pool. A
new baby-changing area has been
incorporated into the ladies toilet.
Greene King.
🐎 ♣ 🕸 🖼️ ⊃ *not Sun* ♡ ▽

Patchetts Green

The Three Compasses
Hillfield Lane (01923 856197).
Large, lively and friendly, this
pub welcomes families in the
conservatory. Perhaps you might
call in here when visiting the

nearby Aldenham Country Park, which has a lake and a small children's zoo. The pub garden has a slide, swings and a climbing frame, and there is a bench for nappy changing in the toilets. Good food, and a separate children's menu.

Benskins, Morland and Tetley, with guests such as Adnams, Greene King and Marston's.
🏃 ❀ 🏠 ◐ *not Sun or Mon evening* ☕ 🍴 ▽ ⏰ *21.00*

Spellbrook

The Three Horseshoes
Spellbrook Lane East (01279 722849). *On the A1184 between Harlow and Bishop's Stortford.* A popular pub dating from 1535, with an open fire and a most unusual stone tile floor. There is a large play area in the garden with sand, and a bouncy castle and crazy golf. Clowns and children's discos are often seen here. Baby changing is located in the disabled area. Children are welcome in the pub except at six tables and the bar.
Greenalls and Tetley, plus a

monthly guest beer.
🏃 ❀ 🏠 ◐ ☕ 🍴 ▽ 🍷 ▶ River Lea

Water End

Old Maypole
Near North Mimms (01707 642119). A fine 16thC pub complete with an inglenook fireplace and a large garden.
Greene King.
🐴 ♣ ❀ ◖ *not Sun* ◗ *varies, more often in summer* ☕ 🍴

Wilstone

Half Moon
(01442 826410). This comfy 17thC pub is entered through a wildly leaning front door. Haggis is an autumn speciality, when the landlord returns from his Scottish holiday. There is a climbing frame, castle and swings in the garden.
Bass, Flowers and Tetley, plus guests
❀ 🏠 ◐ *not Mon eve* ☕ 🍴 ▶
Grand Union Canal

ISLE OF WIGHT

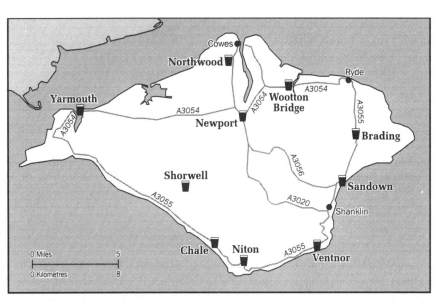

Bonchurch

The Bonchurch Inn
Bonchurch Chute, Bonchurch (01983 852611). *Just east of Ventnor.* A fine stone pub tucked away in a courtyard. The floors are built from old decking, and the chairs are from a liner.
Courage, with Theakston as a typical guest.
🐴♣◑👄📫

Brading

The Bugle Inn
56 High Street (01983 407359). Refurbished at great expense, this pub has been provided with many family-friendly attributes,

including an adventure playground. It is also very well placed for visits to some of the island's premier attractions. Baby-changing facilities in both the ladies and gents toilets.
Bass and Flowers, with Boddingtons and Marston's as guests.
♣❀🏠◑👄✂▶ Isle of Wight Wax Works, Animal World, Lilliput Museum of Antique Dolls

Chale

The Wight Mouse Inn
(01983 730431). *On the B3399 Chale to Shorwell road.* This splendid, friendly and welcoming 17thC coaching inn has a warm

and cosy bar, an open fire and a choice of 365 malt whiskeys (once you have sampled their ales). Children's facilities are excellent, with an indoor play area (£1), a bouncy castle, swings, slide, pony rides, toddler trikes and a pets' corner, plus pool, pinball and a juke box. Excellent food, including a children's menu with a free lucky bag. Fine gardens with extensive views over the Downs and the sea. Their adjoining hotel, The Clarendon, commemorates the wreck of a sailing ship of the same name, driven ashore at Blackgang in 1836. The oak beams in the hotel were salvaged from the wreck. Visitors have included Queen Ena of Spain, Earl Mountbatten, Alexander Fleming and Edward Heath. Live entertainment each evening, and Punch & Judy and a magician occasionally during the summer.

Boddingtons, Gale's, Marston's, Theakston, Wadworth and Whitbread, with guests such as Adnams, Greene King and Timothy Taylor.

Blackgang Chine, beaches, local church

Newport

Wheatsheaf Hotel

16 St Thomas Square (01983 523865). A handsome 17thC town hostelry, where Oliver Cromwell once held parliament. It has open fires and a friendly atmosphere. *Boddingtons, Flowers and Wadworth.*

Niton

Buddle Inn

St Catherine's Road (01983 730243). *Off the main Niton to Ventnor Undercliffe road. Follow signs to the lighthouse.* One of the island's earliest pubs, once run as a farm and first granted a licence in 1850. The bars are rich with stone floors and oak beams. Pool, bar billiards and shove ha'penny are played here.

Bass, Brakspear, Flowers, Greene King, Theakston and Young's, with guests such as Adnams making a total of about 15 real ales on offer, along with Hamstead Isle of Wight cider. Lighthouse

Northwood

The Travellers Joy

Pallance Road (01983 298024).

On the Cowes to Thorness road.
This is a well renovated country
inn, which has a fine garden with
swings, slide and a climbing
frame. There is a pool table, and
petanque can also be enjoyed
here.
***Goddards, Theakston, Ringwood
and Ruddles, with guests such as
Fullers and Greene King, and
Godshill real cider.***

Sandown

Culver Haven Inn
Culver Down (01983 406107).
*From Sandown follow signs to
Bembridge. Culver Haven is the
first right-hand turn after the
junction just beyond Yaverland
church.* An isolated and friendly
pub on the top of Culver Cliffs,
enjoying fine sea and coastal
views. Toys are planned for the
garden.
Hall & Woodhouse.

Shorwell

The Crown Inn
Walkers Lane (01983 740293). *On
the Newport to Brighstone road.*
Once associated with smugglers,
this 17thC pub has fine unspoilt
bars, a Jacobean dresser, stone

walls and oak beams, and is situated in a pretty village. The lovely garden has a trout stream, with
a dovecot on an island, and
swings, a slide and a Wendy
house. Good food.
***Boddingtons, Flowers and
Wadworth, with Badger as a
typical guest.***

Ventnor

The Chequers Inn
Niton Road, Rookley (01983
840314). *On the Niton road
between Newport and Godshill.*
There is a flag-stoned public bar
in this characterful pub at the
heart of the island, set in an idyllic spot with good local walks
and riding facilities. The garden
has a large adventure playground,
bouncy castle, toboggan run,
Wendy house and swings and
slides. The nappy changing area
has baby-wipes and so on. High
chairs and bibs are available.
***Courage, John Smith's,
Marston's and Theakston, with
guests such as Goddards.***

Wootton Bridge

The Cedars Hotel
2 Station Road (01983 882593).

Pool is played here, and the garden is well equipped with a Wendy house, slides, swings and climbing frames. Children are welcome, except in the public bar. You can enjoy a ride on the nearby electric railway, which was built on the island in 1880, and was amongst the first in the world.

Gale's, plus a guest, which varies.

The Wheatsheaf Inn
Bridge Road (01983 760456).
From the ferry turn left and then right into Wheatsheaf lane. Warm and cosy, but deceptively large, this pub welcomes children in the Harbour Lounge and conservatory.

Flowers, Goddards, Theakston and Wadworth.

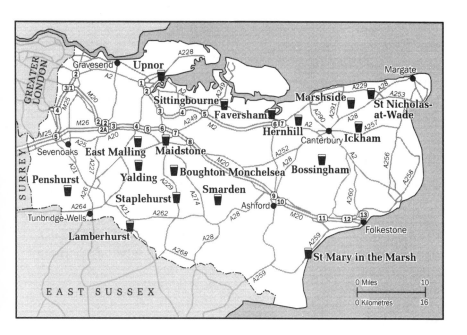

Bossingham

Hop Pocket

The Street (01227 709866). *Off the B2068 (Stone Street) near Stelling Minnis.* A candlelit 19thC pub, where the ceiling is hung with hops. Plenty of games, such as dominoes, dice and shuttlebox, but no pool. A one-acre meadow adjoins the garden, and there is a slide and swings. Children are welcome in the conservatory and dining area.

Harveys and Shepherd Neame, with guests from Fullers, Wadworth and many others. They also keep Engelfield real cider, from Devon.

🐎 ♣ ❀ ⌸ ◑ ⌣

Boughton Monchelsea

The Red House

Hermitage Lane (01622 743986). *Turn south off the B2163 at Marlpit onto Wierton Road. Go over the crossroads, then turn left into East Hall Hill.* This friendly pub has a good choice of real ales and an extensive range of imported bottled beers. There is pool and table football, and a camping and caravan site adjoining.

Excellent choice, including Burton Bridge, Cotleigh,

Eldridge Pope, Greene King, Hop Back, Otter and Viking, with bottled beers such as Chimay, Duval and Hoegaarden Grand Cru.
🐎 ♣ ✿ ◑ ⌁

East Malling

Rising Sun
125 Mill Street (01732 843284). If you are touring the Weald of Kent, or visiting Leeds Castle, this pleasant village local amongst the Kentish orchards makes a pleasant stop.
Goacher's and Shepherd Neame, along with two varying guests.
✿ ◖

Faversham

The Albion Tavern
Front Brents, Faversham Creek (01795 591411). This pub, which is opposite the Shepherd Neame Brewery, has a pleasant airy bar .
Shepherd Neame, plus guests.
✿ ◑ ⌁

The Crown and Anchor
41 The Mall (01795 532812). A friendly welcoming pub on the outskirts of town.
Shepherd Neame.
♣ ◖*not Sat & Sun* ⏱ *20.00*

Hernhill

Red Lion
The Green (01227 751207). *Turn off the A299 Thanet Way to Hernhill.* Standing by the church and the village green, this is an old 14thC pub in a fine village. Boules are played, and the garden has swings, a slide and a Wendy house.
Courage, Hancock's and Shepherd Neame, guests such as Gale's, and Symond's Scrumpy Jack cider.
♣ ✿ 🏯 ◑ ⌁

Ickham

The Duke William
The Street (01227 721308). *About 1½ miles off the A257 Canterbury to Sandwich road.* This 16thC pub has a bright bar with a large open fireplace and a refreshing no-smoking conservatory, where families are welcome. There is also a pleasant garden.
Adnams, Fuller's, Shepherd Neame and Young's, with various guests.
🐎 ♣ ✿ ◑ *not Sun evening or Mon lunch* ⌁ ⚄

Lamberhurst

Brown Trout

Lamberhurst Down (01892 890312). *Off the A21 south of Lamberhurst, near Tunbridge Wells.* A very pretty pub with a fine sign and its front covered with flowers, opposite what were once oast houses. The garden has trampolines and swings.
Fuller's and King & Barnes, and Symond's Scrumpy Jack cider.
🏵 🎖 ◑ ⌣

Maidstone

The Ringlestone Inn

Ringlestone Road, nr Harrietsham (01622 859900). *From the M20, junction 8, turn left off the A20 through Hollingsbourne, and turn right at the crossroads at the top of the hill.* Dating from 1533, when it was a hospice for monks, it became an ale house in 1815. An inscription, carved on the oak sideboard in 1632 states 'A Ryghte Joyouse and welcome greetynge to ye all'. It is not out of place in this friendly and comfortable medieval tavern, warmed with log fires. The candle-lit dining room, a later addition, contains tables made from timbers from an 18thC Thames barge. Excellent food, traditional pies and fruit wines. Eight acres of landscaped gardens, with ponds and a hop-scotch area.
Fullers, Greene King, Harveys, Shepherd Neame, with guests such as Adnams and Badger, and Biddenden's real cider
🏵 🎖 ◑ ⌣ 🛏

Marshside

Gate Inn

Chislet (01227 860498). Featured in the 'Good Beer Guide' for over 20 years, this is a very fine, and lively, country pub. Duck racing, cricket, rugby, food theme evenings and an August beer festival are just some of the activities here. Spare plates are offered so that you can share food with your children.
Shepherd Neame, with bottle conditioned Spitfire.
🐗 🏵 🎖 ◑ ⌣ 🍴 ⏰ *20.30*

Penshurst

The Bottle House

Coldharbour Road (01892 870306). A very fine old pub, built in 1492. It has a polished copper bar, oak beams and an open fire.
Ind Coope, Harveys and Larkins.
🏵 ◑ ⌣ 🔻 ⏱ *21.00*

St Mary in the Marsh

The Star Inn

(01797 362139). On the wide-open expanse of Romney Marsh you will find this friendly and attractive 15thC village pub. *Shepherd Neame and Wadworth*.

St Nicholas-at-Wade

Bell Inn

The Street (01843 847250). With plenty of nooks and crannies, this is a fine pub with Tudor origins. Children are welcome in the snug and games room, where pool and bar billiards are played. *Bass, Bateman's, Flowers and Wadworth, with guests such as Greene King and Young's*.

Sittingbourne

The Ship Inn

22 East Street (01795 425087). This popular and sociable town local has two bars. Pool and video games are played here. *Shepherd Neame and Theakston*.

🐎♣ ◖ *evening meals to order* ☕ ▽

Smarden

The Bell Inn

Bell Lane, Smarden Bell (01233 770283). A large 15thC Kentish inn with a fine interior of low beams and three separate bars. *Boddingtons, Fullers, Goacher's, Harveys, Marston's, Shepherd Neame and Theakston, with guests such as Ringwood, and Biddenden real cider*.

🐎♣❀◖☕✄🚗▶ Classic car rally each month

Staplehurst

The Lord Raglan

Chart Hill Road (01622 843747). *Off the A229, 2 miles north of Staplehurst*. This traditional country pub has log fires in winter. There is an orchard garden. *Goacher's and Harveys, with Badger and Hop back as typical guests, and Biddenden real cider during the summer*.

❀◖ *not Sun eve* ☕

Upnor

The Tudor Rose

29 High Street (01634 715305). A 400-year-old country pub right next to Upnor Castle and overlooking the River Medway. *Shepherd Neame, Swale, Viking*

and Young's, with Goacher's as a typical guest, and Young's bottle conditioned Ram Rod.
 not Sun or Mon eve

Yalding

Woolpack Inn
Benover Road (01892 730356).

There is quite literally a skeleton in the cupboard of this 17thC country pub, which also has an unusual double-inglenook in the main bar area. Children are welcome in the dining area.
Shepherd Neame.

Ashton-under-Lyne

The Station
2 Warrington Street (0161 330 6776). This Victorian pub has a pleasing railway theme. Children are welcome in the conservatory. *Boddingtons and Marston's, with as many as ten guest beers each week, draught and bottled.*
🏃 ❀ ◖ ♡

Belmont

Black Dog
2-4 Church Street (01204 811218). *Take the A666 from Bolton, turning left onto the A675.* A traditional homely village pub with plenty of rooms, all decorated with antiques. There is no jukebox: only classical music is played. Pool and shove ha'penny are available. *Holts.*
♣ ❀ ◖ *not Mon or Tue eve* ♡ 🛏

Bilsborrow

Owd Nell's Tavern
Guy's Thatched Hamlet (01995 640010). *Leave the M6 at junction 32 and head north on the A6, following the brown signs.* An extensive thatched canal-side tavern which is part of a pub/restau-

rant/motel complex around Mitton Hall, built circa 1514. A ring game, and bowls, can be played in the large garden, and there is a cricket ground. Every Saturday Uncle Martin and Guy's Friends entertain. *Boddingtons, Jennings, Timothy Taylor and Wadworth, with guests such as Brakspear, Flowers and Mitchell's.*
🎠 ♣ ❀ 🏠 ◖ ♡ ✄ 🛏 ♉
▶ Lancaster Canal

Blackley

The Pleasant Inn
Chapel Lane (0161 740 3391). A small three-room community pub in a fine old village. *Robinson's.*
❀ 🕐 20.00

Boothstown

The Moorings
Quayside Close (0161 702 6251). *From junction 13 on the M62 follow signs for Boothstown.* Overlooking the Bridgewater Canal, this is a large new pub splendidly situated on the edge of the Bridgewater Park Nature Reserve. Children should keep clear of bar areas. There is a baby-changing room. *Boddingtons, Cains and*

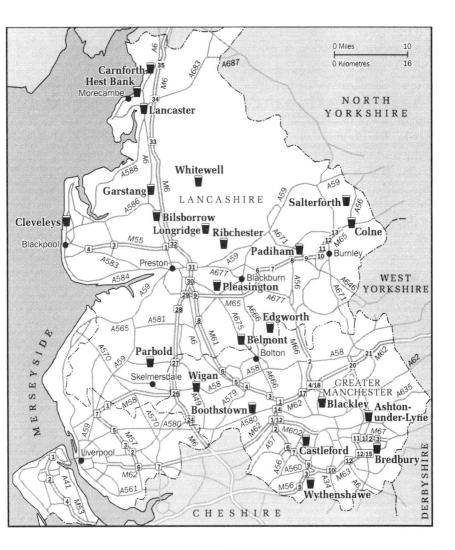

Greenalls.
❀ ⌸ ◑ ⌣ ✄ ▶ Bridgewater
Canal, Nature Reserve

Bredbury

Arden Arms
Ashton Road (0161 430 2589).
*From junction 15 on the M63
head towards Denton. The pub is
on the A6017.* This pub is situat-

ed in a green belt area, where people can walk in the Tame Valley, with the charming Peak Forest Canal not far away. 'It is a little bit of country between the major towns of Stockport and Hyde'. Children are welcome, as long as they are properly supervised. Pool is played here, and the garden has a slide, swings and a climbing frame.
Robinson's.
♣ ❀ 田 ◖◷ *20.00*

Broadheath

The Old Packet House
Navigation Road (0161 929 1331). *On the A56 just outside Altrincham, travelling towards Manchester.* Open fires, exposed bricks and timbers create a fine atmosphere in this inn, which dates from the 17thC. It takes its name from the packet boat services which used to operate close by, on the Bridgewater Canal.
Boddingtons, Webster's and Wilson's.
❀ ◖ *not Sun eve* ⌣ ✂ ⊨
▶ Bridgewater Canal

Carnforth

Royal Hotel
15 Emesgate Lane, Silverdale (01524 701266). Friendly village

local with a pool table, and swings, a slide and a climbing frame in the garden.
John Smith's, with guests such as Courage, Marston's and Theakston.
🐎 ♣ ❀ 田 ◖ ⌣ ⊨ ▽

Castleford

Dukes 92
14 Castle Street (0161 839 8646). There are canals on three sides of this very well situated and pleasant pub, which not surprisingly has a canalside terrace. There is children's entertainment on each summer Sunday.
Boddingtons and Timothy Taylor, with a guest beer changing fortnightly.
❀ ◖ ♗ ▶ Canalscape, locks, lift bridges and boats

Cheadle

Queens Arms
177 Stockport Road (0161 428 3081). A traditional pub with plenty of rooms, which can get busy at lunchtime. Plenty of family events, including a children's quiz, a 'conker knock-out', and a Guy Fawkes party. The large garden has playthings.
Robinsons.
🐎 ❀ 田 ✂ ◷ *20.30*

Cleveleys

The Royal
North Promenade (01253 852143). At one time a seafront hotel, this is now a pub divided into four areas, with one for games. The family room is actually a sea-front sun lounge, so you can watch all the outside activities from here. *Boddingtons and Theakston, with a different guest each week.*
○ ☞ ⏱ *21.30* ▶ The seaside

Colne

The Hare & Hounds
Black Lane Ends, Skipton Old Road (01282 863070). *2 miles beyond Colne when travelling towards Skipton.* This is a fine pub with a warm atmosphere and open fires, serving good food and excellent beer. *Timothy Taylor.*
♣ ❀ ○ *not Tues* ☞ ⏱ *22.00*

Edgworth

Strawbury Duck
Overshores Road, Entwistle (01204 852013) *Off the Edgeworth to Darwen old road.* Isolated but busy old pub next to the station. Pool can be played

here.
Flowers, Moorhouse's, Ruddles and Timothy Taylor, with guests such as Greene King, Cains, Theakston and others.
🐴 ♣ ❀ ○ *not Mon lunch* ✗ 🛏

Garstang

Kenlis Arms Hotel
Wray Lane, Barnacre (01995 603307). This was once a shooting lodge, then the station hotel (but the station closed!) and now it is a sociable country local. The garden has a large lawn and a climbing castle. *John Smith's and Tetley.*
♣ ❀ ▦ ○ ☞ 🛏 ⏱ *21.00*

Th 'Owd Tithebarn
The Wharf, Church Street (01995 604486). *Half a mile from the A6 between Preston and Lancaster.* An ivy-covered building completed in 1710 with open fires, a flagstone floor and plenty of beams, built on the site of a tithe barn dating from 1110. There is a 35-foot long table in the restaurant, which has pews salvaged from a Blackpool church. Both the restaurant and bar are decorated with hundreds of farming implements. At Christmas time they have the tallest indoor Christmas tree in Lancashire. A large patio fronts the canal. Children are

welcomed in the restaurant.
Mitchell's.
❀ ◑ ☂ ▽ ▶ Lancaster Canal,
Christmas tree (at Christmas!)

Hest Bank

Hest Bank
2 Hest Bank Lane (01524 824339).
A very fine old coaching inn
beside the Lancaster Canal,
which dates from 1554, and still
retains the window for a guiding
light, showing the way across the
sands. It has sheltered monks and
abbots, soldiers and highwaymen,
dukes and princes. Excellent
food, with a separate children's
menu.
*Boddingtons and Marston's, with
Gale's and Jennings as typical
guests.*
♣ ❀ ▦ ◑ ☂ ▶ Lancaster Canal,
ducks.

Lancaster

Farmhouse Tavern
Scale Hall, Morecambe Road
(01524 69255). *On the left-hand
side of the road heading towards
Morecambe.* This is a very handsome and highly recommended
inn, in a 350-year-old building,
with comfortable bars and log
fires, decorated with the wood
panelling from a luxury German

liner, decommissioned at the turn
of the century. With the feel of a
baronial mansion (note the
antlers above the fireplace, and
stained glass), it represents the
product of much hard work and
worry for ex-soldier Stephen
Hunt and his wife Diane, who
took it on when it was the Scale
Hall Restaurant, and converted it
to its present fine state by January
1995. Since then it has gone from
strength to strength. Pool and
dominoes are played here, and in
the garden you will find a boules
area, a tree house, swings, a slide
and other amusements. There is
also a conservatory, and a nappy-
changing mat in the ladies toilet.
Good traditional farmhouse cooking.
*Boddingtons and Marston's, with
guests from Flowers, Wadworth
and others.*
🐴 ♣ ❀ ▦ ◑ ☂ ✂ 🛏 ⏱ 21.00

Longridge

Alston Arms
Inglewhite Road (01772 783331).
This splendid family pub is beautifully decked with flowers in
summer. The garden has a double
decker bus: eating on the upper
deck, play on the lower, and a
tractor, an adventure play area
and some small farm animals.

Lion and Theakston, plus a guest.

Padiham

Hare & Hounds
58 West Street (01282 774749). A small, friendly and very old pub remote in the Pennines.
Tetley.

Parbold

Railway
1 Station Road (01257 462917). Typical friendly village local, with a pool table, dominoes and board games.
Burtonwood.
♣ ✿ ◖ *meals at other times on request* ☞

Pleasington

The Railway
Victoria Road (01254 201520). *Just half a mile from the A674 Preston Old Road.* Quiet and pleasant, this village pub was converted from a farmhouse in 1870. Crown green bowls is played here.
Theakston, Wilson's and Younger's, with Boddingtons and Tetley as typical guests, and bottle conditioned *Norman's Conquest.*
✿ ◖ *not Sun eves, and bar menu only Tue, Wed & Thur eves during winter* ☞ ⏰ *21.00*

Ribchester

White Bull Hotel
Church Street (01254 878303). There is a swing and climbing frame in the garden of this pub.
Boddingtons, Flowers and Marston's.
✿ ▤ ◖ ▽ ▶ Site of 1stC Roman Fort, and museum

Salterforth

Anchor Inn
Salterforth Lane (01282 813186). An interesting traditional pub, where a second building was built on top of the first – so where you now drink was once bedrooms with a buried pub and stalactites in what is now the cellar. The garden has slides, swings and a sand pit.
Bass, John Smith's, Theakston and Worthington.
♣ ✿ ▤ ◖ ☞

Stockport

Arden Arms
23 Millgate (0161 480 2185). *In the town centre, near the Asda car park.* A very fine traditional town-centre pub, with a collection of grandfather clocks and a splendid snug. There are children's toys, pets, and horses in the stables, with pool, cribbage and dominoes played in the bar. *Robinson's, with bottle conditioned Old Tom.*
♣ ✿ ⊞ ◑ ➦ ⏰ *19.30*

Whitewell

The Inn at Whitewell
Forest of Bowland (01200 448222). A large and homely country house inn, with cosy furnishings and open fires. *Boddingtons and Marston's.*
✿ ◑ ➦ ⊨

Wigan

Swan & Railway
80 Wallgate (01942 495032). *Opposite Wigan railway station.*

This traditional Victorian pub has been splendidly renovated. Children are welcome in the snug and restaurant. *Banks's, with Marston's as a guest.*
⚓ ◖ ⊨ ▶ Wigan Pier Complex

Wythenshawe

Airport Hotel
Ringway Road (0161 437 2551). This multi-roomed pub has two advantages for families. It makes a change from the airport lounge if you are waiting for a flight, and it also offers wonderful views of the aircraft taking off and landing, and taxiing past. Naturally there is a fair bit of noise associated with all of this, but young people are rarely bothered. Children are welcome in the Runway Room, and there is a climbing frame and tree house outside. *Robinson's, in bottles as well.*
🐎 ♣ ✿ ⊞ ◑ ➦ ⊨
▶ Aeroplanes

LEICESTERSHIRE

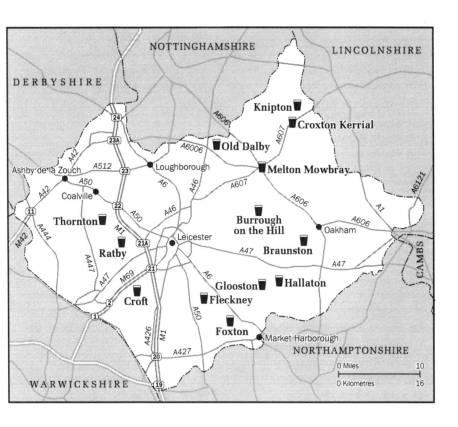

Braunston

Blue Ball

6 Cedar Street (01572 722135).
This handsome 17thC pub stands
at the centre of the village, opposite the church. Inside there are
oak beams, cosy log fires and a
friendly atmosphere.
*Courage, Ruddles and John
Smith's, with guests such as
Theakston.*

Burrough on the Hill

Stag & Hounds

4 Main Street (01664 454181). A
traditional and homely country
pub, with open fires. There are
rabbits, guinea pigs and an aviary
in the garden.
*Ruddles and John Smith's, with
guests such as Courage and
Wadworth.*

Croft

The Heathcote Arms

Hill Street (01455 282439). Up on a hill overlooking the village, this 300-year-old pub extends a friendly welcome to both locals and visitors.

Everards, with guests from Gale's and Greene King.
❀ ◖ ☙ ⏱ 21.00

Croxton Kerrial

Peacock Inn

1 School Lane (01476 870324). Pool and skittles can be played in the games room here.

Adnams, Bateman's, Courage and Fullers, with Mansfield and Charles Wells as guests.
♣ ❀ ◑ ☙ ⅟ ⌸ ⏱ 21.00

Fleckney

The Old Crown

High Street (0116 240 2223). Books line the walls of the bar in this friendly and welcoming traditional village pub. Skittles, pool and table skittles are played here, and there is a bouncy castle and play house in the garden. Visiting clowns, face painting and games provide entertainment from time to time.

Adnams and Everards, with Bateman's and Theakstons as guests. Bottle conditioned Everards Tiger is also kept.
♣ ❀ ▦ ◑ *not sun evening* ☙ ⏱
21.00

Foxton

The Black Horse

94 Main Street (01858 545250). Very handy for exploring the remarkable flight of locks, the remains of the inclined plane boat lift and museum on the nearby canal, this pub is noted for its fine selection of home-cooked food. The very large garden contains sheep, goats, chickens and other animals.

Marston's, with fortnightly guests.
❀ ▦ ◑ ☙ ⅟ ▶ Grand Union Canal, with Foxton Locks, Boat Lift and Museum nearby

Glooston

The Old Barn Inn

St Andrews Lane (01858 545215). This is a very fine 16thC rural inn, with oak beams, an open fire, wooden tables and chairs and no piped music. Excellent seasonal food is cooked to order. Children are welcome in the bar, sitting at a table. Under-eights are allowed in the restaurant on Sundays

only. There are roadside tables during the summer.
Morland and Theakston, with Adnams, Bateman's, Everards, Fuller's, Hook Norton and others as guests.
 weekends only ❱ not Sun evening ☞ ✂ 🛏

Hallaton

The Bewicke Arms
1 Eastgate (01858 555217). A 400-year-old thatched country inn, situated on the village green. Inside there is a log fire with copper kettles and wooden settles. The garden has a climbing frame and slide. Baby-changing facilities in the disabled toilet.
Marston's and Ruddles, with guests such as Bass, Greene King and Mansfield.
⚘ 🏠 ◑ ☞ ▽

Knipton

The Red House Inn
6 Croxton Road (01476 870352). *Off the A607 at Croxton Kerrial.* This is a sturdy 250-year-old former hunting lodge with a fine conservatory. Pets corner and aviary in the garden.
Tetley and Marston's, with guests such as Fuller's, Mitchell's and Wadworth.

 Belvoir Castle

Melton Mowbray

The Crown
10 Burton Street (01664 64682). This popular two-roomed traditional town pub welcomes children at lunchtimes.
Everards, with guests such as Greene King and Elgood's.
❌ ♣ ⚘ (*not Sun or Mon*

Old Dalby

Crown Inn
Debdale Hill (01664 823134). *Off the A46 Leicester to Newark road.* Beers are served from the wood in this cosy 17thC pub which has small intimate rooms, each with a coal fire during the winter. Children are welcome, except in the bar area.
Bateman's and Marston's, with Greene King, Timothy Taylor and Smiles as guests.
🐎 ⚘ ◑ ✂

Ratby

The Plough Inn
Burroughs Road (0116 239 2103). A large and very old pub, with a restaurant.
Bateman's and Marston's.
❌ ⚘ 🏠 ◑ ☞

Thornton (Coalville)

Bricklayers Arms

213 Main Street (01530 230808).
Traditional village local overlooking Thornton Trout Fisheries.
Part of the building dates from
the 16thC. The bar is quarry tiled:
the lounge is cosy. There is
wheelchair access around the
back. In the garden are a climbing
frame, swings, slide and petanque
area.
Everards.

LINCOLNSHIRE

Alford

Half Moon Inn
25-28 West Street (01507 463477). In a craft-oriented market town which is ideally placed for exploring The Wolds, this is a popular and welcoming pub *Bass, Everards, Morland and Worthington, with a choice of guests.*
♣ ✿ ◑ *not Sun or Mon evenings* ✆ ⊁

Caythorpe

Red Lion Inn
62 High Street (01400 272632). A friendly 17thC country inn renowned for its 'beer and curry' festivals. Bar skittles, solitaire and shove ha'penny can be played here. There is a large cleanable bench in the ladies toilet suitable for baby-changing. *Bass and Bateman's, with lots of guests such as Eccleshall, Glentworth and Highwood, and Westons draught cider.*
🐴 ♣ ✿ ◑ *not Mon lunch* ✆ ⊁ ▽☼ 21.00

Cleethorpes

Kings Royal
20-21 Kingsway (01472 691012). *On the seafront, between the pier* and the leisure centre. Fine seafront pub, with a Victorian-style theatre bar. *Ruddles, Theakston and Younger's, with Bateman's, Shepherd Neame and Charles Wells as typical guests.*
✿ ◑ ✆ 🛏☼ 20.00

Deeping St James

The Goat Inn
155 Spalding Road, Frognall (01778 347629). *One and a half miles from Market Deeping on the Spalding Road.* The patio of this friendly pub is draped with hop and grape vines. Standing in 1½ acres of grounds, it welcomes children in all areas except the lounge bar. These areas are all 'no-smoking', but note that this pub does get busy at weekends. The garden has an 'action tree', swings, slide and an adventure frame. There is also a special area for the under 5s. Varied menu, and a separate selection for children. *Since June 1993 they have had over 900 different real ales. Guests come from independents, micros or brew pubs all over Great Britain. So you should find something you will like!*
✿ ▦ ◑ ✆ ⊁

Dogdyke

The Packet Inn

Belle Isle (01526 342294). *Follow signs for 'The Battle of Britain' and continue to the sharp bend in the road.* Parts of this pub are at least 300 years old, and it was at one time a stopping-point for the packet boats which plied the river. There is a pleasant waterside patio, a large garden with swings, and free fishing. Good choice of food, including some Indian dishes. Pool and dominoes are played here.
Theakston.
♣ ❀ ⌸ ◑ ➷ ⅄ ▶ River Witham, and Tattershall Castle is not far

Dyke

The Wishing Well Inn

Main Street (01778 422970). *One mile north of Bourne, off the A15.* This fine country inn does indeed feature a well, inside the restaurant. Oak beams, stone walls and plenty of brass complement the huge inglenooks. The garden has a children's activity centre, and a beer festival is held each August in the adjoining paddock. Excellent food.
Everards, Greene King and their own 'Going Down Well', alongside a splendid array of guest

ales – over 800 so far!
❀ ⌸ ◑ ➷ ⅄ 🛏

Freiston

Castle Inn

Haltoft End (01205 760393). Handy if you are travelling near Boston. The garden contains some imaginative play equipment.
Bateman's, plus a guest.
❀ ◑ ➷ 🛏

Grantham

Castle Inn

33 Vicarage Lane, Eaton (01476 870949). *Not easy to find, but it's adjacent to the church and cemetery.* A fine old rural pub with a 3 acre grass field suitable for caravans and camping, and with sweeping views over the Vale of Belvoir. Skittles and pool can be played in the games room, and there are a slide and swings in the garden. Good walks in the area.
Mansfield, with guests such as Hook Norton.
🐴 ♣ ❀ ⌸ ◑ ➷ ⅄ 🛏

Horbling

Plough Inn

4 Spring Lane (01529 240263).

LINCOLNSHIRE

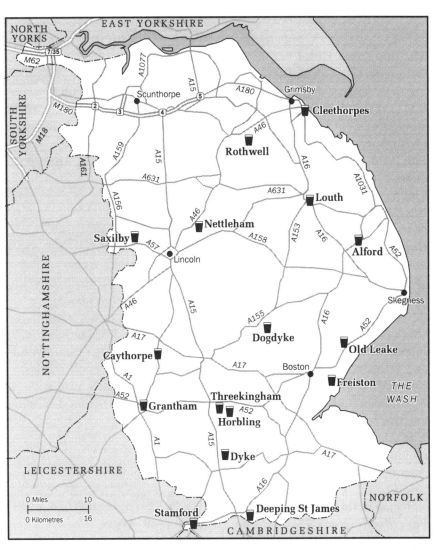

Look out for Fred, the friendly resident ghost who wanders around this late 17thC building in search of a late drink. There are baby changing facilities in the disabled toilet.

Bateman's, with Shepherd Neame, Wadworth's and Worthington as typical guests.
♣ ⚘ ◐ ⌣ ▽

Louth

Masons Arms Hotel

Cornmarket (01507 609525). Lovingly and carefully restored, this former 18thC posting inn serves excellent food: indeed it has an entry in CAMRA's *Good Pub Food* guide. There is a large annexe in the ladies toilet, handy for changing baby.

Bass, Bateman's, Highwood and Marston's, with guests such as Cains, Fullers, Charles Wells and Theakston.
◐ ⌣ ⅄ 🛏 ▽ ⓣ *21.00*

Wheatsheaf Inn

62 Westgate (01507 601968). A charming and traditional 16thC inn situated in a Georgian terrace, and warmed by coal fires. It was National Wine Pub 1989/90, and holds an annual 'Beer 'n' Bangers' Festival during late May each year – featured sausages have included Stilton & Leek, Aberdeen Angus with Plum and Grimsby Smokey. Children are welcome in the lounge bar.

Bass, Boddingtons, Flowers and Tipsy Toad (from Jersey), with Black Sheep, Orkney, Wood's and Woodforde's as typical guests.
🎏 ❀ ◖ *not Sun lunch* ⌣ ⓣ *21.00*

Nettleham

The White Hart

14 High Street (01522 751976). This very handsome pub incorporates a restaurant. Children are welcome in the Beckside Room, and pool is played.

Bateman's, with Bass, Marston's and other guests.
🎏 ♣ ❀ ◐ ⌣

Old Leake

The Bricklayers Arms

Wainfleet Road (01205 870657). *On the A52 Boston to Skegness Road.* Standing under wide Lincolnshire skies, The Bricklayers is a large friendly pub with an open fire. Pool, skittles, dominoes and bull's nose are played here, and the food is home cooked.

Bateman's.
♣ ❀ ◐ ⌣ ⅄

Rothwell

Nickerson Arms

(01472 371300). *Off the A46 at Caistor.* A charming, beamy village inn warmed by a cosy coal fire. À la carte restaurant. Swings and play-park in the garden.

Bateman's and Courage, with guests such as Fuller's and

Marston's. Belgian Trappist bottled beers are also kept.
 21.00

Saxilby

Anglers
65 High Street (01522 702200).
Just up the road from the
Fossdyke Navigation, this basic
but sociable pub has skittles, cribbage and dominoes.
*Home and Theakston, with
guests from Scottish Courage,
Charles Wells and others.*
Fossdyke Navigation

Stamford

The George of Stamford
71 St Martins (01780 755171).
Built on the site of a Norman hospice, this is a fine 16thC coaching
inn. The crypt is under the cocktail bar. A friendly place, it welcomes children in the York Bar.
The ladies toilet has a chaise
longue, handy for changing baby.
Adnams and Fuller's.

Threekingham

Three Kings Inn
Saltersway (01529 240249). *On
the A52 mid-way between Boston
and Grantham.* The pub, and the
village, are named to commemorate three Danish Chieftains
killed in the 9thC Battle of Stow
Green close by. Pool can be
played here.
*Bass, with guests such as
Adnams and Robinson's.*
20.00

E7

The Old Spotted Dog

212 Upton Lane (0181 472 1794).
During the 15thC this building
was once used by Henry VIII as
kennels for his hunting pack, and
there is a legend that it was connected to Boleyn Castle, the home
of his beloved Anne, by a tunnel.
The castle is of course no more,
its site occupied by Upton Park,
home of West Ham United
Football Club. The oldest secular
building still standing in
Newham, it became a pub in the
early 17thC, and was associated
with local highwaymen, since
this area was at the time part of
Epping Forest. The Bow Street
Runners, who pursued these mis-
creants, also used the pub, and
their spy-hole survives in the Dog
Bar, an ancient place with a stone
floor and a cooking range. At the
back of the building is a mid-
Victorian extension built as tea-
rooms for the extensive grounds
which were used by the local
gentry, who played football and
cricket here. Clapton Football
Club have occupied these
grounds since 1870. The bar here
contains many old prints, and
leads to the conservatory, where
children are welcomed. Bar billiards are played, and there is

music on Thursday and Friday
evenings.
*Courage and Marston's, plus
two guests, which change weekly. They also keep two guest
farmhouse scrumpies.*
🏃 ♣ ❀ 🈲 ◑ ⌂ ♀ ▶ West Ham
United Football Club matches

E9

Falcon & Firkin

360 Victoria Park Road (0181 985
0693). When your children have
fed the ducks, and run their legs
off, in Victoria Park, this is a
pleasant place to relax and enjoy
some of their house ales. Table
football, chess and Jenga can be
played here.
House ales, plus Dogbolter.
♣ ❀ ◑ ▶ Victoria Park and the
canal

Greenford

Black Horse

425 Oldfield Lane North (0181
578 1384). Regular appearances
in the Good Beer Guide and a
charming canal-side position
ensure that this handsome pub
maintains its popularity.
Cribbage, dominoes and pool are
played here. Children are welcome in the food area. The huge
garden has a play area, and boun-

cy castle on summer weekends. *Fuller's, with guests such as Cains, and some nice bottle conditioned ales from Fuller's.* ♣❀❖◐☞✁▶ Grand Union Canal

Hayes

Blue Anchor
Printing House Lane (0181 569 3396). This grand half-timbered and tile-hung canalside pub welcomes children in the back bar. *Fuller's, Theakston, Wadworth and Young's.* ➤♣❀◐☞✁⏰ *20.00* ▶ Grand Union Canal

NW1

The Albert
11 Princess Road (0171 722 1886). Very handy for refreshment if you are visiting London Zoo, Regent's Park and the Grand Union Canal or Camden Lock. Children are welcome in the conservatory, and you will receive a friendly London welcome. *Bass, Fuller's and Greene King.* ➤❀◐☞✁⏰ *leave before it gets very late!* ▶ London Zoo, Regent's Park, Grand Union Canal, Camden Lock

Old Isleworth

The Castle Inn
18 Upper Square (0181 560 3615). Built prior to 1930, this building replaced an earlier pub which served nearby Isleworth Docks, on the Thames. It is a handsome place, with a long-standing Good Beer Guide entry. There is a large comfortable bar, a games room, and a conservatory where children are welcome. *Young's.* ❀◑▶*Mon-Fri* ☞⏰ *19.00*

SE22

The Grove Tavern
522 Lordship Lane, East Dulwich (0181 693 3661). *At the corner of the South Circular Road and Lordship Lane.* Just half a mile from the Horniman Museum, so a handy stop if you have been for a visit. There is quite an emphasis on food, and in this respect a wide choice is offered for children. Children are welcome in the restaurant. On the first Saturday of each month there are entertainers, and children eat free. *Bass, with guests such as Fuller's and Ruddles.* ◐☞✁♣

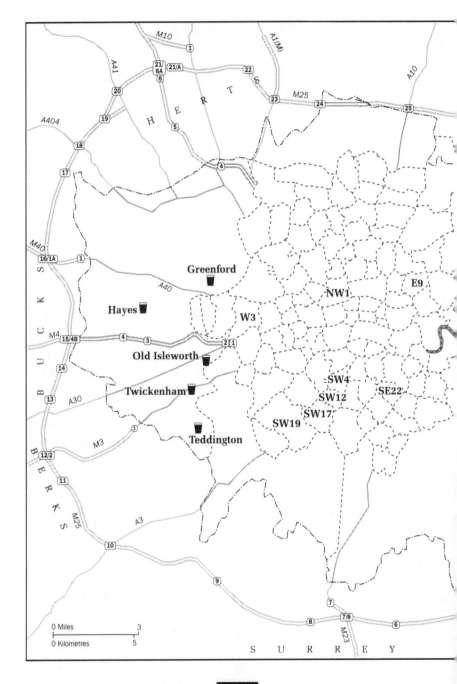

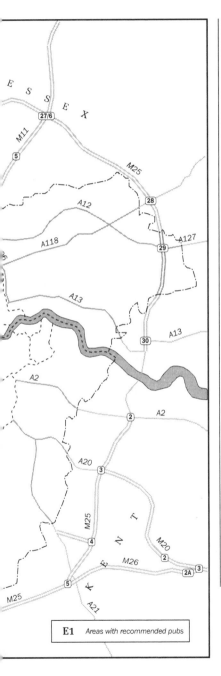

E1   Areas with recommended pubs

SW4

Tim Bobbin

1-3 Lillieshall Road (0171 652 1990). *Off North Street, close to Clapham Common.* Children are welcome in the Garden Room of this well established pub, which has a nice shady part which is especially good for babies. The pub itself has nicely etched windows and is decorated with an array of interesting artifacts. The garden is enclosed and safe, but it is not large.
Adnams and Woodforde's, with Nethergate as a guest.

SW12

The Nightingale

97 Nightingale Lane, Balham (0181 673 1637). You will find this pub between Clapham and Wandsworth Commons, and its atmosphere is that of a friendly and caring country local. Children are welcome in the conservatory.
Young's.
🚶 ❀ ◑ *not Sat or Sun evenings*
☂ ✄

SW17

Prince of Wales
646 Garratt Lane, Tooting (0181 944 0460). Refreshingly consistent two-bar pub, which is comfortable, spacious and handy for Wimbledon Dog Stadium. There is a pin table.
Young's.
♣ ✿ ◖ ▽

SW19

Hand in Hand
6 Crooked Billet, Wimbledon Common (0181 946 5720). Patrons often spill out from the small front garden of this pub onto the common, so if you are with young children, they can run off some of their excess energy while you recoup some of yours. Children are welcome in the family room, which itself looks out over the green.
Young's.
🐴 ✿ ◑ ▶ Wimbledon Common

Teddington

The Anglers Hotel
3 Broom Road (0181 977 4178). Well placed next to Thames Television studios, so who knows, you could end up drinking alongside the rich and

famous. Pool, pin-ball, fruit machines and quiz machines are provided, and there is a fenced-off play area in the large riverside garden, with slides, a climbing frame, bouncy seats and a Postman Pat ride. Nappy changing unit in the disabled toilet.
Burton, Tetley and Young's, with Marston's and Morland as guests.
♣ ✿ 🏠 ◑ ➽ ✂ ▽ ⏰ *21.30*
▶ The River Thames

Twickenham

The White Swan
Riverside (0181 892 2166). An extremely attractive black and white balconied pub right by the riverside, where you can watch the boats go by.
Marston's, Morland and Wadworth.
✿ ◑ ➽ ▶ The River Thames, Marble Hill House

W3

Duke of York
86 Steyne Road (0181 992 0463). Friendly London pub, just off the High Street.
Fuller's, with guests such as Cains, Shepherd Neame, Wadworth and Young's.
🐴 ✿ ◑ ➽ ⏰ *21.00*

NORFOLK

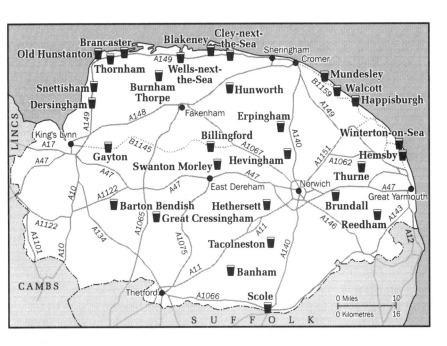

Banham

Banham Cider Shed

The Appleyard, Kenninghall
Road (01953 888593). *Opposite
Banham Zoo.* Cider has been
made here since 1991, using
locally grown fruit to make this
traditional drink in a variety of
blends and styles. Now the adjacent barn has been converted into
a cider and wine bar, built with
redwood pine and brick and furnished with leather and beautiful
antique wooden cider presses,
and warmed by a wood-burning
stove. As well as being able to
enjoy a meal and a drink here,
you can see cider-making during
the season, participate in cider
'talk and taste' sessions, witness
traditional wood turning demon-
strations, or just enjoy a game of
bar billiards or chess. The peaceful cobbled courtyard has antique
oak presses and other artifacts,
and there is a field to run around
in. Monster ploughman's lunch-
es, and cider off-sales. Caravan
and camping close by.
***Adnams and Chalk Hill, plus
bottled Czech Budvar and the
full range of Banham real
ciders***.
♣ ✿ ◑ ▶ Banham Zoo

Barton Bendish

Spread Eagle Country Inn

Church Road (01366 347295). *Off the A1122 between Downham Market and Swaffham.* There are two churches in the village, one of which is thatched. When you have had a look at them, why not visit this charming 17thC inn with log fires and well priced, homely accommodation. Children are welcome in the restaurant. There is a play house and slide in the garden. *Greene King and Marston's, with guests such as Wadworth and Whitbread.*
⚔ ✿ 🏠 ◑ *not Mon lunch* ⌣ ⅄ 🛏️⏱️ *21.00*

Billingford

The Forge Inn

Bintree Road (01362 668720). *Between Fakenham and Dereham.* Once a blacksmith's forge, this long, low brick building is now a quiet and friendly village local, with open fires. Children are welcome in the dining room. *A selection of four real ales is usually available.*
⚔ ✿ 🏠 ◑ *not Mon* ⌣ ⅄

Blakeney

The Kings Arms

Westgate Street (01263 740341). This traditional family-run Norfolk inn has a splendidly tiled roof. There are books and toys for children, and a large, safe garden with swings. *Morland and Woodforde's.*
🐕 ♣ ✿ 🏠 ◑ ⌣ ⅄ 🛏️ ▽ ▶ The seaside, bird-watching

Brancaster

Ship Inn

Coast Road (01485 210333). A fine traditional inn with a wood-panelled bar. There are swings in the garden, and children are welcome in the restaurant. *Flowers, with Greene King and Tetley as guests.*
⚔ ✿ 🏠 ◑ ⌣ 🛏️ ▶ The seaside is nearby

Brundall

The Yare

Station Road (01603 713786). *Next to the railway station.* Brundall is one of the Norfolk Broads favourite cruiser embarkation points, and this pub is a fine watering hole if you are in the area. It is decorated with plenty of local artifacts and pictures relating to these famous water-ways, and there is a sun lounge for long lazy summer afternoons and evenings. Pool and table football are played here.

Courage, John Smith's and Woodforde's, along with Black Sheep, Marston's, Wadworth and other guests.

🐎 ♣ ❀ ◐ ❧ ▶ The Norfolk Broads

Burnham Thorpe

Lord Nelson

Walsingham Road (01328 738241). This village was the birthplace of Lord Nelson in 1758. In 1793 he held a farewell party in this building, which was then known as The Plough, before returning to sea in the 64-gun warship 'Agamemnon'. It remains a very handsome 17thC pub with a stone flagged floor, original wooden settles and *no* bar. Dominoes and shove ha'penny can be played, and there are toys, a climbing frame and basketball in the garden. Children are welcome in all but one bar area.

Greene King and Woodforde's, served straight from the barrel.

🐎 ♣ ❀ 🏠 ◐ ❧ ✄ ❖

Cley-next-the-Sea

George & Dragon Hotel

(01263 740652). This splendid hotel was rebuilt in the Edwardian style in 1897 on the site of an earlier inn. They keep a 'Birds Bible', where sightings of birds rarely seen on Cley marshes and the scrape (lake) are recorded – these include purple heron, crane, night heron, black stork, snowy owl and penduline tit. Good food.

Greene King.

❀ ◐ ❧ 🛏 ▶ Windmill dating from 1713, church, bird-watching

Dersingham

Feathers Hotel

Manor Road (01485 540207). *Just ¼ mile from Sandringham.* A fine Jacobean inn built from locally quarried garstone. It has royal connections, having been visited by the then to be Edward VII. Plenty of dark woodwork, and cosy open fires when the weather is cool. Pool and dominoes can be played. The garden has an ornamental carp pool, a large children's play area, a sand pit, Wendy house and swings.

Adnams and Bass, with guests such as Shepherd Neame, Thwaites and Woodforde's amongst over one hundred each year.

♣ ❀ 🏥 ◑ ↩ 🛏▶ Sandringham (there is a Visitor Centre, and the grounds are open during the summer, if the Royal family isn't there)

Erpingham

The Spread Eagle Inn
Eagle Lane (01263 761591). *Off the A140, 6 miles from Cromer.* This 16thC village pub has a one acre garden with a pavilion. Plenty of games and machines. *Woodforde's.*
🐎♣❀🏥◑↩✄

Gayton

Crown Inn
Lynn Road (01553 636252). Bar billiards are played in this fine village local.
Greene King.
🐎♣❀🏥◑↩✄▽

Great Cressingham

The Olde Windmill Inn
Water End (01760 756232). *Just off the A1065 Swaffham to Brandon road.* A large old country pub, with plenty of beams and cosy open fires, and a spacious conservatory. There are three

family rooms and a games room. Adventure play area, pool and shove ha'penny. Country music Tue evening, jazz & folk on Thur. *Adnams, Bass, Bateman's, Greene King, with two or three guest ales each week, including local brews, national favourites and bottle conditioned real ales.*
🐎♣❀🏥◑↩

Happisburgh

The Hill House
(01692 650004). *On the coast road, near the church. It is pronounced 'Haze-borough'.* Built as a coaching inn during the 16thC, The Hill House has a timbered lounge with a pool area, and an inglenook with a wood-burning stove to keep out the chilly winds. In 1903 Sir Arthur Conan Doyle wrote one of his Sherlock Holmes stories in the pub. During the summer there is a separate children's bar, and this has toys for all ages. You will also find a good range of books in the main bar. There is no road between the pub and the beach, so it is nice and easy to drift between the two. *Adnams and Shepherd Neame, with Burtonwood as a guest.*
🐎♣❀◑↩✄🛏🕙 21.00
▶ The beach

NORFOLK

Hemsby

Kings Head
North Road (01493 730568). This traditional Norfolk pub has a fine garden suitable for families. Children are welcome in the lounge and dining room.
Greene King, Shepherd Neame and John Smith's, and Westons Scrumpy cider.
🏄 🌸 ◑ ➷ ✄ ▶ The seaside

Hethersett

Kings Head
36 Norwich Road (01603 810206). A friendly 17thC ale house with a cosy snug and a beamed lounge with a log fire. Good food is available but 'does not dominate'. Swings and climbing frames.
Courage, Marston's, Morland and John Smith's, with Woodforde's as a guest.
🐎 🌸 🏯 ◑ *not Sun evening* ⏱ 21.00`

Hevingham

Marsham Arms
Holt Road (01603 754268). *Just 4 miles north of Norwich Airport on the B1149 Holt road.* Situated in a splendid part of rural Norfolk, but still handy for Norwich, The Broads and the air-

port, this friendly pub caters well for families, with an attractive room which is decorated in keeping with the rest of the pub. There are facilities for nappy-changing (just ask at the bar) and a slide, swings, see-saw and Wendy house in the garden.
Adnams and Bass, with two guests such as Greene King, Highgate or Morland.
🐎 🌸 🏯 ◑ ➷ ✄ 🛏 ▽

Hunworth

Bluebell
The Green (01263 712300). There is a log fire in this comfortable pub when the weather is chilly. Swings and children's castle in the garden. Children are welcome in the eating areas.
Adnams, Bass and Greene King, with Theakston as a guest.
🏄 🌸 🏯 ◑ ➷

Mundesley

The Royal Hotel
30 Paston Road (01263 720096). An inglenook fireplace and leather chairs add to the atmosphere in this cosy pub.Children are welcome in the lounge.
Adnams and Greene King, with Badger & Flowers as guests.
🏄 🌸 ◑ ➷ ✄ 🛏

Mundford

Crown Hotel
Crown Road (01842 878233). A handsome traditional 17thC inn with a large open fireplace in its beamed bar.
Courage, Theakston and Woodforde's, with guests such as Everards, Iceni and Scottish Courage.
♣ ❀ ◑ ⌒ 🛏

Old Hunstanton

The Ancient Mariner Inn
Le Strange Arms Hotel, Golf Course Road (01485 534411). Nautical decor, bare boards and family rooms. The garden has swings, a slide and a climbing frame.
Adnams and Bass, with guests such as Bateman's, Mansfield and Theakston.
🐂 ❀ 🏯 ◑ ⌒ ✄ 🛏 ▶ The seaside, bird-watching

Reedham

The Reedham Ferry Inn
Ferry Road (01493 700429). *By the river, on the B1140 between Acle and Beccles.* Right by the famous chain ferry, this friendly pub, with its riverside patio, is popular with boaters during the summer. There are baby-changing facilities in the ladies toilet.
Adnams and Woodforde's, with Elgood's and Ruddles as guests.
🐂 ❀ ◑ ⌒ ✄ ▽ ▶ The Broads, boats

Scole

Scole Inn
Norwich Road (01379 740481). *Halfway between Norwich and Ipswich on the A140.* A fine 17thC coaching inn of great character, which can name Charles II and Nelson amongst its past patrons. Fine fireplaces, oak tables, oak settles and an iron-studded door.
Adnams, with guests from Charles Wells, Shepherd Neame and Marston's.

Snettisham

The Rose & Crown
Old Church Road (01485 541382). Just a stone's throw away from some of west Norfolk's most beautiful beaches, the Rose & Crown makes an excellent stop (or stay) if you are exploring this area. Dating from the 14thC, it is an inn of great character, with all you would expect within the three bars: open log fires, beamy

ceilings, old brick walls and a fine collection of old tools and antique prints. During the summer you can watch your food being cooked on the barbecue in the Garden Room. There is also a large play area in the garden, with swings and two forts. A wall-mounted nappy-changing unit will be found in the ladies toilet.
Adnams, Bass and Woodforde's, with Wolf's as a guest, and Shepherd Neame in bottles.
🐎🕸🎖◑👓🍴🛏▽▶ The seaside

Swanton Morley

Darbys Freehouse
1 Elsing Road (01362 637647). *On the B1147 in the centre of Swanton Morley.* Fine family pub in two beautifully converted cottages with beamed ceilings and a log fire: the eight hand-pumps at the bar make a heartwarming sight. It is part of Park Farm, which has holiday accommodation, excellent walks and fishing. Horse riding is available locally. A children's Christmas party is held. Caravan and camp-site nearby.
Adnams, Badger and Woodforde's with guest ales such as Robinson's, Wadworth

and Wychwood's.
🐎🕸🎖◑👓🍴🛏▶ Fine church nearby

Tacolneston

The Pelican
Norwich Road (01508 489521). The single bar has a welcoming open fire. In the garden you will find aviaries, and there are also rabbits, chickens, climbing frames and a slide.
Flowers and Wadworth, with Tetley as a guest.
🐎🕸🎖◑👓🍴⏱ 21.00

Thornham

The Lifeboat Inn
Ship Lane (01485 512236). *6 miles east of Hunstanton on the A149. Take the first left in the village.* Much of the original character of this old inn has been retained in the cosy Smugglers Bar. 'Penny-in-the-hole', a game dating from the 1600s, can be played here. Indeed, it is a fine 16thC pub, with welcoming open fires when the weather is cold. Fine views across Thornham Harbour.
Adnams, Greene King and Woodforde's, with guests such as Bass, Shepherd Neame and Tolly Cobbold, and Westons real

cider.

🐎 ♣ ❀ ◑ ☕ 🛏 ▶ The seaside, Holme Nature Reserve, windsurfing, dinghy sailing

Thurne

The Lion Inn

(01692 670796). Large village pub on the Norfolk Broads. Pool can be played inside: outside there is a Wendy house, rides and crazy golf. Children are welcome in the large family area.

Boddingtons, Flowers, Greene King and Woodforde's, amongst others.

🐎 ♣ ❀ 🏨 ◑ ☕ ⚔ ▽ ▶ Norfolk Broads

Walcott

The Lighthouse Inn

Coast Road (01692 650371). This lively and handsome pub holds outdoor family discos and barbecues Tue and Thur evenings during the summer, and Hallowe'en and Guy Fawkes parties. Pool, children's rides and various toys available. Good food and fresh fish.

Adnams and Tetley, with guests such as Greene King and Marston's.

🐎 ♣ ❀ ◑ ☕ ⚔ ♀ ▶ The seaside

Wells-next-the-Sea

Crown Hotel

The Buttlands (01328 710209). An extremely attractive 16thC hotel, in a listed building, overlooking The Buttlands, or village green, which was used in medieval times for archery practice. Charming bars, open fires and a sheltered courtyard. Children are welcomed away from the bars, or in the sun lounge.

Adnams, Bass and Marston's.

🏯 ❀ ◑ ☕ 🛏 ▶ The harbour, and boats

Winterton-on-Sea

Fishermans Return

The Lane (01493 393305). A cosy and friendly 300-year-old brick and flint seaside pub, warmed by a log fire in winter.

Woodforde's, with guests such as Mauldons, and James White's cider.

🐎 ♣ ❀ 🏨 ◑ ☕ ⚔ 🛏 ▶ The seaside

Ashby St Ledgers

The Olde Coach House Inn
(01788 890349). *North of Daventry on the A361*. This handsome creeper-clad pub was converted from a farmhouse in the late 19thC. It has oak beams, open fires and a welcoming atmosphere. Excellent food, a children's menu, and a fine play area in the garden, with slides, ropes and climbing frames. There is a baby-changing tray in the disabled toilet. On Sundays, during the summer holidays, they have a bouncy castle and a clown. *Everards and Flowers, with guests which include Fuller's, Jennings and Sarah Hughes.*
🐕 ❀ 🏥 ◑ ☞ ✂ 🛏 ♀

Brackley Hatch

Green Man Inn
Strensham (01280 850209). *On the A43, a mile south-west of Silverstone*. Very child-friendly and welcoming, this hotel is well placed for those with motor-racing-mad offspring, as it is just a short way from Silverstone Race Circuit. Those who yearn for a quieter time can visit Sulgrave Manor, the Washington family home, or Stowe School (but who wants to go to school on a day off!) which has gardens landscaped by Capability Brown. The Green Man is run by experienced and caring licensees, and you can enjoy wide ranging and well thought out prize-winning food, with a special menu and quiz for the youngsters. The garden is well equipped for play, with novelty slides, swings and a 'Dr Who' time capsule. Come on a Sunday and you will see face painters, balloon modellers, clowns and magicians. If baby needs a nappy changed, ask at the reception. *Worthington plus a weekly guest – Caledonian, Tolly Cobbold or Wadworth for example.*
🐕 ❀ 🏥 ◑ ☞ ✂ 🛏 ♀ ▶ Silverstone Motor Racing Circuit, Sulgrave Manor, Stowe School

Braunston

The Admiral Nelson
Dark Lane, Little Braunston (01788 890075). Originally a farmhouse, this building, warmed by a log fire in winter, still retains much of its traditional charm. The safe garden has swings, slides and a climbing frame. *Marston's (during the summer), John Smith's and Theakston.*
❀ 🏥 ◑ ☞ 🛏 ▶ The Grand Union Canal, locks, and Braunston Tunnel

The Mill House

Canalside (01788 890450). A family pub, once 'The Rose & Castle', in a splendid canalside position at Braunston Turn. There is a slide and climbing frame in the garden. Baby-changing facilities. *Bass, Hancock's & Worthington.* ❄️🏠◑🍴🍽️▽⏰ *21.00*

▶ The Grand Union Canal, locks, and a tunnel a short walk away

The Old Plough

82 High Street (01788 890000). *150 yards from bridge no. 1 on the nearby canal, in the centre of the village.* An attractive and friendly pub, with plenty of brass and beams, at the heart of this famous canal village. Children are welcome in the lounge bar and skittle room.

Ansells and Burton, with a 2-week rotation of guests from Tetley, Whitbread and others. 🎖️♣️❄️◑🍴⏰ *21.30* ▶ The Grand Union Canal, Braunston Turn and locks, and a tunnel

Clipston

Bulls Head

Harborough Road (01858 525268). The beams in the bar of this fine village pub are crammed with coins, a tradition started by American airmen, who left their money there when ordering drinks. The bar has a cosy fire, the walls are hung with old artifacts, and there are comfy seats and wooden stools. Skittles and pool are played here.

Bateman's, Ruddles, Timothy Taylor and Wychwood, with guests such as Fremlins and Worthington. 🐎♣️❄️◑🍴🍽️🍴⏰ *21.00*

Crick

The Wheatsheaf

15 Main Road (01788 822284). *On the A428, one mile east of junction 18 on the M1.* A traditional old pub just up the road from the canal, and not far from Crick Tunnel. There is a swing and climbing frame in the garden. *Mansfield and Marston's.* 🐎♣️❄️🏠◑🍴

Deanshanger

Fox & Hounds

71 High Street (01908 569267). *Just off the A422.* A friendly country local in the High Street, where the former stables have been converted into a barbecue area. Good, reasonably priced food. Garden and patio. *Boddingtons and Flower's, with various guests.* ♣️❄️◑🍴🍽️

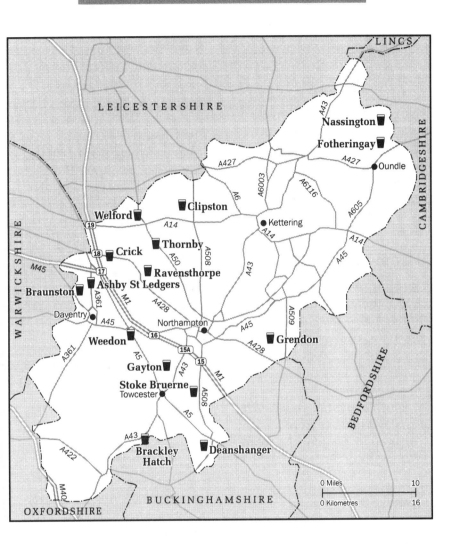

Fotheringhay

Falcon Inn

(01832 226254). There is an open fire in each of the bars of this very handsome 18thC pub. *Elgood's and Ruddles, with guests such as Bass, Greene King and Nethergate.* ♣ ❀ ◑ n*ot Mon* ☙ ⚒ ▶ Castle ruins to explore, and a fine church

NORTHAMPTONSHIRE

Gayton

Queen Victoria Inn
10 High Street (01604 858438). This large and sociable pub and restaurant was once a bakery. Pool and skittles are played here. *Hook Norton, Ruddles and Theakston, with a guest which changes every three days.*

Grendon

The Half Moon
42 Main Road (01933 663263). *Off the A45 at the Earls Barton exit.* 17thC country pub, with beams and plenty of brass and copper. Pool and cribbage, and there are swings in the garden. *Badger, Theakston and Charles Wells, with guests from Mansfield & Shepherd Neame.* not Sun evening

Nassington

Black Horse Inn
Fotheringhay Road (01780 782324). *2 miles from the junction of the A1 and A47.* There are secluded seating and dining areas in this quiet village local, which has a large open fire. *Courage, John Smith's and Theakston.*

River Nene, and a playground 200 yards away

Ravensthorpe

The Chequers
Chequers Lane (01604 770379). Skittles can be played at this friendly and sociable pub, and there is a climbing frame and slides in the garden. *Fuller's, Samuel Smith's, Mansfield and Thwaites, with a variety of guests such as Greene King and local ales, along with bottled Gale's.*

Stoke Bruerne

The Boat Inn
Canalside (01604 862428). This fine thatched pub, with two low-ceilinged bars, has been in the same family for over 100 years. It stands at the heart of this picturesque canal village, opposite the Waterways Museum. It can get busy during the 'canal season', but during the rest of the year it is very much a local. Northamptonshire skittles is played here, and informal music sessions are encouraged. *Fuller's, Marston's, Robinson's and Theakston, with at least two guest real ales.*

♣ ☸ ◑ *including breakfast from 09.00* ☞ ⅟ ▶ Stoke Bruerne is one of the finest surviving examples of a canal village in the country. The double locks contain boat scales, and there are always plenty of traditional narrowboats moored here. Boat trips into Blisworth Tunnel (the second longest currently open to navigation) are available during the summer, and The Waterways Museum is well worth visiting. It is a good family day out.

Thornby

Red Lion
Welford Road (01604 74028). *One mile from junction 1 on the A14.* Warmed by a log-burner during chilly weather, this friendly pub has a fine display of plates and jugs. Children are welcome in the restaurants.
Fuller's, Robinson's and Thwaites.
▣ ☸ ◑ ☞ ⓣ *20.00*

Weedon

The Globe Hotel
High Street (01327 340336). *3 miles west of junction 16 on the M1, at the A45/A5 crossroads.* A relaxed, informal and friendly hotel. An en-suite bedroom can

be used for baby changing.
Marston's and Webster's, with guests such as Bateman's, Fuller's and Greene King. Also bottled Marston's.
☸ ◑ ☞ ⅟ ⛂ ▶ The Grand Union Canal is nearby

The Heart of England Hotel
Daventry Road (01327 340335). *3 miles west of junction 16 on the M1.* Dating from 1740, this family pub claims to be haunted by the ghost of a very naughty and noisy child. Indoor ball pool can be played here, and The Real People Punch & Judy Show visits. Children are welcome away from the main bar area.
Mansfield.
🐎 ♣ ☸ 🏢 ◑ ☞ ⅟ ⛂ ⚕

Welford

Shoulder of Mutton
12 High Street (01858 575375). *On the A5199, north of junction 1 on the A14.* Friendly low-beamed 17thC village pub, which has a large garden with swings, a slide and a giant shoe house. Skittles can be played here.
Bass and Worthington, with guests such as Gale's, Shepherd Neame and Theakston.
🐎 ♣ ☸ 🏢 ◑ *no food Thur* ☞ ▶ Grand Union Canal

Alnwick

Old Cross Inn (Dirty Bottles)

Narrowgate (01665 602735). *In the town centre, near the castle.* This pub is known locally as 'Dirty Bottles', as it has a window full of them. A notice inside the pub explains that these bottles are supposedly cursed. The building is over 200 years old – there is no garden but a small patio can be used during summer. Sandwiches are served (no meals), or you can bring your own!

Mordue's and Theakston, with guests such as Bass, Butterknowle and Mansfield.
♣⏰ 21.00

Bamburgh

The Victoria Hotel

Front Street (01668 214431). Excellently placed for visits to Bamburgh Castle, this is an imposing and historic hotel. There is a changing room where babies can be attended to.

Theakston, with Ruddles as a guest.
🐎♣❀◑➷🛏▽▶ Bamburgh Castle, the seaside

Chatton

Percy Arms Hotel

(01668 215244). *5 miles west of Belford on the B6348.* A handsome and imposing hotel, which was advertised in 1880 as 'a romantic retreat – with well-aired beds'. It was formerly a hunting lodge and now stands, creeper-clad, at the heart of a conservation village. It was purchased by the Duke of Northumberland in 1873 and remained in his family until 1977.

Theakston, with Border (Farne Island Ale) as a guest, and bottle conditioned Caledonian 80/-.
🐎♣❀◑➷🛏

Craster

Jolly Fisherman Inn

(01665 576218). *6 miles from Alnwick.* This friendly and welcoming pub overlooks the harbour, and has splendid sea views. Home-made speciality soups, paté, sandwiches and sweets are served until *21.00.*

Vaux and Ward's.
♣❀

Greenside

White Swan

Lead Road Folly (0191 413 4255).

Children are welcome in all rooms except the bar of this friendly and welcoming village pub. Pool and dominoes are played here, and there is a round-about, and ducks and fancy pigeons, in the garden. No meals, just snacks. They have a firework display in November, and a Christmas party.
Banks's and Camerons.
♣ ❀ 📷 ♠

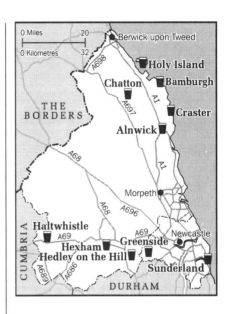

Haltwhistle

Grey Bull Hotel
Wapping (01434 321991). *Just off the A69 between Carlisle and Newcastle.* This friendly and welcoming 18thC coaching inn has a busy front bar: it is often quieter at the back. Quoits are played here during the summer. *Federation and Stones are the permanent real ales: the landlord dispenses many guests 'which may take (his) interest at any time'.*
🐎 ♣ ❀ ◑ ☙ ⏲ 21.00

Hedley on the Hill

Feathers Inn
(01661 843607). A traditional and friendly village pub, with stone walls, plenty of beams and cosy wood-burning stoves. Dominoes,

skittles and shove ha'penny are played here.
Boddingtons, Mordue's and guests which may be Big Lamp, Butterknowle, Fuller's, Marston's or Wadworth.
🐎 ♣ ❀ ◖ *weekends only* ▶ *Tue to Sun only* ☙ ⏲ 21.00

Hexham

Carts Bog Inn
Langley (01434 684338). This unspoilt family-run pub was built in 1730 on a site where brewing began in 1521. The interesting menu extends to Chinese, Indian, Japanese and Thai dishes.
Marston's and Theakston, with

*guests such as Adnams,
Butterknowle, Durham, Four
Rivers and Fuller's*.
🐎 ♣ ❀ ◑ ⌣

Holy Island

The Ship

Marygate (01289 389311). *Turn
left at the T junction in the
village*. This very attractive 400-
year-old pub is on Holy Island,
linked to the mainland by a tidal
causeway (read the notice and
note the tide times, to ensure you
don't get stuck!). There is a family room, and children over 5
years old are welcomed.
*Border and Holy Island Blessed,
with Theakston as a guest.
Border Darling in bottles*.
🐎 ❀ ◑ ⌣ ⚒ 🛏 🕐 *21.00*

▶ Seaside and castle

Sunderland

The Shipwrights Hotel

Ferry Boat Lane, North Hylton
(0191 549 5139). *To the west of
the city, near the A19*. On the
river's edge, this 350-year-old
pub has excellent views from its
first-floor restaurant.
*Vaux and Ward's, occasional
guests*.
❀ ◑ ⌣ 🛏

NOTTINGHAMSHIRE

Caunton

Caunton Beck

(01636 636793). Built in 1820, this is a friendly pub and restaurant, which wishes to be used as 'a meeting place or eating house, reading room or watering hole'. Well restored using the original Elizabethan frame trusses, it has a large fireplace and a viewing window to the cellar, where you can see the casks of beer. Food is served from 09.00 until 23.00 all year.

Adnams and Timothy Taylor.

Edingley

The Old Reindeer Inn

Main Street (01623 882253). This traditional village pub dates from the 18thC. The friendly tap room is popular with rugby fans and there is a play area in the large garden.

Mansfield.
🐎 ❀ ◑ *not Sun evenings or Mon* ☙ ⏱ *21.30*

Epperstone

The Cross Keys

Main Street (0115 966 3033). A classic country pub, with simply furnished bars and a comfy

lounge, where children are welcome. Excellent food.

Hardy's & Hansons.
🐎 ❀ ◑ ☙ ⏱ *22.00*

Gunthorpe

Anchor Inn

80 Main Street (0115 966 3291). *Off the A6097 at Gunthorpe Bridge.* Friendly and lively riverside pub which has a skittle alley, and swings, a slide, climbing frame and bouncy toys in the gar-

den. Two rooms are available for children's parties. There are baby-changing facilities in the disabled toilet: nappy vending and a changing table.

Six real ales are usually available, including: Courage, Mansfield, Marston's, Theakston and Wells.

♣❀Ⓗ◑☞▽▶ The river

High Marnham

The Brownlow Arms
(01636 822505). *Turn off the A1 north of Newark on Trent onto the B1164 at Carlton-on-Trent. Look out for signposted directions on your right. It is just beyond Normanton on Trent.* Recently refurbished, this family pub has a large garden and plans a long skittle alley. The disabled toilet includes baby-changing facilities.

Mansfield, with guests such as Greene King, Marston's and Theakston.

🐂♣❀Ⓗ◑☞✂▽

Laneham

Ferryboat Inn
Church Laneham (01777 228350). A friendly pub with access from the River Trent.

Darktribe and others.

🐂♣❀◑☞▽

Nether Langwith

The Jug & Glass Inn
Queens Walk (01623 742283). *On the A632 between Bolsover and Cuckney.* Standing by the village green, with the River Poulter in front, this is a fine stone-built pub which was first mentioned in 1179 when Welbeck Abbey was being built. In 1879 Albert Beeley took the licence. A large man with a prodigious appetite, it is said that when he died his coffin was so large it had to be taken out through a window. Children are welcome in the eating area and restaurant. On warm summer days it is pleasant to sup beer beside the water.

Hardy's & Hansons, plus guests.

⊠♣❀◑☞🛏⏰ 21.00

Newark on Trent

The Castle Barge
Town Wharf (01636 706333). *On the River Trent, adjacent to Trent Bridge.* A fine floating pub in a former 94ft-long Spiller's grain barge. Downstairs things are suitably nautical, with lots of polished wood and pictures. Outside you can enjoy the river.

Mansfield.

🐂❀◑☞⏰ 20.30 ▶ A boat on the river

NOTTINGHAMSHIRE

Newark on Trent

The Old Malt Shovel
25 North Gate (01636 702036).
This sociable town pub serves
Mexican and Portuguese food,
together with the usual dishes.
Skittles can be played here.
Timothy Taylor and Theakston,
with guests from Adnams,
Greene King and Rudgate's.
🐎 ♣ ✿ ◑ *not Mon or Tue*
evening ☞

Normanton on Trent

Square & Compass
Eastgate (01636 821439).
Signposted off the B1164 south of
Tuxford. On cool days a large
wood-burning stove is a welcoming sight in this low-beamed traditional village pub, which is
over 400 years old. Skittles and
pool can be played here, and in
the large garden there is a Wendy
house, a Mother Hubbard shoe,
swings and a slide.
Adnams, and guests including
Springhead, Timothy Taylor
and Theakston, with bottle con-
ditioned Adnams as well.
♣ ✿ 🏠 ◑ ☞ 🛏

Orston

Durham Ox
Church Street (01949 850059). A
pleasant split-level village pub
with traditional values. It has a
large garden with a 'drinking
boulevard'. Children are welcome
in the no smoking Garden Room
and skittle alley. Table skittles
can also be played here. They
reckon the rolls they serve are
'the best in the county'.
John Smith's and Theakston,
with Home, Marston's and
Wadworth as typical guests.
🐎 ♣ ✿ ✄

Sandiacre

The Plough Inn
Town Street (0115 949 9191).
This smart canalside pub has a
pleasant garden.
Bass.
✿ ◑ ☞ ⏱ 21.00 ▶ Erewash Canal

Stoke Bardolph

The Ferry Boat Inn
Riverside (0115 987 1232). *From*
Nottingham, turn off the A612 at
Burton Joyce. Overlooking the
River Trent, this pub has a large
heated courtyard, popular with
families. Inside they have an
'Adventure Island' playroom,

which costs £1 for admission during the week, and £1.50 at weekends. Clowns, balloons and face-painting are featured at advertised times. Children are welcome in the family dining area. *Greenalls, Shipstone's and Tetley, with a different guest each week, from Courage to Wychwood's.*
🐎♣❀▦◑🍽️✂️▽▶ River Trent

Upton

The Cross Keys

Main Street (01636 813269). *On the A612 between Southwell and Newark.* Standing opposite the British Horological Institute at Upton Hall, so you will surely find time to visit this pleasingly restored 17thC inn, where the upstairs restaurant is in what was formerly a dovecot. Families are welcome in an area off the bar, and in the restaurant. There are two beer festivals held here each

year – one during the week before Easter, and one in October, and both feature 40 beers and ciders, and live music. There is a small garden.
Boddingtons, Marston's and Springhead, with guests such as Barnsley, Church End, Glentworth, Oldershaw and York.
♣❀◑🍽️✂️🎤

West Stockwith

The White Hart

Main Street (01427 890176). This friendly country inn overlooks the confluence of the rivers Idle and Trent – you will often see gravel barges travelling to and from Girton Wharf, upstream on the Trent. Pool is played here, and there are swings outside in the garden.
John Smith's and Theakston.
♣❀▦◑🍽️🛏️▶ River Trent, and West Stockwith Basin a short walk away

OXFORDSHIRE

Bampton

The Romany Inn
Bridge Street (01993 850237). *On the A4095 Witney to Faringdon road.* There are Saxon arches in the cellar of this fine 17thC inn, which was once a grocer's shop. The garden has a children's play area with swings, slides and a tree-house.
Archers, Courage, Donnington and Hook Norton, with guests from Scottish Courage and Theakston.
❄️🏚️🌓☕✂️🛏️⏰ *21.00*

Barford St Michael

The George Inn
Lower Street (01869 338226). *Off the A361 between Chipping Norton and Bloxham.* A thatched 17thC stone pub, warmed by open fires when the weather is cool. Pool, giant chess, Aunt Sally and dominoes can be played, and there is a full adventure playground in the garden.
Ruddles, Theakston and Wadworth, with a guest.
🐎♣️❄️🏚️🌓 *not Sun, or Mon evening* ☕

Bicester

Littlebury Hotel
Kings End (01869 252595). Friendly and comfortable hotel, where many functions are held.
Marston's.
❄️🌓☕✂️🛏️

Blewbury

Red Lion
Nottingham Fee (01235 850403). *You will find this pub 'down the lane with the tree in the middle'.* A friendly and cosy 18thC beamy pub with a fine open fire in cold weather. Children are welcome in the Elbow Room.
Brakspear.
🚶❄️🌓☕✂️🛏️⏰ *20.30*

Buckland

The Trout
Tadpole Bridge (01367 870382). *Just off the A420, halfway between Bampton and Buckland.* This very handsome 17thC riverside pub is set in pretty grounds. Children are welcome in the dining areas.
Archers, Fuller's and Morland, with a large variety of guests such as Gibbs Mew, Hampshire, Vale and Wychwood.
🚶♣️❄️🌓☕▶ River Thames

145

Burcot

The Chequers

(01865 407771). A very fine and totally civilised thatched black-and-white pub, where you can nestle into settees in front of roaring log fires, and sample some decent beer and good food. There is often a pianist at the grand piano, and the occasional sing-song, as well as New Year, Valentine's Day and other celebrations. Excellent food and bread baked on the premises. A new patio area has night lighting. *Brakspear, Flowers and Marston's, with Archers, Hook Norton, and Ruddles as guests.* ❀ ◗ *not Sun evening* ✂

Burford

The Lamb Inn

Sheep Street (01993 823155). *Sheep Street is on the left as you descend Burford High Street.* A very distinctive sign announces this particularly handsome honey-coloured Cotswold stone inn. Inside the 15thC building you will find cosy bars with log fires, gleaming brass and flagstone floors, and comfortable lounges, replete with antiques. Excellent food. There is also a very pretty walled garden.

Adnams, Hook Norton and Wadworth. ❀ ◗ *lunch, but no bar meals, on Sun* ♥ 🛏

Chadlington

The Tite Inn

Mill End (01608 676475). *On the edge of the village.* Built during the 1600s, this has been a pub for over 200 years, and takes its name from a stream which runs beneath the building. Warmed by log fires in winter, the cosy bar offers all the traditional comforts and this, together with the cellars, is the oldest part of the building. The ghost of a woman, as yet unidentified, has been seen here. Perhaps she is connected with the Battle of Edge Hill in 1642. Troops took refreshment in the village before leaving to fight in the first mêlée of the Civil War. Just a short walk from the pub is Knollbury Camp, where you can enjoy fine views over the Evenlode Valley. The camp is thought to have been an ancient dwelling and later a Roman Camp – flint arrow heads and tools have been uncovered here. Excellent food and fine cheeses. There is a fine mature garden. *Closed on Mon except Bank Holidays. Archers, Fuller's and*

OXFORDSHIRE

NORTHAMPTONSHIRE

WARWICKSHIRE

Banbury

BUCKINGHAMSHIRE

GLOUCESTERSHIRE

Barford
St Michael

Chipping Norton

Chadlington

Shipton-under-
Wychwood

Ramsden

North Leigh

Burford

Whitney

Enslow

Bicester

Stanton St John

Oxford

Newbridge

Cumnor

Bampton

Northmoor

Buckland

Kelmscott

Fyfield

Sandford-
on-Thames

Thame

Lewknor

Burcot

Roke

Wantage

South Moreton

East Hendred

Blewbury

Wallingford

Stonor

Nuffield

Stoke Row

Goring

Henley-o-T

Shiplake

BERKSHIRE

WILTSHIRE

0 Miles   5

0 Kilometres   8

*Wychwood, with guests from
Cottage. Real draught cider is
also available.*

Chipping Norton

The Albion Tavern
90 Burford Road (01608 642860).
This is the last pub on the left of

the A365, heading towards Burford. If you are visiting the Chipping Norton area, (it is the highest town in Oxfordshire at 700 feet), this makes an excellent stop for refreshment. Pool and dominoes can be played. While you are here, you can reflect upon the fact that if you had visited the town before the 13thC, you would be in 'Norton'. The 'Chipping', or 'cheapening', means market, and this was added when the town was granted one.

Hook Norton.

♣ ❀

Cumnor

The Vine Inn
11 Abingdon Road (01865 862567). *Off the A420 Oxford to Swindon road.* You will see the vine growing prolifically over the front wall of this friendly pub. Children are welcome in the conservatory. There is a play frame and Aunt Sally, and on summer bank holidays you may see bungee jumping in the garden!

Adnams, Greene King and Morland.

 🗙 ♣ ❀ 🏠 ◑ ⌣ ⅄ 🛏

East Hendred

The Wheatsheaf
Chapel Square (01235 833229). A 14thC timbered country pub, with a cosy bar warmed by a stove. Aunt Sally can be played here, and the garden is pretty.

Morland, Ruddles and Theakston, with guests such as Gale's.

🐎 ♣ ❀ ◑ *not Sun evenings* ⌣ ⅄

Enslow

The Rock of Gibraltar
(01869 331223). *On the A4095, north of Oxford (Kidlington) airport.* This fine canalside pub, in a beautiful setting, was once owned by Henry Baker, a contractor who helped build the canal, and now has a lock named after him. This lock is a couple of hundred yards along the tow-path towards Oxford. The pub is now run by a couple who were living on a narrowboat moored close-by, and took over when new management was needed. Their traditional Cornish pasties are *highly* recommended. Swings and a slide are to be found in the garden.

Courage, Fullers and Marston's.

♣ ❀ 🏠 ◑ *not Sun evening or all day Mon, although salads are*

available Mon lunchtime ⬤ ✿
🕙 *21.00* ▶ Oxford canal

Fyfield

The White Hart
(01865 390585). *Just off the A420,
5 miles south-west of Oxford.*
This very fine pub was built during the reign of Henry VI by the
executors of Sir John Golafre,
Lord of the Manor of Fyfield, as
the Hospital of St John the
Baptist, to provide accommodation for a chantry priest and five
alms-men. All chantries in
England were put up for sale in
1548, and in 1580 this building
became the property of St John's
College, Oxford, who leased it to
tenants who converted it into a
public house. Extensive renovations in 1963 restored the original
character of the building. The
priest's lower room is now the
dining room, and the kitchen is
now the public bar. The garden
has a play area.
*Bass, Boddingtons, Hook Norton,
Theakston and Wadworth, with
various guests.*
🐎 ✿ 🏚 ◑ ⬤ ✿

Goring

The Catherine Wheel
Station Road (01491 872379).

Children are welcome in the
Forge Bar of this attractive 15thC
pub, which has foreign food
evenings about once a month. It's
a good place to stop if you are
visiting this Thames-side town,
where you will see lots of pretty
brick and flint cottages. The
handsome church, down by the
river, contains one of the oldest
bells in the country, dating from
1290. The fine mill by the bridge
is in fact a replica of an earlier
building, and was built in 1923.
In prehistoric times there was a
ford at Goring, linking the
Icknield Way with the Ridgeway.
Brakspear.
🚶 ✿ ◑ *not Sun evening* ⬤ 🛏
▶ River Thames

Kelmscot

The Plough Inn
(01367 253543). This very fine
17thC inn has flag floors. Bar billiards can be played here.
Bass, Greene King and Fuller's
♣ ✿ ◑ ⬤ 🛏 🕙 *21.00* ▶ River
Thames

Lewknor

Ye Olde Leathern Bottel
1 High Street (01844 351482).
Open fires, low beams and a
friendly reception await you at

this inviting family-run village pub. Children are welcome in the snug and lounge bar. The big garden has a toy car, a slide and some smaller toys.
Brakspear, with Theakston as a guest.

Newbridge

The Maybush
(01865 300624). *On the A415 Whitney road*. A fine riverside pub with a terrace overlooking the Thames, and an attractive grassy garden.
Morland, with guests from Flowers and Marston's.
River Thames

North Leigh

Woodman Inn
New Yatt Road (01993 881790). *Off the A4095 between Woodstock and Witney*. Smallish turn-of-the-century local in a village which is set amidst fine countryside, with excellent views. A mile away, at the other end of the village, you can explore some important Roman remains. Dominoes and cribbage are played in the pub, and there is a large terrace and garden. Beer festivals are held here on Easter

and August Bank Holidays.
Hampshire, Hook Norton and Wadworth, with guests such as Shepherd Neame and Wychwood.
not Mon evening

Northmoor

The Ferryman Inn
Bablockhythe (01865 880028). *North of the village, down the lane to the river*. This lively and welcoming pub marks the famous ferry crossing, mentioned by Matthew Arnold in 'The Scholar Gypsy', 1853, who was seen:
'in hat of antique shape
and cloak of grey,
crossing the stripling Thames
at Bab-lock-hithe'
There has been a ferry here since AD904, and it was still operating at the last visit. Skittles, pool and Aunt Sally can be played here, and there is a bouncy castle in the garden. A full calendar of events includes a July beer festival, August raft racing, September steamboat rally (excellent), and a grand Guy Fawkes bonfire. The canal-boat based Micron Theatre also visits. There is a fold-down baby-changing table in the disabled toilet.
Greene King, Shepherd Neame and Theakston, together with

various guests.
 River Thames

Nuffield

The Crown
(01491 641335). *On the main Henley to Wallingford road.* A sociable brick-and-flint pub with warming log fires when the weather is cool. Children are welcome in the small family room. *Brakspear.*

Oxford

Turf Tavern
Bath Place (01865 243235). *Off Holywell Street.* Pleasantly situated away from the hustle and bustle of Oxford, and quite distinctive, this 13thC tavern was popularised in Hardy's 'Jude the Obscure'. It is patronised by both students and tourists. Children are welcome in any area away from the bars.
Flowers and Whitbread, with guests such as Archers, plus Bulmers real cider.
The delights of Oxford
The Waterman's Arms
7 South Street, Osney Island (01865 248832). A very fine riverside pub, once used by bargees and in spite of its prime Thamesside location, still very popular with locals. The Osney Island Raft race starts here on the first Saturday in July.
Morland's.
not Sun evenings
River Thames and the delights of Oxford

Ramsden

The Royal Oak
High Street (01993 868213). A friendly 17thC coaching inn with a cosy open fire when the weather is cold. Good food.
Archers, Hook Norton and Morrells, with Adnams and Arkell's as typical guests.

Roke

Home Sweet Home
(01491 838249). A fine thatched country pub, with wooden settles, large fireplaces and low beams – all 'nice and old'.
Eldridge Pope.

Sandford-on-Thames

The Kings Arms
Church Road (01865 777095). *Follow signs to Rose Hill round-*

about on the ring road – turn towards Littlemore and, after 2½ miles, turn left opposite The Fox. The ceiling beams in this fine lock-side pub were made from barge timbers, and pictures in the bar recall 19thC Oxford University Boat Race crews.
Theakston.
🐎 ❀ ◖ ☕ ⚒ ▽ ⏱ *21.00* ▶ River Thames

Shiplake

The Plowden Arms
Reading Road, Shiplake Cross (01189 402794). *On the A4155 between Reading and Henley.* Heavily beamed and with a log fire, this fine old pub dates from the 15thC, and all the decorations and renovations have been executed with great sympathy. The family room is in the former stable and coach house. Nearby is the 12thC Church of SS Peter and Paul, which contains some exquisite medieval Belgian glass. Alfred Lord Tennyson married Emily Selwood in the church here in 1850.
Brakspear, from the brewery in nearby Henley-on-Thames.
🐎 ❀ ◖ *not Sun or Mon evening* ☕

Shipton-under-Wychwood

Shaven Crown Hotel
(01993 830330). Overlooking the village green, this splendid 14thC pub, with soaring beams and a fine staircase, was at one time a hospice. Shove ha'penny and other games can be played here. The courtyard garden was once used by monks.
Hook Norton and Morland, with Greene King and Hampshire as guests.
♣ ❀ ◖ ☕ 🛏

South Moreton

The Crown
High Street (01235 812262). A genuinely friendly and enthusiastic village local. Bar billiards.
Adnams, Badger, and Wadworth, with guests such as Hoskins & Oldfield, Shepherd Neame and Smiles.
🐎 ♣ ❀ ◖ ☕

Stanton St John

The Star Inn
Middle Road (01865 351277). This country local has a fine inglenook and a family room.
Wadworth, with Badger as a guest.
🐎 ❀ ◖ ☕ ⚒

Stoke Row

The Cherry Tree
(01491 680430). A very attractive
village local opposite the Maharajah's Well, which you will certainly enjoy visiting. This opulent
domed strcture was built in 1863
as a gift from the Maharajah of
Benares in what was then a poor
rural backwater. It is 365 feet
deep, and was, astonishingly, dug
by hand. In a pleasant garden setting, the pub can supply booklets
about the well. There are swings,
a slide and lots of lawn. Pool,
dominoes and cribbage can be
played inside.
Brakspear.
♣ ❀ 🏠 ⌡ *no meals on Mondays*
▶ Maharajah's Well

Stonor

Five Horseshoes
Maidensgrove (01491 641282).
*Take the A4130 from Henley and
turn right on the B480 along the
Stonor Valley. Turn left at Stonor,
going through beech woods.*

Established in the 17thC, this is a
friendly pub where you can enjoy
some of the best views over the
Chilterns in Oxfordshire. Fine
food.
***Brakspear, with Theakston as a
guest.***
❀ ◑ ⌂ ⏰ *children under 8-years-
old should leave by 19.00*

Thame

The Swan Hotel
9 Upper High Street (01844
261211). Built in the 16thC, The
Swan was completely redesigned
in 1987, with bare boards, rugs
and interesting fittings giving the
pub a new start. A medieval ceiling does survive, however, in the
fresh-food restaurant. Children
are welcome as long as they stay
away from the bar.
***Brakspear and Hook Norton,
with guests such as Shepherd
Neame and Timothy Taylor.***
🚶 ❀ ◑ ⌂ 🛏 ⏰ *20.00*

Bishop's Castle

The Three Tuns Inn & Brewery

Salop Street (01588 638797). This timber-framed building was probably a late-16thC open hall, and many of its original features have been retained – oak beams, a Jacobean staircase and a large open fireplace with a wall painting, circa 1600, above. Beer has probably been brewed here since the first licence was granted in 1642, although the present brewery was built in the 1880s by John Roberts, whose family owned and managed the inn until 1976. The brewery is a classic Victorian four-storey tower, and much of its original equipment is still in use. It is Grade II listed and a rare survival of a working rural brewery. Tours can be arranged by appointment. Children are welcome in the pub, but preferably not in the public bar. There are visits by Morris dancers.
Own brews, and occasionally Six Bells, also from Bishop's Castle, plus their own Cleric's Cure bottled real ale.
❀ ◑ ➷ *by Spring 1998* ♟ ▶
Brewery, ancient buildings and museum

Bridges

The Horseshoe Inn

Ratlingthorpe (01588 650260). A 16thC country pub, which was the local CAMRA Pub of the Year in 1995. It is well situated by the River Onny, and is used by walkers tackling the Long Mynd and Stiperstones. Children are welcome in the lounge area.
Adnams, Shepherd Neame, with guests from Enville, Hobsons, Hughes and Wood, bottled real ales and Westons real cider.
🖾 ➹ ♣ ❀ ◖ *not Mon or Tue in summer, or Mon to Thur in winter* ✗ ⌚ *21.00*

Bridgenorth

The Red Lion o'Morfe

Upper Farmcote (01746 710678). *About 3 miles east of Bridgenorth, off the A458, signposted to Claverley.* A traditional public bar with an open fire, a smart lounge and conservatory make this a comfortable country pub. Pool is played, and there is a floodlit boules piste. The garden extends to an orchard.
Banks's, with guests from Bass, Everards, Mansfield, Marston's, Ruddles, Shepherd Neame and Wood.
♣ ❀ 🖾 ◑ ➷ ✗ ⌚ *21.30*

SHROPSHIRE

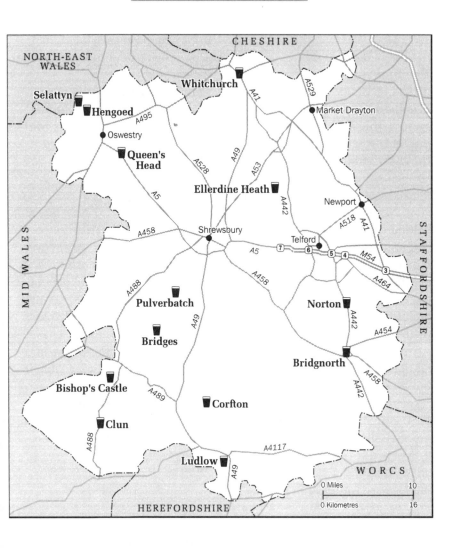

Clun

The White Horse Inn

The Square (01588 640305). This friendly pub is in the centre of this charmingly timeless village. Children are welcome if eating, or in the games room. Skittles and pool are played here.

Courage and Home, with guests from Hook Norton and Wye Valley.

🏃 ♣ 🐾 ◐ 🍴 ⌚ *22.00* ▶ Clun Castle

Corfton

The Sun Inn

(01584 861239). *On the Ludlow to Bridgnorth road*. With many awards, this greatly acclaimed pub in beautiful Corvedale was first licensed in 1613. It has strong connections with Molly Jones, local heroine and girl made good, who was born in a cottage behind the pub in 1762. Having had an illegitimate child, and then getting married and having another, she moved from Corfton to Cold Weston. When some hemping yarn was stolen from the Sun Inn, Molly's house was searched and the yarn found. She and her husband were arrested, but he escaped, and Molly was taken to the Sun and locked up for the night. In despair she cut her own throat, but was successfully sewn up and later transported to Australia. Eventually she managed to return to England, only to go back to Australia where she did well as a farmer, and gained a reputation for her sexual exploits. Eventually she became known as 'The Queen of Hunter Valley', and recently a wine has been named in her honour. The food at The Sun Inn has a good reputation, with all tastes catered for. Fresh local produce is used whenever possible. There are swings and climbing ropes in the garden.

Flowers, with over 120 guest ales each year, and including Wye Valley, plus Westons real cider.
♣ ❀ ⌘ ◑ ⌣ ✄

Ellerdine Heath

Royal Oak (The Tiddly)

(01939 250300). *Midway between the A53 and A442, north-west of Telford*. It is worth seeking out this very fine traditional country pub, where a cosy, simple bar adjoins the games room. The garden has a slide and swings, and there is a baby-changing table in the ladies toilet.

Brains, Hanby, Hobsons and Wood, with guests from Adnams and Felinfoel, and real cider from Westons.
♣ ❀ ⌘ ◑ *not on Tue* ⌣ ▽

Hengoed

The Last Inn

(01691 659747). *On the B4579 between Oswestry and Weston Rhyn*. The food in this large and welcoming country pub close to the border is excellent: well priced, but not 'fancy' – the pub features in CAMRA's *Good Pub*

Food Guide. There is a fine collection of beer trays. Pool is played in a separate games room. **Bass and Boddingtons, with guests such as Burton Bridge, Pembroke, Vale and Wye Valley, plus Westons real cider.** ♣ ▶ *plus Sun lunch* ♥

Ludlow

Unicorn Inn
Corve Street (01584 873555). A huge log fire warms the bar of this charming 17thC inn, which has a terrace beside the River Corve.
Bass and Worthington.

Norton

Hundred House Hotel
Bridgnorth Road (01952 730353). *On the A442 between Telford and Bridgnorth.* Taking its name from the medieval administrative subdivisions of the shires, parts of this inn (the thatched courthouse barn) date from the 14thC, although the main part of the building is Georgian. Opposite the old courthouse are what remains of the stocks and whipping post – just down the road is an old ducking pond. The landlord of the Hundred House was at one time responsible for feeding the ducks on the pond, and keeping the keys to the stocks, but both responsibilities have disappeared into the mists of time. Warm and welcoming, the hotel has oak beams and wood panelling, and excellent food is served. There are baby-changing mats in the toilets.
Smiles, with guests such as Brains and Charles Wells, and Bulmer's real cider.
 Two donkeys

Pulverbatch

White Horse Inn
(01743 718247). *8 miles southwest of Shrewsbury, between the A49 and A488.* A 13thC coaching inn with plenty of oak beams, warmed by a coal-burning range and decorated with pewter mugs and brass knick-knacks.
Boddingtons, Flowers and Wadworth, with Marston's as a guest.
🎠 ♣ ❀ ◑ ♥

Queen's Head

Queen's Head
Near Oswestry (01691 610255). *3 miles south-east of Oswestry, just off the A5.* Right by the newly opened section of the

Montgomery Canal, this is an attractive pub with a conservatory. A breach in the canal bank in 1936, about 3 miles north-east of here and close to Perry Aqueduct, resulted in the canal's closure, and it's abandonment, in 1944. Extensive campaigning and a good deal of work by enthusiasts, local councils and British Waterways have led to this, and other stretches of the Montgomery Canal, re-opening. It is hoped they will all link up early in the next century, when navigation should extend a good way towards Newtown. Excellent choice of food, a children's menu, and baby-changing facilities in the ladies toilet.

Theakston, with guests from Jennings, Wadworth, Wood and others.

🦋 ◑ ➷ ✂ ▽ ▶ The Canal

Selattyn

Cross Keys

(01691 650247). *On the B4579 between Oswestry and Glyn Ceriog.* A very fine 17thC village local with several rooms – a focus for village life and popular with those walking Offa's Dyke path. Skittles can be played here. No meals, but sandwiches are available. They have self-catering

accommodation in a converted granary attached to the pub. *Banks's.*

♣ 🦋

Whitchurch

Old Town Hall Vaults

St Mary's Street (01948 662251). *Well hidden at the bottom of the High Street.* Known as the 'Back Street Vaults', this attractive 18thC pub was the birthplace of Sir Edward German (1862-1936), composer of *Merrie England* and *Tom Jones*.

Marston's.

🦋 ◑ *not Wed or Sun evenings* ➷

Willeymoor Lock Tavern

Tarporley Road (01948 663274). *About 2 miles north of Whitchurch on the A49.* This pub, well situated beside the Llangollen Canal, occupies what was once the lock-keeper's cottage, built in the late 1790s. Inside there are fine old beams, lots of brasses and a fascinating collection of teapots. The garden has a climbing frame, swings and a slide. Children are welcome, except in the bar area.

Theakston, plus 3 guests such as Bushy's, Wadworth, Weetwood, Wychwood and many others.

♣ 🦋 🖼 ◑ ➷ ▶ Llangollen Canal

SOMERSET

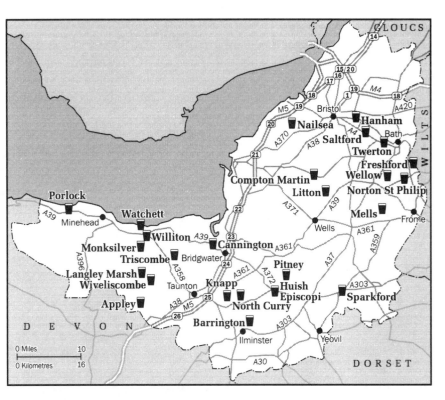

Appley

The Globe Inn

(01823 672327). This is a very fine and traditional 500-year-old country inn, where the bar is a hatchway in a flagstoned corridor, with several cosy rooms leading off. There is a skittle alley, and the attractive garden has a children's play area. Good food. Hidden in a maze of country lanes, it is well worth seeking out.

Cotleigh, with guests from Butcombe's, Eccleshall and Teignworthy, and Lane's real cider.

Barrington

The Royal Oak Inn

(01460 53455). A friendly village pub with a busy public bar and a quieter lounge. Children are welcomed in the lounge, upstairs function room and skittle alley. There is a patio outside.

Courage, Otter, Smiles,

Marston's, Morland and Theakston are amongst the beers rotated here.
🏹 ♣ ❀ ◑ ⌣ ⏰ *21.00*

Cannington

The Malt Shovel Inn
Blackmoor Lane (01278 653432). *4 miles from Bridgwater off the A39.* Friendly and comfortable. *Butcombe's, John Smith's and Theakston, with guests such as Cotleigh, Cottage or Exmoor, and draught ciders from Lane's and Rich's.*
🐎 ◑ *not Sun evening in winter* ⌣ 🛏

Compton Martin

Ring 'o' Bells
(01761 221284). *On the A368 near the Chew Valley Lake.* A lovely 200-year-old roadside inn with a large, safe garden and a fine family room. Table skittles and shove ha'penny can be played here. *Butcombe's and Wadworth, with Adnams, Bateman's, Timothy Taylor and Wickwar as guests.*
🐎 ♣ ❀ 🏠 ◑ ⌣ ✄ ▽

Freshford

The Inn at Freshford
The Hill (01225 722250). Situated by an old stone bridge and overlooking the River Frome, this is a splendid and traditional village pub. Pleasant garden with pretty flowers. *Bass, Courage, Marston's and Theakston.*
❀ ◑ ⌣ ✄

Hanham

The Old Lock & Weir
Hanham Mills (0117 967 3793). *At the end of Abbots Road, turn right into Ferry Road.* A fine rural free house overlooking Hanham Lock. It was CAMRA Local Pub of the Year in 1996. Children are welcome away from the bar. There is a large garden and patios. *Bass, Exmoor and Marston's.*
❀ ◑ ⌣ ▶ River Avon and Hanham Lock

Huish Episcopi

Rose & Crown
(01458 250494). *On the A372, one mile from Langport.* This thatched country inn has been in the same family for four generations, and is known locally as

Eli's. This is (almost) the description they supplied to us: 'The pub has been in the family for 130 years and, in what has now become a rarity, it has no bar, just a cellar where the beer is served and the customers mingle. There are no specific no-smoking areas but as there are five rooms as well as the cellar, there is generally one without smoke. We have no visiting clowns, but children usually find amusement by trying to catch fish in the stream, climbing trees or kicking a football in the adjoining paddock. In summer we play a form of cricket in the paddock against a local pub. We don't specifically serve children's portions of food, but we do try to accommodate people's wishes if we can. Likewise we have no specific baby-changing facilities but that has proved no obstacle in the past. We have always welcomed children and they may go into any of the rooms except the cellar (due to practicality). Families genuinely feel part of the pub as opposed to being stuck in the 'dreaded' family rooms. We have an enclosed children's play area as well as a lawn and patio. Well behaved dogs are also made welcome'. Sounds OK? Skittles, pool and shove ha'penny are played, with a climbing frame, sit-on car

and sand-pit in the garden. *Bass and Boddingtons, plus guests from local breweries such as Moor, Smiles and Teignworthy, and Burrow Hill's real cider, served from wooden barrels.*

Knapp

The Rising Sun Inn
(01823 490436). *Just east of Taunton and junction 25 on the M5.* Fine surviving example of a 15thC Somerset longhouse, with two inglenooks and many other original features. Extensive fish menu, which has won many awards.
Bass, Boddingtons and Exmoor.

Langley Marsh

The Three Horseshoes
(01984 623763). *Just north-west of Wiveliscombe, off the B3227.* A traditional 'no nonsense' pub, with plenty of games – bar skittles, skittles, shove ha'penny, cribbage and dominoes. Children are welcome away from the bar, and there is a full play area in the garden.
Otter, Palmers and Ringwood, with guests from Harveys,

Ridleys and Young's plus Ridley's real cider.
🐎♣🦟🈂️◑🍴

Litton

The Kings Arms
(01761 241301). *On the B3114, between West Harptree and Chewton Mendip.* This friendly 15thC pub has a flagstoned entrance hall leading to the bars, where you will find a large fire and cosy seats. Children are welcome in the Old Kitchen and Garden Room. The garden has a slide, swings and a climbing frame.
Bass, Courage and Wadworth.
🐎🦟🈂️◑🍴

Mells

The Talbot Inn
High Street (01373 812254). *Just north-west of Frome, between the A361 and A362.* The village of Mells was at one time owned by Glastonbury Abbey. In 1543, at the time of the dissolution of the monasteries, the village was purchased by the Horner family for £1832, a considerable amount of money at the time. Tradition has associated the family with 'Little Jack Horner' of nursery rhyme fame, but there is great doubt

about this. Next to the inn is the Manor House, owned by the Earl of Oxford and Asquith, a direct descendant of the Horners' and the freeholder of the inn. This is a 15thC coaching inn of great character, with open fires and oak beams in the bars, and a very pleasant cobbled and planted courtyard. Excellent food, and a sunny cottage garden.
Bass, Butcombe's and guests such as Hook Norton, Palmers, Timothy Taylor and Wadworth.
🦟◑🍴🛏️

Monksilver

The Notley Arms
(01984 656217). At the heart of a village close to Exmoor, this charming pub has a nicely decorated family room, thoughtfully furnished with toys and books. The pleasant garden is edged by a stream, so take care if your children are young.
Exmoor, Morland, Smiles and Wadworth.
🐎🦟🈂️◑🍴

Nailsea

The Blue Flame Inn
West End (01275 856910). *Just south-west of Nailsea.* A very fine 'cottagey' pub, with a wide

appeal. In the garden you will find swings, a Wendy house and a truck. No meals, but rolls are served.

Bass, Fuller's and Smiles, with guests from Oakhill and Bath, and traditional local cider.

North Curry

The Bird in Hand
1 Queen Square (01823 490248). *Off the A378, 5 minutes from junction 25 on the M5.* Very well renovated, this country inn has a low-beamed ceiling and cosy open fires, when the weather is cool. Children are welcome in the dining room, away from the bar. The pub is *closed Mon lunchtimes.*

Badger, Butcombe's and Otter, with guests such as Bath, Branscombe, Exmoor and Juwards, plus Rich's real cider.
⚑ ♣ ✿ ◖ *not Mon* ▶ *Fri & Sat only* ♥ ⚒ ⊙ *21.00*

Norton St Philip

The Fleur de Lys
(01373 834333). An ancient stone building, where parts date from the 13thC. It has been refurbished with great consideration for all except the ghost, who now has to pass through the bar which now blocks the passageway, on his way to the gallows. Skittles and shove ha'penny are played here, and there is a patio.

Bass, Oakhill, Wadworth and Worthington.
✿ ◖ ♥ ▶ A ghost

Pitney

Halfway House
(01458 252513). *On the B3153 mid-way between Langport and Somerton.* A wonderful CAMRA 'gem'. Open fires, wooden furniture and flagstone floors, with a range of local beers and tasty home-cooked curries.

Butcombe's, Hop Back and Teignworthy, with guests from Cotleigh and others. Plus real cider from Wilkins of Mudgley.
✿ ◖

Porlock

The Ship Inn
High Street (01643 862507). One of the oldest inns on Exmoor, 13thC and thatched. There is a fine traditional bar with a stone floor and roaring log fires when the weather is cold. It is free from piped music, has a separate games room with skittles and pool, and swings and a climbing

frame in the garden.
Bass, Courage and Cotleigh, with guests such as Exmoor, and Perry's real cider.
🐎 ♣ ❀ 🎇 ◑ ⌣ 🛏 ▶ Close to the sea and Exmoor

Saltford

Riverside Inn

(01225 873862). *Off the A4 between Bath and Bristol at Saltford Marina.* A smart riverside bar and restaurant, with a climbing frame in the field car park. Children are welcome in the upstairs bar and restaurant.
Bass and Wadworth with guests such as Smiles.
🎇 ♣ ❀ 🎇 ◑ ⌣ ▶ River Avon

Sparkford

The Sparkford Inn

(01963 440218). *In Sparkford village, just off the A303.* Corridors lead to several rooms, including one for families, in this 15thC coaching inn, which still retains many original features. A supervised soft play area with a 25ft bouncy castle, wobbly log, punch bag and balls, trampoline and see-saws is open Sun lunchtime (£1), and the garden has a log-style adventure train.
Badger, Bass, Butcombe's

Wadworth and Worthington, with Morland as a guest.
🐎 ♣ ❀ 🎇 ◑ ⌣ ✄ 🛏 ▽
▶ Super play area every Sunday lunchtime

Triscombe

Blue Ball Inn

(01984 618242). *Off the A358 Taunton to Minehead Road at Flaxpool.* This very pretty thatched pub, with a cosy interior, offers very fine views over the Brendon Hills from the garden, amongst other delights. Children are welcome in the conservatory. Cribbage and dominoes are played in the pub.
Butcombe's, Cotleigh and Otter, with Exmoor as a typical guest, and Sheppy's real cider.
🎇 ♣ ❀ ◑ *not Sun evening* ⌣ ✄
🛏 ⏰ *21.00*

Twerton

Dolphin Inn

103 Locksbrook Road, Lower Weston (01225 445048). *Off the A4 to the west of Bath, take the second turning left after Royal Victoria Park. Locksbrook Road is on the left.* Close to Weston Cut on the River Avon, this sociable pub has a bouncy castle, a slide, swings and climbing frame in the

garden.

Flowers, Marston's, Smiles and Wadworth.
🐎 ❀ 🈳 ◑ ↩ ▶ River Avon, with Weston Lock a short walk downstream

Watchet

West Somerset Hotel
Swain Street (01984 634434). A former coaching inn, now a lively local in this historic port. The food is good value. Skittles and pool are played here.
John Smith's, with guests from Courage and Wadworth.
🐎 ♣ ❀ ◑ ↩ 🛏 ▶ The seaside

Wellow

Fox & Badger
Railway Lane (01225 832293). *3 miles south of Bath.* This is a fine two-bar local in a very pretty village. Cosy settles and log fires, flagstone floors and flowers, skittles and shove ha'penny.
Bass, Butcombe's and Wadworth.
❀ ◑ ↩ ✗ 🕐 *21.00*

Williton

Foresters Arms
55 Long Street (01984 632508). *Near the West Somerset railway station.* Haunted by the ghost of a 14-year-old girl from the workhouse, which once stood nearby, this is a fine 17thC coaching inn. Bar skittles and dominoes are played here.
Cotleigh and Exmoor, with Morland as a guest.
🐎 ♣ ❀ ◑ ↩ 🛏 ▶ West Somerset Railway, and ghost

Wiveliscombe

The Bear Inn
10 North Street (01984 623537). *On the B3228, 11 miles from Taunton.* A 17thC coaching inn of great character, close to the town centre. It has a skittle alley, and other games are also played. Good, home-cooked food.
Bear Bitter, Exmoor and Otter, with guests such as Bunces and Cotleigh, and real ciders from Inch's and Sheppy's.
❀ ◑ ↩ 🛏

STAFFORDSHIRE

Acton Trussell

The Moat House
Lower Penkridge Road (01785 712217). *Turn north off the M6 at junction 13, then turn right down Mill Lane. It is at the far end (south) of the village.* This very handsome 14thC pub is in a Grade II listed building, set in 6 acres of fine canalside grounds, with two lakes.
Morland, Morrells and Shepherd Neame, with guests such as Banks's.
❀ ◑ ➳ 🛏 ▽ ▶ Staffordshire & Worcestershire Canal

Brewood

Bridge Inn
High Green (01902 850778). Pronounce Brewood 'brood' and you won't be far off – 'bre' derives from the Celtic 'hill', so it means 'the wood on the hill'. It is a charming and fascinating village, with plenty of interesting buildings to see, especially in Dean Street, below the tall elegant church. Look out for Old Smithy Cottages, which date from around 1350 and was once a hall house, open to the roof.
Speedwell Castle, which stands on the square, is a wonderfully ornate building, erected by an apothecary who financed it with his winnings on a horse named 'Speedwell'. Nearby is a chemist's shop with an 18thC frontage, which was the birthplace of Thomas Walker, the Victorian engineer who built the Severn Railway Tunnel. This fine pub stands beside the Shropshire Union Canal, which was built by Thomas Telford during the latter period of canal construction, and demonstrates his 'straight and level' principles (earlier canals 'wiggled about' more, following contours). You can play dominoes here, and there is a climbing frame in the garden.
Burtonwood.
♣ ❀ 🍴 ◑ ➳ 🕐 *20.30*
▶ Shropshire Union Canal

Burton upon Trent

The Bass Museum
Horninglow Street (01283 511000). This fine museum covers all aspects of brewing during the late 19thC, so your children will see brewing as a craft rather than an industrial process. There is a children's trail, and an all-year programme of activities, plus vintage vehicles and shire horses. Climbing frame and slide. The World Barrel Rolling Championships are held here

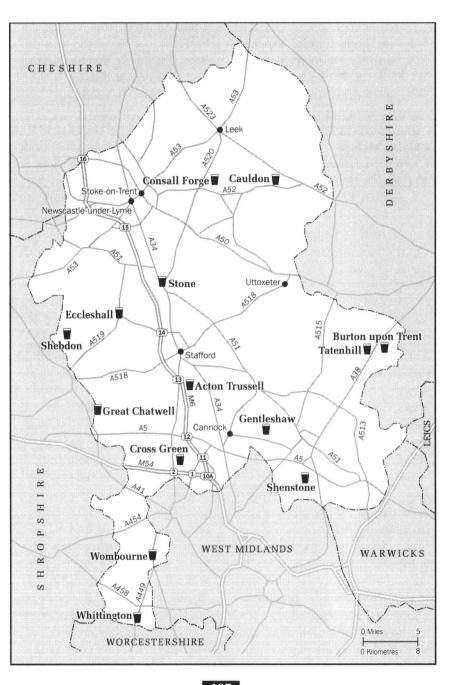

CHESHIRE

DERBYSHIRE

A523
A53

Leek

16

Consall Forge   Cauldon

A52   A52

Stoke-on-Trent

Newscastle-under-Lyme

15

A34

A50

A53   A51

Stone

Uttoxeter

A518

Eccleshall

Shebdon

A519

A515

Burton upon Trent

Tatenhill

14

Stafford   A51

A38

A518

13   Acton Trussell

Great Chatwell

M6   A34

A513

LEICS

A5   Cannock   Gentleshaw

12

Cross Green

M54   A5   A51

11

2   1   10A

Shenstone

A41

A454

WEST MIDLANDS   WARWICKS

Wombourne

SHROPSHIRE

A458   A449

Whittington

WORCESTERSHIRE

0 Miles   5

0 Kilometres   8

each September.
Museum, including P2 Imperial Stout and No 1 Barley Wine.
🐌 ✿ 🏛 ◖ ⟷ ▶ The Bass Museum, steam fairs, classic & vintage car rallies, heavy horse parades, World Barrel Rolling Championship.

Coopers Tavern
43 Cross Street (01283 532551). Genuinely traditional pub with a splendid tap room, with a 'top bench' seat, and an open fire. Children are welcome in the front room.
🗙 ◖ ⟷

Cauldon (Waterhouses)

Yew Tree Inn
(01538 308348). *Just west of the junction between the A52 and A523, north-west of Ashbourne.* Families are welcome in the Polyphon Room – and there are very few, if any, other pubs where you can enjoy this privilege. This wonderfully eccentric and award-winning place is simply crammed full of mainly Victorian paraphernalia and antiques, from musical boxes to ancient guns, and from pianolas to swordfish blades. Totally fascinating and very enjoyable. Skittles, cribbage, dominoes and shove ha'penny are played here.

Snacks are available most of the time.
Bass, Burton Bridge and M&B, with cider 'from flagons'.
🗙 ♣ ▶ The pub itself!

Cooper's Tavern
43 Cross Street (01283 532551). A traditional ale house noted for its tap room, with stillaged casks, barrel tables and a 'top bench' seat. No evening meals, but cold cobs are available. There is a patio.
Bass, Kimberley and Marston's
✿ ◖

Consall Forge

The Black Lion
Wetley Rocks (01782 550294). *Turn off the main Leek to Cheadle road through Consall village and continue down the gravel track, ignoring the 'Residents Only' sign. Do not be put off!* This is a fine pub in a remote and beautiful setting in the Churnet Valley, with the Caldon Canal, river and Churnet Valley Railway just a stone's throw away. The interior is splendidly straightforward, with a warming coal fire when the weather is chilly. During the summer the place is busy with boaters, back-packers and families. Excellent garden.
Marston's and Morland, with

guests from Charles Wells and Mansfield.
❀ ◑ ⌒ ⏱ *20.00*▶ Caldon Canal

Cross Green

Anchor Inn
Brewood Road (01902 790466). *North of Wolverhampton. Turn off the M54 at junction 2 and head north on the A449, then turn right at the first roundabout.* Well situated by the Staffordshire & Worcestershire Canal, this is a family-friendly pub, tastefully decorated with wood and stained glass. Toys are available, there are pictures to colour, plus activity packs for children who are sharing a meal with their parents – they also keep an eye on costs, with reasonably priced children's food and drinks. A special menu is available for blind and partially sighted people. Good vegetarian options, and a Balti choice. There is a slide in the garden, but no dogs inside, please. Wesley, Big Steak's children's character, is featured. Children are welcome in the restaurant and raised bar areas. Baby-changing room. *Ansells, Holt and Tetley.*
🏊 ❀ ⊞ ◑ ⌒ ✄ ▽ ♥ ⏱ *21.30*
▶ Staffordshire & Worcestershire Canal

Eccleshall

The George Hotel
Castle Street (01785 850300). A friendly family run hotel, with nine comfortable bedrooms, once a town-centre coaching inn. After a 100-year break from ale-making in Eccleshall, brewing began here in 1995. *Eccleshall (brewed here), with guests from small local breweries. Also Grays or Green Valley real cider.*
❀ ◑ ⌒ 🛏

Gentleshaw

Old Windmill
Windmill Lane (01543 682468). Situated on the edge of Cannock Chase, next to an old windmill, this sociable pub welcomes families in the lounge at lunchtime, and in the upstairs restaurant during the evening. There is a slide in the garden, and a crown bowling green, which you can use if you bring your own bowls. *Bass, plus a different guest each week.*
🏊 ❀ ⊞ ◑ ⌒

STAFFORDSHIRE

Great Chatwell

Red Lion Inn
(01952 691366). There are video machines, pool and table soccer inside this pub, and slides, a climbing frame and ropes in the garden.
Bass, Everards and Wells, with guests such as Greene King, Hook Norton, Morland, Shepherd Neame and Wood.
🐎♣❀🏠🌙☕⌦

Shebdon

Wharf Inn
(01785 280541). Canalside pub which stands by an aqueduct at one end of the great Shebdon Embankment on the Shropshire Union Canal. The garden has a swing and a climbing frame.
Tetley, plus two constantly changing guests.
❀◖Sun only▶☕▽
▶ Shropshire Union Canal

Shenstone

The Bull's Head
Birmingham Road (01543 480214). This striking 17thC coaching inn was once the local courtroom, with the cellars being used as a lock-up. It is said that a young girl, bricked up there and

left to die, still haunts the place. The small wood-panelled upstairs meeting room has an inglenook. The garden has climbing frames, a slide, see-saw and rocking toys.
Bass, Fuller's and M&B.
🐎❀🏠◑☕⌦▶ A ghost

Stone

Star Inn
21 Stafford Street (01785 813096). This is a superb old canalside pub, parts of which date from the 14thC. Apparently none of its 13 rooms are on the same level, and all those which constitute the pub seem to exude character, with low beams, tiled floors and open fires. The lounge has recently been extended, so there is now more space. The bars attract locals and visitors from the canal, who all congregate to enjoy its unique atmosphere, which is not sullied by bleeping machines. The Star is situated right beside Star Lock, so in summer drinkers spill out onto the canal-side to watch the boats passing through.
Banks's, Camerons and Marston's.
❀◑☕⌦▶ Trent & Mersey Canal and lock

170

Sutton Stop

The Greyhound

Hawkesbury Junction (01203 363046). *Leave the M6 at junction 3 and take the B4113 under the motorway. Take the first right, follow this around to the right, then turn left towards the canal. Cross the canal and turn left. Or ask.* This is a famous and fascinating canalside pub, decorated with Toby jugs, rugby memorabilia and, of course, items connected with the canal. At one time the buildings at the rear of the pub were used to store corn, oats and maize, which fed the towing horses. There is always plenty to see here: lots of boats, a stop lock, and an old pumping house, which once contained a Newcomen-type atmospheric steam engine, installed in 1821 and used to pump water into the canal from a well. Prior to this the engine had seen 100 years of service at the nearby Griff Colliery. It was known as 'Lady Godiva', and is now kept at the Dartmouth Museum. The building which faces the junction was Sephtons Boathouse, where narrowboats were built. Hawkesbury Junction is often referred to as Sutton Stop, taking this name from a family who lived here in the 1800s, and collected the tolls. *Banks's, Camerons and Banks's, with a different guest each week.*
✿ ◑ ⌣ ▶ Coventry and Oxford Canals, lock, boats and buildings

Tatenhill

The Horseshoe Inn

Main Street (01283 564913). A fine unspoilt 16thC coaching inn. The Forge Room, where families are welcome, retains the character of the rest of the pub. The large enclosed garden has an activity area and a slide. Good food.
Marston's.
🐴 ✿ 🏢 ◑ ⌣ ✂

Whittington

Whittington Inn

(01384 872110). *On the A49 near Kinver.* Dating from 1310, this timber-frame building was once the home of Dick Whittington's grandfather, and later Lady Jane Grey (1537-54), who was Queen of England for a few days until Mary Tudor, the legal claimant, moved in and had her executed. Jane's ghost is sometimes seen. The building has priest holes, a tunnel which connects with Whittington Hall nearby, and a

walled Tudor garden. It is full of character, and has open fires on chilly days. Families are welcome in bar three, overlooking the garden, where boules is played.
Banks's and Marston's, with regularly changing guests.
🎿 ❀ 🎠 ◑ ♿ ✂ ◁

The Round Oak
Ounsdale Road (01902 892083). This well modernised canalside pub caters well for families. The large garden has swings and a climbing frame. Children's videos are shown.
Banks's, with guests such as Camerons and Marston's.
🎠 ❀ 🎠 ◑ *not Sun evening* ♿ ✂
♟ ▶ Staffordshire & Worcestershire Canal

SUFFOLK

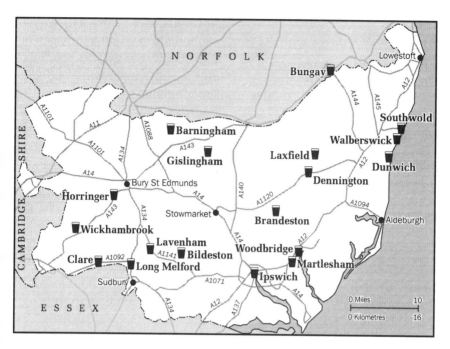

Barningham

Royal George

Church Street (01359 221246).
There are plenty of beams and a
splendid inglenook in this very
fine 17thC thatched pub. Pool
and cribbage are played here, and
the pleasant garden has shady
areas.
Greene King.
♣ ❀ ◑ ⌣ ⚡

Bildeston

Kings Head Inn

132 High Street (01449 741434).
Opposite the Market Square. This
is a rambling old 15thC heavily
timbered inn. Skittles and pool
are played, and there is a climbing frame and a swing in the garden. During the summer, they
often have a bouncy castle, Punch
& Judy show or a juggler at weekends. Live music played Fri & Sat
evenings and Sun lunchtime.
*Brett Vale ales brewed on the
premises, plus guest such as
Fuller's, Mauldons, Old
Chimneys and Woodforde,
together with some bottle conditioned ales.*
♣ ❀ 🏠 ◑ ⌣ ▽ ⚑

Brandeston

Queens Head
The Street (01728 685307). A 400-year-old family run country pub, with extensive gardens containing a 'play tree' and a climbing frame. Children are welcome in the family room.
Adnams.
🐴 ❀ 🏠 ◐ *not Sun evening* ♥ 🛏

Bungay

Green Dragon
Broad Street (01986 892681). Once The Horse & Groom, this friendly pub now fronts a microbrewery, where its own award-winning beers are brewed. Curry is served Wed evening, and fish & chips on Fri evening, but there are no other evening meals.
Green Dragon own ales, with Adnams as a guest.
❀ ◖ *not Sun* 🍴 *Wed & Fri only* ♥ 🚭 ⏰ 21.00

Clare

The Bell Hotel
Market Hill (01787 277741). Recorded as a coaching inn in the 16thC, parts of the building have revealed earlier origins. Today it is a smart, timbered pub, hotel

and conference centre with a garden room, comfortable lounge and friendly bars, with open fires during chilly weather. Good food, and afternoon teas.
Courage, Nethergate and Theakston, with Marston's as a typical guest.
❀ ◐ ♥ 🚭 🛏

Dennington

Queens Head
(01728 638241). *On the A1120 between Stowmarket and Yoxford.* An atmospheric pub right by the church, with fine timbers and a handsome fireplace. An area is set aside for families, but under 7s are not allowed on Sat evening. There is a slide and swings on the playing field at the back.
Adnams, with guests such as Morland, and bottle conditioned Adnams.
🏠 ❀ 🏠 ◐ ♥

Dunwich

The Ship Inn
St James Street (01728 648219). Thankfully not amongst those parts of the village which have tumbled into the sea due to coastal erosion, this a fine traditional brick-built village pub.

Warmed by a stove, the cosy bar has wooden settles and chairs on a tiled floor. The garden contains a wonderful old fig tree. Babies can be changed in the bathroom upstairs. It is sometimes hard to imagine that Dunwich was, during medieval times, one of the east coast's busiest ports.
Adnams.
🐕 🐾 ◑ ⌖ 🛏 ▽ ▶ The seaside, church and monastery ruins

Gislingham

Six Bells
High Street (01379 783349). *A mile or so from Thornham Walks.* Spacious pub in the centre of the village and adjoining the playground. Pool, bar billiards and cribbage are played here. Good food. No visiting theatre or clowns – 'only the landlord'.
Buttles and Margarets (brewed specially for this pub by Old Chimneys), with guests such as Adnams.
🐕 ♣ 🐾 ▦ *next door* ◑ *not Mon* ⌖ ⅃

Horringer

The Beehive
The Street (01284 735260). A pretty Victorian flint-walled cottage pub, with lots of cosy cor-

ners, and a fine terrace and garden to the rear. Good, interesting food.
Greene King, with Morland as a guest.
🐕 🐾 ◑ ⌖

Ipswich

The Lord Nelson Inn
81 Fore Street (01473 254072). This is a distinctive 16thC oak-beamed pub, with barrels behind the bars, situated next to the Fore Street swimming pool (and remember, it is swimming *followed* by beer, if you wish to enjoy the two). The quiet lounge is decorated with Nelson memorabilia. There is a small terrace to the rear.
Adnams.
🐾 ◑ ⌖ ⅃ 🛏

Laxfield

The Kings Head (The Low House)
Gorams Mill Lane (01986 798395). This is a rare and little-changed rural gem, where beer is served straight from the barrel. High-backed settles in the front room.
Adnams and Greene King, plus bottle conditioned Adnams.
🐕 ♣ 🐾 ◑

Lavenham

Angel

Market Place (01787 247388).
Facing the market cross, the
Angel was first licensed in 1420
and continues to offer warm hos-
pitality in the comfortable bars.
There is a sheltered garden and a
terrace by the Market Place.
Board games, dominoes, scrabble
and Trivial Pursuit can be played.
*Adnams, Mauldons and
Nethergate, with guests such as
Woodforde's, and bottle condi-
tioned real ales.*
♣ ❀ ◑ *not Christmas or Boxing
Day* ➷ ✄ ▽ ▶ Fine medieval
buildings in the town

Long Melford

The Bull Hotel

Hall Street (01787 378494). Once
a manorial hall, it has been an
inn since 1580. As you would
expect, the bar contains fine tim-
bering, old wooden furniture and
a large open fireplace. There is
also a pleasant paved courtyard
for fine days.
*Bass and Nethergate, with
Morland as a guest.*
❀ ◑ ➷ ✄ 🛏
The Crown Hotel

Hall Street (01787 377666). It was
in 1885, from the steps of The

Crown, that the Riot Act was last
read in Suffolk – if your children
are playing up, you might read
your own version before retiring
to the extremely comfortable bar
here for a calming pint. The hotel
was built in 1610, and still
retains Tudor cellars. There are
plenty of exposed beams around,
and roaring log fires during cold
weather. Long Melford claims the
longest village street in England,
plus a very fine parish church.
When you have seen the town,
you could visit the nearby vineyards of Cavendish Manor, to
sample their wine. Those who are
interested in Constable's work
can visit the locations of a couple
of his most famous paintings:
Flatford Mill and Dedham Lock.
*Bass and Greene King, plus a
couple of guests, which change
every two weeks.*
♣ ❀ ◑ ➷ 🛏 ⏱ *21.00*
▶ The village, Cavendish Manor

Martlesham

Black Tiles

Main Road (01473 624038). *200
yards from the A12 roundabout,
by the Police HQ.* A good family
pub with a positive attitude, in
what was originally a tea-room
next door to the historic RAF station. Children are welcome in the

restaurant, garden room and lounge (but not after *21.00* in the lounge). Baby changing facilities in the disabled toilet.
Adnams.
🐴 ❀ ▦ ◐ ↶ ⚲ ▽ ⏱ *21.00 in lounge*

Southwold

The Lord Nelson
East Street (01502 722079). *Off the Market Place, next to the sea.* A traditional late-18thC seaside pub where children are welcome away from the main bar. There is a patio to the rear.
Adnams.
❀ ◐ ↶ ▶ The seaside

The Red Lion
2 South Green (01502 722385). *Straight through the town onto South Green.* Built in the 17thC and once a fisherman's pub, it was tastefully extended in the 20thC. Popular with families during the summer, it serves locally caught fresh fish.
Adnams.
🐴 ❀ ◐ ↶ 🛏 ▶ The seaside

Walberswick

The Bell Inn
Ferry Road (01473 723109). With its origins in the 15thC, this is a fine country pub, yet it is close to

the sea. Warmed by a stove, the bar has a flagged floor and old settles.
Adnams.
❀ ◐ ↶ 🛏 ▽ ▶ The seaside

Wickhambrook

The Greyhound
Meetings Green (01440 820548). *On the Haverhill to Bury St Edmunds road.* A real, and very friendly, drinkers' pub, with lots of pub games – pool, bar billiards, dominoes and cribbage. Children are welcome away from the bar, and there is a climbing frame, rubber rings and swings in the garden, with a bouncy castle on bank holidays. They also have a 'pig pets' corner.
Greene King.
♣ ❀ ▦ ◐ ↶ 🛏 ⏱ *20.30*

Woodbridge

Ye Olde Bell & Steelyard
103 New Street (01394 382933). Calculated as possibly being Britain's twelfth oldest pub, this is one of three Grade I listed buildings in the town. It takes its unusual name from the 17thC weighbridge that used to be controlled by the publican, and now stands, minus its weight, in front of the pub. Children are welcome

in the dining room.
Greene King.
⚡ ◑ *not Sun, Mon or Tue*
evenings ➤ ✗ ⏰ *21.00*

Seckford Arms

Seckford Street (01394 384446).
Mayan Indian wood-carvings
from South America make unusual decor for a Suffolk pub, but
these are momentos of the own-

ers' travels before they settled
here. Once a small cottage, the
pub has been extended to include
a large conservatory, and families
are welcome there. There is
pleasant parkland opposite.
Adnams.
🐎 ♣ ◑ ➤ ✗ 🛏 ⏰ *20.00*

SURREY

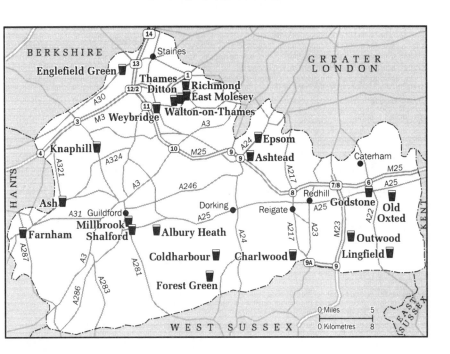

Albury Heath

William IV

Little London, Albury Heath
(01483 202685). This traditional
16thC pub has several separate
rooms, one of which has a warm
fire when the weather is cold.
Another is used for dining. Shove
ha'penny can be played here.
*Greene King, Fuller's and
Wadworth, plus a guest.*
♣ ❀ ◑ *not Sun evening* ♡

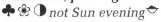

Ash

The Dover Arms

31 Guildford Road (01252
326025). This is a traditional two-
bar pub with pool and a pin-
table.
*Marston's and Wadworth, with
Ballard's and Hogs Back as
guests.*
♣ ❀ ◑ ↶ ⚡ ⏰ *21.00*

Ashtead

The Brewery Inn

15 The Street (01372 272405). *On
the A24 between Epsom and
Leatherhead.* A 19thC pub built
on the site of Sayers' Ashtead
Brewery, hence the name.
Children are welcome in the
restaurant, and there is a climb-

ing frame, slide and swings.
Burton, Friary Meux, King & Barnes and Tetley, with guests such as Eldridge Pope and Marston's.
🏃 🌢 🌂 ◐ 🍴

Charlwood

Greyhound Hungry Horse

12 The Street (01293 862203). If you are on your way to Gatwick Airport, or are visiting Gatwick Zoo, this is a good stop for a meal and a pint. Big plates, big helpings, and a children's menu. There is a small terrace garden.
Greene King, plus a guest, such as Courage.
🌢 ◐ 🍂 ⏱ *21.00*▶ Gatwick Zoo

Coldharbour

The Plough Inn

(01306 711793). *3½ miles southwest of Dorking, on the eastern slope of Leith Hill.* There are two friendly bars here, one of which has an open fire. The wide choice of real ales includes a couple brewed on the premises. Pool, cribbage and shove ha'penny.
Adnams, Badger, Hardy, Leith Hill (their own brews), Ringwood plus others, and Hardy bottle conditioned ale.
♣ 🌢 ◐ 🍂 🍴 🛏 ▽ ⏱ *20.00*

East Molesey

Kings Arms

Liongate (0181 977 1729).
Opposite the entrance to Bushy Park. Superbly situated, this is a traditional pub, with a family room, and bar billiards and chess for your amusement.
Badger, with Mauldons as a typical guest.
◐ 🍂 ▶ The Thames, Bushy Park

Englefield Green

The Sun

Wick Lane (01784 432515). Friendly and compact pub providing a refuge in this busy part of the country. The food is recommended, and children are welcome in the patio bar.
Courage and Fuller's, with Morland as a guest.
🐎 🌢 ◐

Epsom

Barley Mow

12 Pikes Hill (01372 721044). *Off the Upper High Street.* An excellent back-street local, with a conservatory at the rear, where children are welcome. Cribbage and dice can be played here.
Fuller's.
♣ 🌢 ◐ 🍂 ⏱ *20.00*

Farnham

Bat & Ball

Bat & Ball Lane, Boundstone (01252 794564). *Vehicle access is off Upper Bourne Lane – it is not easy to find, but worth the effort.* Noted for its fine Balti curries, this friendly pub has a Wendy house and a climbing frame in the garden.

Archers, Brakspear and Young's, with four different guests each week. Bottle conditioned Gale's is also kept.

Forest Green

The Parrot Inn

(01306 621339). A rambling and friendly village pub, with a bouncy castle and a slide in the garden. Baby changing can be carried out in the new area.

Courage, Fuller's, Hogs Back and Morland.

Godstone

The Bell

128 High Street (01883 743133). Children are welcomed 'under strict supervision' in this former coaching inn, dating from 1393.

Tetley and Morland, with guests such as Adnams and Ruddles.

Knaphill

Robin Hood Inn

88 Robin Hood Road (01483 472173). This is a good traditional local, where a part of the bar is allocated to families. Pool is played, and there are swings and a slide in the garden.

Courage, with guests such as Greene King, Hogs Back, Sharp's and others.

Lingfield

The Star Inn

Church Road (01342 832364). Spacious and well renovated, this is a village pub, with open fires, flagged floors and plenty of beams. There is a special children's area. Giant Jenga can be played, while in the garden there is play equipment plus goats, chickens and rabbits. Excellent food, including pasta and Lebanese dishes.

Boddingtons, Flowers, Fuller's, Greene King, Wadworth and Whitbread, with guests such as Morland and Young's.

Millbrook

Jolly Farmer
Shalford Road (01483 538779).
South of Guildford on the A281.
An imposing and sociable river-
side pub, with a terrace and
patio.
*Friary Meux and Tetley, with
guests from Greene King and
Morland.*
🐝 ◑ 👟 🍴 🕐 *21.00*▶ Godalming
Navigation, and a field opposite

Old Oxted

The Crown Inn
High Street (01883 717853). *Just 3
miles from junction 6 on the M25,
in the old village, off the A25.* We
can do no better than quote the
landlord's description:
'Traditional free-house dating
from the 16thC set in the centre
of the old village High Street,
with lots of period cottages. It is
rumoured to be haunted, and was
recently featured on national television in The Paranormal World
of Paul McKenna, when a medium contacted the spirit of Emy,
who worked here, and killed her-
self, in the 1850s. The pub has
been extensively refurbished to a
high standard, and has a separate
dining area. The downstairs bar
has a log fire, and the garden con-

tains a floodlit petanque pitch,
with boules, plus a large draughts
board painted on the patio. Logs
are used for pieces'. Children will
also enjoy the adventure playground with a log cabin and play
towers. Inside you can play
chess, draughts and backgammon. Well-behaved children are
welcome at anytime.
*Adnams, Badger and Fuller's,
with guests from Pilgrim,
Marston's and Morland.*
♣ 🐝 🏠 ◑ 👟 🍴

Outwood

Bell Inn
Outwood Lane (01342 842989).
Typically charming 16thC inn,
with plenty of beams, and open
fires when the weather is cold.
Pleasant garden with good views.
*Boddingtons, Harveys, Hogs
Back and Young's, with guests
such as Eldridge Pope, Fuller's
and Young's.*
🐝 ◑ 👟 🍴 🕐 *21.30*

Richmond

The White Cross
Water Lane (0181 940 6844). A
comfortable upstairs room, with a
balcony overlooking the Thames,
is usually available for families
(sometimes it is used for wed-

dings) in this traditional Victorian riverside pub, which has open fires. There is no children's menu, but smaller portions can be arranged.
Young's.
🏃 ❀ ◖ ▶ River Thames

Shalford

The Parrot Inn
Broadford Road (01483 561400). Winner of the Guildford in Bloom Pub of the Year competition, this is a fine Victorian pub by the village green, just up the road from the Godalming Navigation. There is a pleasant walled garden.
Brakspear, Morland and Wadworth, along with other guests.
❀ ◑ ➻ ✂ 🛏▶ Godalming Navigation

Thames Ditton

The Crown Inn
Summer Road (0181 398 2376). Very handy for lunch if you are visiting Hampton Court or the River Thames. There has been a pub on this site for over 300 years, although this one is not *so* old, dating from 1925. It is a

friendly place, with a good lunchtime menu.
Bass.
❀ ◖ ➻ ⏰ *17.00*▶ Hampton Court Palace, River Thames

Walton-on-Thames

The Swan
50 Manor Road (01932 225964). An imposing and friendly mock-Tudor pub with a large riverside garden. Children are welcome in the hallway and food areas.
Young's.
❀ ◑ ➻ ✂ ▶ River Thames

Weybridge

The Old Crown
83 Thames Street (01932 842844). Grade II listed, rambling, weather-boarded pub by the old course of the River Wey. Inside, the decor is charmingly nautical, and you can play bar skittles, cribbage or dominoes. Children are welcome in the lounge bar, and there is a patio and a riverside garden.
Courage and Young's, with guests such as Brakspear and Marston's.
🏃 ♣ ❀ ◑ ➻ ⏰ *21.00*▶ River Wey nearby

Alfriston

Sussex Ox

Milton Street Village (01323 870840). *To the east of Alfriston, off the A27 west of Polegate, and worth seeking out.* This has been an unspoilt family inn for about 20 years, so you will often find young families coming here, who had been, in turn, brought by their parents years ago. There is a large family room with toys and plenty of old pine chairs and tables, where the french windows open onto a large garden with a 'wicked' assault course, complete with a slide and swings. There are also plenty of picnic benches, and a large area for campers. A children's menu is available and, thoughtfully, beakers of fruit squash at reasonable prices in the summer. Splendid walks on the South Downs from the pub, visiting the Long Man of Wilmington, and across the hills to Seaford and Eastbourne. Drusilla's Zoopark is also not far away. Morris dancers perform here. Nappy changing in the ladies toilet.

Greene King and Harveys.
🐎 ♣ ❀ 🏥 ◑ ↶ ⚹ ⚑ ▶ South Downs, Drusilla's Zoopark

Arlington

Old Oak Inn

(01323 482072). *'Pass the speedway stadium and turn left'.* Traditional 17thC beamed pub with log fires and a pleasant garden.

Badger and Harveys, with Caledonian as a guest.
❀ ◑ not Sun or Mon evenings ↶

Berwick

The Berwick Inn

By Berwick Station (01323 423082). *From the A27 at Drusilla's roundabout just north of Alfriston, take the north turning and after about a mile The Berwick will be found next to Berwick station.* This charming Victorian country pub and restaurant, set amidst fine countryside, extends a warm and friendly welcome to families. Indeed, children will certainly enjoy the garden, which contains an exciting adventure playground with a wooden treehouse-cum-slide, climbing frame and swing. The pub interior is very cosy, with a low beamed ceiling and pine furniture, warmed by a log fire. There is an excellent choice of food, with children's specials. Table football and pool are

played, and quiz night is Wed.
*Flowers, Harveys and
Wadworth, amongst others.*
🛏♣❀🏨◑👄✒

Brighton

The Prestonville Arms
64 Hamilton Road (01273
701007). When you have 'done'
the Pavilion, spent all your loose
change in the slot machines and
enjoyed a spell on the sands, why
not call in for a pint?
Gale's.
❀ ◖ *Sat & Sun only* ▶ *Mon-Fri
only* 👄 🕒 *20.00* ▶ The seaside

Sir Charles Napier
50 Southover Street (01273
601413). This Victorian back-
street local welcomes children in
the back bar.
*Gale's, plus guests from regional
brewers.*
🖼❀ ◖ *Fri-Sun* ▶ 🕒 *20.00* ▶ The
seaside

Burwash

The Bell Inn
High Street (01435 882304).
Opposite the church. There is an
old and cosily decorated bar,
with an open fire when the
weather is cold. Plenty of games,
including table skittles, dominoes, cribbage, ring the bell and

toad in the hole. There is a patio
in front of the pub, and baby-
changing facilities in the ladies
toilet.
Bateman's and Harveys.
♣❀ ◑ *not Sun evening* 👄 ✒ 🛏
▽🕒 *21.00* ▶ Bateman's (once
Rudyard Kipling's home)

Fletching

The Griffin Inn
(01825 722890). A very attractive
brick-built 16thC inn, which was
voted Sussex Dining Pub of the
Year for 1998. Pool is played
here. Four-poster beds.
*Badger, Harveys, Hogs Back and
Marston's.*
♣❀◑👄🛏

Firle

The Ram Inn
(01273 858222). *Just off the A27,
4 miles east of Lewes.* An
unspoilt village pub, with no
piped music or gaming machines.
*Harveys and Otter, with Hop
Back and Cotleigh as guests.*
❀◑👄✒▶ Firle Place

Hartfield

Anchor Inn
Church Street (01892 770424).
Built originally around 1465 as a

farmhouse, the Anchor has been a pub since 1745. It has a fine verandah and plenty of beams. Dominoes are played here, and there are swings in the garden. *Flowers, Fuller's and Harveys, with guests from Bass and Morland.*
🐴♣🕸🎋◑👓🛏

Pevensey

The Moorings
Seaville Drive (01323 761126). As it is situated right by the beach, this is a splendid venue for families. You can enjoy a pint on the patio while your offspring dig like mad on the sands, safely within sight, and if a storm blows up, you can all retreat to the large and comfortable family room. Nappies can be changed in the disabled toilet.
Courage, with Harveys and Morland as guests.
🐴🕸◑👓🍴▽⏱ 21.00▶ The beach

Star Inn
Norman's Bay (01323 762648).
About 1½ miles east of Pevensey.
The Star is situated in a building which has just claim to be as old as the river which passes its door. It began just after the Norman conquest, when Pevensey Marsh was an inland sea, and it was

decided to drain it to reclaim the land. Initially a sea wall was built, but this was overcome during a storm in 1287. Later it was decided that the ultimate answer was to divert the River Ashburn to empty into the sea at Normans Bay, passing through the lands of Stephen Waller of Hooe – hence the river here is known as Waller's Haven. Flood gates were erected in 1402, and a 'Sluice House' was built nearby to house the men who were to control the drainage. It is this sluice house which was to become The Star Inn sometime before 1597. The origins of the name are equally interesting. Opposite the building were two Tudor cottages, where 'lookerers' stayed to tend sheep and cattle on the marsh. It was their patronage which led to the inn being called 'The Star of Bethlehem', which was later abbreviated to the name we see today. Smuggling was rife in this area in the 18thC, and there are records of fights with customs' men in front of the inn. The last recorded major smuggling run took place on 3 January 1828, and this ended with a major showdown near Bexhill. The pub has seen other notable events, one being a severe flooding – the high water mark is recorded on one of the walls! Pool can be played here, and there is a slide and swings over the bridge. Good food. Trad jazz every Tue evening.

Adnams, Harveys, Tetley and Charles Wells, with a variety of guests – there have been over 150 in the last 12 months! Also Biddenden real cider.

 The seaside

Punnetts Town

The Three Cups Inn

(01435 830252). Oak beams, sparkling brass and a warm inglenook will be found in this unspoilt 16thC pub, where you can play cribbage, dominoes and shove ha'penny. It also has three large gardens, and a touring caravan park out back. Morris dancers perform here from time to time.

Bateman's, Beards, Harveys and Wadworth, with guests such as Badger, Fuller's and Gale's.

Robertsbridge

George Inn

High Street (01580 880315). Characterful old coaching inn in

a deceptively large building. Pool and skittles are played here, and there are swings in the garden. *Boddingtons, Flowers and Wadworth.*

Rye

The Standard Inn

The Mint (01797 223393). *The Mint is a continuation of the High Street.* Rebuilt in 1420, a cannonball lies buried somewhere in the walls of this old pub, which are all bare brick, with plenty of timber. There is a pool table.

Old Forge and Young's, with King & Barnes as a guest.

Uckfield

The Alma

Framfield Road (01825 762232). *On the B2102 towards Heathfield.* A fine traditional town pub, which has been in the same family for generations. Quiet, with no music.

Harveys.

not Sun lunch

WEST SUSSEX

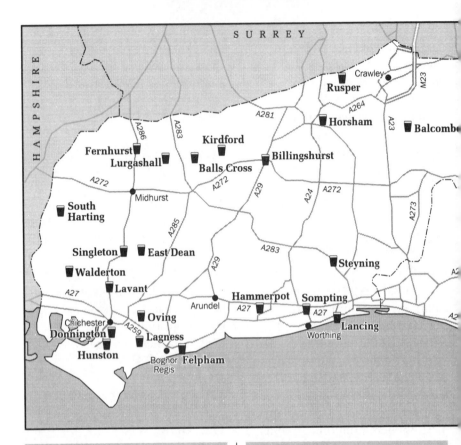

Balcombe

Cowdray Arms

London Road (01444 811280). *At the junction of the B2036 and B2110 north of the village.* Popular roadhouse with a no-smoking conservatory, and plenty of parking space.

Adnams, Beards and Harveys, with three regularly changing guests.
🌼 🈲 ◑ ❤ ✂ ⌚ 21.30

Balls Cross

The Stag Inn

(01403 820241). This 16thC pub retains its cosy inglenook, and stone floor. Children are welcome in the dining and games rooms. Skittles and shove ha'penny are played here.

King & Barnes.
🈲 🌼 ◑ *not Sun evening* ❤ 🛏 ⌚
21.00

WEST SUSSEX

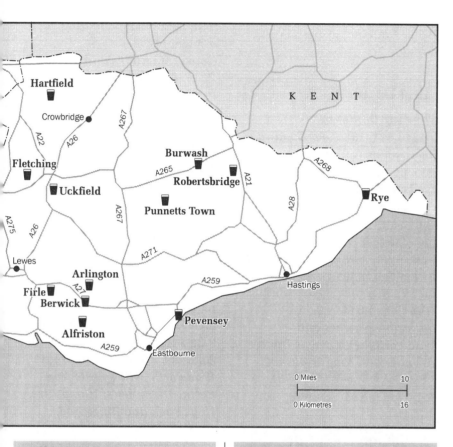

Billingshurst

Limeburners

Newbridge (01403 782311).
*About 1½ miles west of
Billingshurst on the B2133.* This
16thC country pub has a slide,
swings, a climbing frame and a
Wendy house in the garden.
Camping and caravanning.
*Gale's, along with Bulmers
Traditional real cider.*
♣ ❀ ▦ ◐ ⬦ ⏱ *21.00*

Donnington

The Blacksmiths Arms

Selsey Road (01243 783999). Full
with a fascinating collection of
bits and pieces, this is a fine traditional 16thC pub, which welcomes families. The garden has
an enclosed play area, and there
is a changing table and mat, plus
an armchair for baby-feeding.
*Badger, Bass, Coniston and
Fuller's, with guests in summer.*

❀ 🅷 ◑ *not Sun evenings Nov-Easter* ↻ ▽

East Dean

The Hurdlemakers
(01243 811318). *Near Goodwood Racecourse.* A flint-built country pub, popular with walkers and cyclists. The name recalls a rural craft once practiced in the village, which still retains its 'duck crossing'. There is indoor crazy golf, plus a slide, swings, sand pit and basket ball in the garden. During the summer they have barbecues, with live music.
Ballard's, Flowers and Wadworth, with guests from Arundel and King & Barnes.
♣ ❀ 🅷 ◑ ↻ 🛏 ▽ ♟ ⏱ 21.30
▶ Downland Museum

Felpham

The Southdowns
133 Felpham Way (01243 583916). *Just 2 miles to the east of Bognor Regis, on the A259.* This 'Big Steak Family Pub' makes a pleasant port of call if you are visiting Bognor, or South Coast World. There is a pleasant family area set aside, and the large garden is well equipped with hop-scotch, climbing frames, slides and springers, sur-

rounded by safety flooring, for a soft landing.
Gale's, Marston's and Morland.
🐎 ❀ 🅷 ◑ ↻ ✄ ⏱ 21.00
▶ The seaside

Fernhurst

The Red Lion
8 The Green (01428 653304). *On the village green, off the A286 between Haslemere and Midhurst.* Close to the church, this 15thC stone-built pub retains plenty of beams. Excellent food. Dominoes and cribbage are played here, with boules in summer. Children are welcome, as long as they don't roam around.
Adnams, King & Barnes and Wadworth, with guests from Ballard's, Fuller's, Hampshire, Hogs Back and Ringwood.
♣ ❀ ◑ ↻ ✄

Hammerpot

The Woodman Arms
(01903 871240). *Off the A27 between Arundel and Worthing.* Handsome 16thC thatched inn, with an open fire. Children are welcome in the dining area and no-smoking room.
Gale's, with Adnams, Greene King and Hook Norton as guests, plus bottle conditioned Gale's

Prize Old Ale.
⚔ ❀ ◑ *not Sun evening* ☞ ✄

Horsham

Bax Castle
Two Mile Ash (01403 730369).
*About 1½ miles south of
Horsham, on the road between
Christ's Hospital and Southwater*.
A partly 15thC pub adjacent to
the South Downs Link walking
route. Shove ha'penny can be
played, and there is a separate
play area in the garden.
*Bass, Fuller's and John Smith's,
with Brakspear and Weltons as
guests*.
🐎 ♣ ❀ 田 ◑ ☞ ✄ ⏱ *20.00*

Dog & Bacon
North Parade (01403 252176). A
popular suburban pub.
King & Barnes.
🐎 ♣ ❀ ◑ *not Sun or Mon
evenings* ☞ ✄ ⏱ *20.00*

Hunston

The Spotted Cow
(01243 786718). *On the B2145
between Chichester and Selsey*.
Traditional country pub with
open fires and a large, enclosed,
rear garden with garden chess,
boules, a climbing frame and
other garden toys. Children are
welcome in the saloon bar and
restaurant. There is space in the
ladies toilet for baby-changing.
**Gale's, with Fuller's, Greene
King and Shepherd Neame as
guests**.
⚔ ❀ 田 ◑ ☞ ✄ ▽

Kirdford

The Half Moon Inn
(01403 820223). *They suggest you
ring and ask if you can't find the
pub!* Finding a 17thC inn opposite a 13thC church, with flag-
floored bars and a cosy
inglenook, is reward in itself.
Here they also have a boules terrace, and there are opportunities
for tennis, riding, clay-pigeon
shooting, fishing and golf nearby.
The award-winning restaurant
specialises in fish, and there are
often unusual varieties on offer.
Pool, Jenga and backgammon can
be played here, and babies can be
changed in an upstairs room –
just ask.
*Brakspear, Harveys, Hop Back
and Morland, with guests from
Arundel and Gale's.
Addlestone's real cider*.
♣ ❀ 田 ◑ ☞ ✄ 🛏 ▽ ⏱ *21.30*

Lagness

The Royal Oak
Pagham Road (01243 216262). *On*

the B2166 between Chichester and Bognor Regis. Traditional pub which makes a fine stop if you are visiting Bognor Regis, Pagham and the seaside.
Gale's, with Hook Norton and Brakspear as guests. Bottle conditioned Gale's Prize Old Ale should also be available.
❀ ◐ ✌

Lancing

Three Horseshoes

182 South Street (01903 753424). On the seafront opposite the green, this pub provides a welcome retreat from seaside pleasures, with the added attraction of a very large safe garden, with a climbing frame and tyre swings to amuse your children. Inside, pool and a pin table are provided.
Adnams, Courage, Greene King, Marston's, Wadworth and a guest, which varies.
♣ ❀ 🕮 ◐ ✌ ✄ ▶ The seaside

Lavant

The Earl of March

(01243 774751). *On the A286, 2 miles north of Chichester.* A welcoming 16thC pub offering fine views over the South Downs. Secure cycle parking.
Ballard's, Ringwood and

Tanglefoot, with guests such as Bass, Brewery on Sea, Theakston, Weltons and Woodforde's, plus Westons real cider.
♣ ❀ ◐

Lurgashall

The Noah's Ark Inn

The Green (01428 707346). *Situated between Haslemere, Petworth and Midhurst.* Originally built on a marsh in 1537, this fine old pub is beautifully adorned with flowers during the summer. There are plenty of games to play here: pool, bar billiards, bar skittles, cribbage and shove ha'penny, and, when the weather is fine, the village green offers a large safe play area. They are visited annually by an open-air theatre and live bands: suitable for older children.
Greene King, plus bottle conditioned Abbot Ale.
🐎 ♣ ❀ ◐ ✌ ✄

Oving

The Gribble Inn

(01243 786893). *From the A27, take the A259 south-east of Chichester. After a mile, turn left at the roundabout, then take the first right.* Named after its former

owner, Rose Gribble, a schoolmistress and poet, this is a very pretty thatched cottage, with some very low beams, wooden settles, farmhouse tables and cosy inglenook fires.
A selection from Gribble, brewed on the premises, plus a real cider.
🐴 ⚘ ◑ ❤ ⚔

Rusper

The Plough

(01293 871215). In this traditional 17thC pub you will find, not too painfully we hope, *very* low beams, a fine inglenook and warm fires when the weather is cold. The garden is pretty, and there is a fountain out back.
Courage, Fuller's and King & Barnes, with Badger, Ringwood and Charles Wells as guests.
♣ ⚘ ◑ ❤

Singleton

Horse & Groom

(01243 811455). Friendly village pub, with swing boats and a trampoline in the garden. Children are welcome in the dining room. Good food.
Ballard's, Cheriton and Hogs Back, with Burton Bridge as a guest.

▶ Downland Museum

Sompting

The Ball Tree Inn

Busticle Lane (01903 753090). *About 100 yards off the A27 at Hill Barn.* Well placed if you are on your way to or from the south coast beaches. You will get a friendly reception at this family local, which was voted South Coast Pub of the Year in 1997. It has a large garden, with a swing and a climbing frame.
Bass, Morland, John Smith's and Theakston.
🐴 ⚘ 🏠 ◑ ❤ ⚔

South Harting

The White Hart

High Street (01730 825355). Beautiful gardens, with a playhouse, swings and a pond accompany this welcoming 16thC traditional country inn. And when it is too chilly to enjoy the fresh air, you can step inside and sup your pint by a roaring open fir. There is a family room, with a toy box, and pool is played here.
Burton, Friary-Meux and Marston's.
🐴 ♣ ⚘ 🏠 ◑ *not Mon evening* ❤
🕐 *20.00*

Steyning

Star Inn
130 High Street (01903 813078).
At the bottom of the High Street, by the fire station. Jill Adam, previous editor of this guide and now mother of several, recommends this pub highly, so I am delighted to include her description: 'Known affectionately as 'Bottom House', it is a traditionally arranged local which offers a warm welcome to all. The carpeted family room, which is integral to the rest of the pub, can hold about 20 people comfortably; it has a car game and toys for smaller children. There is direct access to the children's toilets and on to the garden. The garden is in fact divided in two: one part is safe for youngsters with a climbing frame, the other has a stream running through it.' Bar billiards are played in the pub, and there are nappy changing facilities. Live music is played every Friday night – suitable 'for all tastes'.
Castle Eden, Flowers, Fuller's and King & Barnes, plus a guest.

Walderton

Barley Mow
(01705 631321). *From Chichester on the B2146, turn right onto the B2147 at Funtington.* Another fine, friendly village pub with cheerful log fires when the weather is cold. There is a skittle alley, and swings in the garden.
Courage, Ringwood, Ruddles and Wadworth.

Barton

The Cottage of Content
Welford Road (01789 772279). A very pretty and award-winning 15thC riverside pub, with a garden at the front, and a large field at the back with a play area containing slides, swings and a climbing frame.
Courage and Theakston.
❀ 🏠 ◑ ⌒ 🍴 ▶ River Avon

Baxterley

The Rose Inn
Main Road (01827 713939). This picturesque pub stands by the village green and duckpond. Here you may feed the ducks, but they do not feed you, being kept firmly *off* the pub menu! There is a family room, and a slide, swings and activity kit in the garden.
Bass, Highgate and M&B, with a various guests.
🐎 ❀ 🏠 ◑ ⌒

Brinklow

The Raven Inn
68 Broad Street (01788 832655). You will find this friendly family pub at the top of the village. The garden has a Wendy house and an animal corner.
Banks's and Marston's.

♣ ❀ 🏠 ◑ ⌒ ▶ Not far from the Oxford Canal

Bulkington

Corner House
454 Nuneaton Road (01203 386159). Very large and friendly, with an orientation towards family eating. It is just down the road from the Ashby Canal, so you can enjoy a waterside walk before or after your visit.
Marston's.
◑ ⌒ 🍴 ▶ Ashby Canal

Corley

Horse & Jockey
Tamworth Road (01203 332643). *On the B4098 Tamworth to Coventry road.* Although it is not far from Coventry, and even closer to the motorway, this is very much a country pub. The family room is equipped with 'child-appeal', and the garden has a rather exciting 'Tarzan Trail' assault course, so keep an eye on young children if they decide to give it a try.
Theakston.
🐎 ♣ ❀ 🏠 ◑ ⌒ 🍴

Coventry

Biggin Hall

214 Binley Road (01203 451046).
Virtually unchanged since it was
built in 1923, this is a large and
distinctive mock-Tudor roadside
pub, where the plush lounge is
home to a very fine central oak
table. The games room doubles as
family room, and here you can
play pool, cards and dominoes.
There is a paved patio area outside.
Banks's and Marston's.
🐎 ♣ 🐾 ◖ ☞ ◷ *21.00*

Nursery Tavern

38-39 Lord Street, Chaplefields
(01203 674530). *A mile west of
the city centre.* This is a lively
and traditional three-roomed tavern, where children are welcome
in the rear lounge. Breakfasts are
available at weekends, and the
Sunday roast lunch is special.
And if you need to change baby,
help will be offered!
*Courage, Morland, John Smith's
and Theakston, with guests such
as Adnams, Greene King and
others. They also keep
Biddenden real cider.*
🐾 ◖ ☞ ◷ *20.00 if under 10 years
old*

Dudley

The Little Dry Dock

Windmill End, Netherton (01384
235369). *Take junction 2 from the
M5 and follow signs to Dudley.
Take left turn at the roundabout,
then turn right at the end of the
road, take the third turning on
the left, turn left at the end of the
road, then take the first right. The
pub is on the right. Or ask (!) –
most people in the area know it.*
This friendly pub, which stands
beside a remarkably interesting
canal area, contains a most unex-
pected interior. The ales are
served from a salvaged Runcorn
six-plank hull set inside an imita-
tion galleon. Ornate tiling covers
the walls, and the bar is further
enhanced with a bizarre collection of Heath Robinson mechani-
cal devices. The food is, as you
might expect, also interesting:
Desperate Dan Cow Pies (finish
one and you get a certificate) and
faggots 'n' paes (peas) are just a
couple of the extensive range of
dishes. The intricate canal network here is particularly interesting, with a couple of branches,
fine cast-iron bridges and a 3027-
yard-long tunnel which you can
walk through (but bring a torch
and do it *before* taking alcohol!).
Cobb's Engine House, which you

WARWICKSHIRE

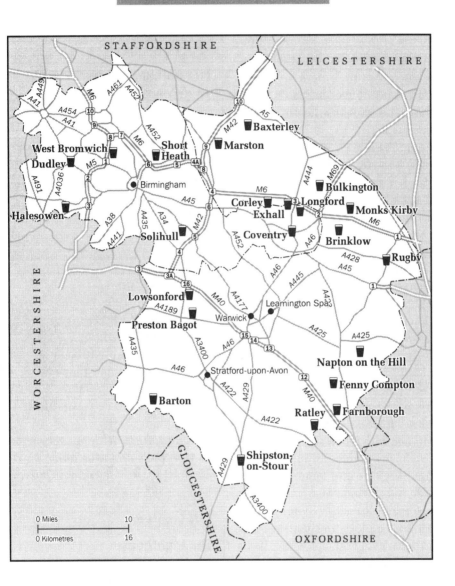

STAFFORDSHIRE

LEICESTERSHIRE

West Bromwich
Dudley
Halesowen
Birmingham
Short Heath
Baxterley
Marston
Bulkington
Corley
Exhall
Longford
Monks Kirby
Coventry
Brinklow
Rugby
Solihull
Lowsonford
Preston Bagot
Leamington Spa
Warwick
Napton on the Hill
Stratford-upon-Avon
Fenny Compton
Barton
Ratley
Farnborough
Shipston-on-Stour

WORCESTERSHIRE

GLOUCESTERSHIRE

OXFORDSHIRE

0 Miles 10
0 Kilometres 16

can see overlooking Windmill End Junction, is now just an empty shell. At one time it presided over a hubbub of industry, with boilers, blast furnaces and brick kilns darkening the sky, and horse drawn canal boats racing to get through the tunnel. The engine used to provide power for a pump in a shaft 522 feet deep by 7 feet in diameter, which lifted 400,000 gallons of water each day to keep the mines here dry. It is said that if it ever missed a beat, a thousand women's hearts missed one also!

Lumphammer and Morrells, with Marston's as a guest.

❀ ◑ ↩ ▶ Dudley Canal, Cobb's Engine House and Netherton Tunnel

Exhall

Greyhound Inn

Sutton Stop, Hawkesbury Junction (01203 363046). *Turn off the M6 at junction 3, and take the B4113. Turn left at the round-about to go under the motorway, then take the first right. Follow the road around to the right, then turn left, cross the canal and turn left again to reach the pub.* Canal and rugby memorabilia decorate this very fine and famous canal-side pub, which also has an extensive collection of toby jugs. There is a pleasant canalside patio, where you can watch boats negotiating the junction, plus an adventure playground.

Banks's and Camerons, with Morrells as a guest.

❀ 🏠 ◑ ↩ ▶ Hawkesbury Junction and the associated canal activity

Farnborough

The Butchers Arms

(01295 690615). There is a play area in the garden of this friendly and homely village inn.

Bass, Fuller's, Hook Norton and Boddingtons, with guests such as Lloyd's, Marston's and Woodforde's.

❀ 🏠 ◑ ↩ ⊙ *21.30*

Fenny Compton

The Wharf Inn

Wharf Road (01295 770332). *On the A423, half-way between Banbury and Southam.* A very fine canalside inn with a large terrace, a garden and play area with climbing frames and a tube. Canal theatre groups visit during the summer.

Bass and M&B, with guests such as Marston's and Morland.

🐴 ♣ ❀ 🏠 ◑ ↩ ▶ Oxford Canal

Halesowen

The Lighthouse

153 Combes Road (0121 602 1620). There is a splendid paint-ing of a lighthouse on the outside wall of this fine and friendly local pub, completed by local artist Russell Lowe. They have a portable skittle alley upstairs, a

bouncy castle in summer, and
children's entertainment on Bank
Holidays, with a party on the
Saturday before Christmas.
Children are welcomed away
from the bar.
*Brains, Crown Buckley and
Everards, with guests such as
Bateman's, Elgood's, Greene
King, Titanic and Wadworth.*
♣ ❀ ◑ *not Sun evening* ↶ ♀
▶ Gosty Hill Tunnel and the
Dudley Canal are just down the
hill

Longford

The Boat Inn
108 Black Horse Road (01203
361438). *Turn off the M6 at junction 3, and take the B4113. Turn
left at the roundabout to go under
the motorway, then take the first
right. It is on the right-hand side.*
This is a fine old pub just a short
walk from the Sutton Stop, on the
canal, with unspoilt rooms, a
cosy lounge and a real fire in
winter. Pool and dominoes are
played here. No meals, but snacks
at lunchtime.
*Ansells, Greene King and
Tetley, and guests including
RCH and Warwickshire.*
♣ ❀ ▶ Coventry Canal close-by

Lowsonford

Fleur de Lys
Lapworth Street (01564 782431).
Once a row of 13thC cottages
incorporating a bake-house, and
converted into a pub in the
15thC. It is now a very pretty
place, with open fires, low beams
and an attractive canalside garden. The famous Fleur de Lys
pies were baked here, but this
process switched to mass production during the 1950s. Children
are welcomed in the family dining area. The garden has an
enclosed playground with a slide,
swings and a climbing frame.
Flowers and Wadworth.
🐎 ❀ 🎦 ◑ ↶ ⚔ ▶ Stratford-on-
Avon Canal, and some locks

Marston

The Dog & Doublet
Dog Lane, Bodymoor Heath
(01827 872374). *From junction 9
on the M42, take the A4097 and
turn left at the roundabout at Lea
Marston. A very fine old red-
brick canalside pub.*
Bass and Highgate.
❀ ◑ ↶ 🛏 ⏱ 21.00
▶ Birmingham & Fazeley Canal
and locks

Monks Kirby

The Bell Inn
Bell Lane (01788 832352). A typical old English inn, with timbers and flagstones, yet the atmosphere has a definite touch of northern Spain, thanks to the friendly landlord. A patio overlooks a small brook and the countryside beyond. Live music, including a Spanish guitarist (naturally).
Boddingtons and Flowers, with Wadworth as a typical guest. Also bottled San Miguel and Alhamba Star.
🐎🎪◐👓♟

Napton on the Hill

The Crown
High Street (01926 812484). *Off the A425 between Southam and Daventry.* Look by the green and you will find this friendly and traditional village pub. Skittles, pool and dominoes can be played, and there are videos to watch.
Banks's, Morrells and Whitbread, with guests from Camerons and Marston's.
🐎🎪◐ not Sun evenings 👓🍴 ▽

Preston Bagot

Crab Mill Inn
(01926 843342). Described as a 'Brewers Fayre themed family concept pub', I remember it as a pretty 300-year-old country pub close to the Stratford-on-Avon Canal, and which was converted from a cider mill. Children are welcome, except in the bar area. There are slides in the garden, plus baby changing facilities in the children's and ladies toilets.
Flowers, Fullers and Marston's, with Morland as a guest.
🐎🎪🏠◐👓🍴▽▶ Stratford-on-Avon Canal, and locks (walk to the left at the bridge)

Ratley

The Rose & Crown
(01295 678148). This fine country inn has its origins in the 11thC. Jenga, draughts, cards, chess, scrabble and cathedral can be played here.
Badger, Theakston and Charles Wells, with another, different guest each week.
🐎♣🎪◐👓🍴 (🛏 *planned for 1998*)

WARWICKSHIRE

Rugby

Three Horse Shoes Hotel
Sheep Street (01788 544585). A
plush old 17thC coaching inn,
which provides a warm and
friendly atmosphere with log fires
and oak beams. Children are welcome in two of the rooms. There
is a patio, and baby-changing
facilities in the ladies toilet.
Boddingtons, Church End,
Judges, Wadworth, Warwick-
shire, plus guests from Adnams,
Cottage and Wychwood.
🐎 ♣ ❀ ◑ ⌣ ⅍ 🛏 ▽ ▶ Rugby
School Museum

Shipston-on-Stour

The Black Horse Inn
Station Road (01608 661617). *Off*
the A3400 beside Pettiphers Car
Showroom. Once a row of sheep-
farmers cottages, this is now a
very fine thatched 800-year-old
inn. Ale was brewed here illegal-
ly until a licence was granted in
1540. It has plenty of beams, and
is decorated with pieces of
Cromwellian armour, and horse
brasses and copper, around an
inglenook.
Courage, Ruddles and
Webster's, with guests from
Fuller's, Wadworth and local
breweries.

❀ ◑ *not Sun or Mon evenings* ⌣
⏲ *21.30*

Short Heath

The Broadway
Lichfield Road (01922 405872).
This is a 'Big Steak Wacky
Warehouse', with a slide, rope
bridge and climbing equipment
outside.
Ansells, Ind Coope and Tetley.
🐎 ❀ 🖽 ◑ ⌣ ⅍ ▽

Solihull

Old Colonial
Damson Lane (0121 705 9054).
Turn off the A45 into Damson
Parkway. After about a mile, it is
50 yards beyond the roundabout.
A modern one-room pub divided
into seven areas – one being a
family indoor sun lounge.
Bass.
🖼 ❀ ◖ *not Sun* ▶ *not weekends* ⌣
⅍ ⏲ *19.00*

West Bromwich

Manor House
Hall Green Road, Stone Cross
(0121 588 2035). Contained within a 13thC manor house built for
the Deveraux and de Marnham
families, this pub retains enough
original features to make each

visit an enjoyable experience. Timbered rooms, knights in armour and life-size effigies lend atmosphere.

Banks's.

✳ ◐ ↩ ⚔ ▶ This building!

The Churchfield Tavern

18 Little Lane (0121 588 5468). *Next to Sandwell General Hospital.* Small three-roomed family pub, with a floodlit crown bowling green, and climbing frames in the garden. Children's discos and parties are occasionally held.

Banks's and Camerons.

🐎 ✳ ⌧ ◐ ↩ ⚔

Alton Priors

The Barge Inn

Honey Street (01672 851705). *Just south of Alton Priors, beside the Kennet & Avon Canal.* Opened in 1810, at the same time as this section of canal, this was a prosperous public house, which also, at that time, incorporated a slaughter house, coach house, stabling, a brew house, hop store, bake house, smoke house and cart shed. Much of this was destroyed during a disastrous fire, which broke out on 14th December 1858, and was followed by what the Devizes & Wiltshire Gazette described as 'disgraceful scenes ... the cellars were entered ... and there was nothing but drunkenness and confusion'. However, such was the importance of the inn, it was rebuilt within six months, and between 1871 and 1957 incorporated a grocery and general store. The inn withstood the demise of traffic on the canal brought about by the coming of the railways and still thrives today, alongside the restored and re-opened canal. More recently crop circles have caused a great deal of interest in this area – unnatural or super-natural, they have been good for business, as has the White Horse of Alton Barnes, visible nearby. Camping and caravanning not far away. *Founders and Ushers.* 🏹 ♣ ❀ ◑ 🥄 ▶ Kennet & Avon Canal

Avebury

The Red Lion

The High Street (01672 539266). A thatched 17thC pub set in the middle of a stone circle. No garden, but there is a patio at the back. *Flowers, Morland and Wadworth, with guests from Marston's and Whitbread.* 🐂 ❀ ◑ 🥄 🥄 ✂ 🛏 ▶ Stone circles

Axford

Red Lion Inn

Kennet Rise (01672 520271). *On the Marlborough to Ramsbury road.* An attractive brick-and-flint pub, with beamy bars. The garden offers extensive views, and there are swings for toddlers. *Fuller's, Hook Norton, Wadworth and Young's.* ❀ 🏹 ◑ 🥄 ✂ 🛏

Barford St Martin

Barford Inn

(01722 742242). *5 miles west of*

Salisbury on the A30. This is a welcoming and atmospheric inn. ***Badger.***
❀ ◐ ➴ ⅟ ⛤ ⏰ 21.30

Bowden Hill

The Bell Inn

(01249 730308). *About 3 miles south of Chippenham, between the A350 and A342.* If you are visiting Lacock Abbey, you will find this fine roadside pub quite handy. There is a large garden, with a swing, a climbing frame and a pets' corner.
Hook Norton, Smiles, Wadworth and Wickwar.
❀ ▦ ◐ ➴ ⛤ ▶ Lacock Abbey

Chilton Foliat

The Wheatsheaf

(01488 682391). *From Hungerford take the Swindon Road.* A friendly and traditional thatched pub.
Morland, with guests such as Bass, Flowers and Marston's.
▦ ➳ ♣ ❀ ◐ ➴ ⅟

Chiseldon

Patriots Arms

6 New Road (01793 740331). *About 1½ miles from junction 15 on the M4.* This is a handy stop if you are using the M4, as well as being worth a visit in its own right. Very much a traditional pub, it offers a friendly welcome to families, who can use the spacious room, which is set aside. Pool is played, and in the garden you will find climbing frames and swings. Chiseldon is just outside Swindon, so it is handy for the GWR Museum.
Courage and John Smith's, with guests such as Brakspear, Theakston and Wadworth.
➳ ♣ ❀ ▦ ◐ *not Mon evening* ➴ ⛤ ▶ GWR Museum, Barbury Castle, Avebury Ring

Dauntsey

Peterborough Arms

Dauntsey Lock (01249 890409). Children are welcome in the games room and skittle alley of this well appointed pub, which also has a large family garden with swings, a see-saw, trampoline and slide.
Archers and Wadworth, with Berkeley and Itchen Valley as guests.
♣ ❀ ▦ ◐ ➴

Devizes

Black Horse

Bath Road (01380 723930). Well placed by lock 48, just above the

WILTSHIRE

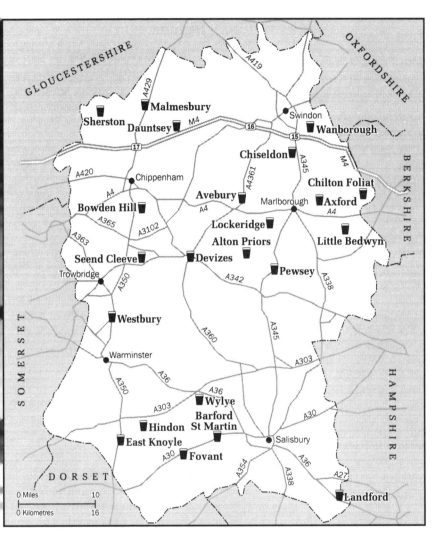

GLOUCESTERSHIRE

OXFORDSHIRE

BERKSHIRE

HAMPSHIRE

SOMERSET

DORSET

Sherston

Malmesbury

Dauntsey

M4

A429

A419

16

Swindon

Wanborough

15

Chiseldon

A345

M4

A420

Chippenham

A4361

Chilton Foliat

Avebury

Marlborough

Axford

A4

Bowden Hill

A365

A3102

A4

Lockeridge

Little Bedwyn

A363

Alton Priors

Seend Cleeve

Devizes

Trowbridge

A350

A342

Pewsey

A338

Westbury

A360

A345

Warminster

A303

A36

A350

Wylye

A36

A303

Barford
St Martin

A30

Hindon

East Knoyle

Salisbury

A30

Fovant

A354

A338

A36

A27

Landford

0 Miles   10

0 Kilometres   16

---

stunning Caen Hill flight of locks
on the Kennet & Avon Canal, and
consequently popular with
thirsty boat crews. The interior is
decorated with some pleasant
waterways' memorabilia. Skittles
and pool can be played here, and

there is a fine canalside garden.
Wadworth.
♣ ❀ ◐ ☞ ▶ Kennet & Avon
Canal and the stunning Caen Hill
flight of 16 locks, each with a
'side-pond'

East Knoyle

The Fox & Hounds

The Green (01747 830573). *Off the A350 between the A303 and Shaftesbury.* A late 15thC thatched inn, originally converted from a row of three cottages but with many later additions. Children are welcome in the conservatory. Views to the west extend for over 15 miles.
Fuller's, Smiles and Wadworth, with guests from Butts, Church End and Ringwood.
❌ ❀ ◑ ☜ ⅍

Fovant

Cross Keys

(01722 714284). *On the A30 between Salisbury and Shaftesbury.* Built in 1485 and full of interesting nooks and crannies, this friendly old coaching inn makes a good stop if you are touring in the area, or having a look at the Fovant Emblems, badges carved in the chalk of the local hills. The beer here is served straight from the barrel.
Adnams and Horndean, with Wadworth as a guest.
❀ ◑ ☜ ⅍

Hindon

The Lamb at Hindon

High Street (01747 820 573). Although the building here dates from the 17thC, there was certainly an earlier building on this site, as the Assizes are recorded as being held in The Lamb during the 15thC. Petty Sessions were held here until the 19thC. An important posting-inn, about 300 horses were once stabled here. Silas White, an ancestor of the Hindon family, a notorious smuggler and leader of the Wiltshire Moonrakers, once used The Lamb as his headquarters – indeed in 1954 blocked up passages were discovered in the cellars, no doubt once used for contraband. Prime Minister Pitt stopped here in 1786, and was upset to find no fresh horses available. Between 1798 and 1825 'The Masonic Lodge of Innocence and Morality No. 592' met here, and in 1812 William Beckford, a parliamentary candidate who built Fonthill Abbey nearby, spent £90 14s 2d on drinks to woo the voters. Author W H Hudson stayed here in 1909 while writing 'A Shepherd's Life'. A friendly and welcoming place, it is warmed by log fires, and offers fine bar and restaurant meals. Cards and

Scrabble can be played.
Entertaining regulars, as well!
Real ales include Ash Vine,
Wadworth and guests such as
Bateman's, Cottage, Hampshire,
Hop Back and Otter.
♣ ❀ ◑ ❤ ✁ ⛌

Landford

The Cuckoo Inn
Hamptworth (01794 390302)
From the A36, take the B3079
between Salisbury and
Southampton. Turn west at the
school in Landford, towards
Redlynch. Sited on the edge of
the New Forest, this is a very
handsome and rustic traditional
thatched pub. The small rooms
have a friendly and welcoming
atmosphere. Dominoes and cribbage are played. Excellent large
garden with an enclosed play
area, containing a Wendy house,
climbing frame and swings. Very
well priced traditional menu, and
take-away snacks can be provided
if you are off on a walk or cycle
ride.
Adnams, Badger, Cheriton, Hop
Back and Wadworth, with
guests from Bunces, Ringwood
and Smiles, plus bottle condi-
tioned Hop Back.
🐎 ♣ ❀ ⊞ ◑ ❤ ✁

Little Bedwyn

The Harrow Inn
(01672 870871). *In the eastern*
part of the village, which is
bisected by the Kennet & Avon
Canal, just a mile from the A4
near Hungerford. A handsome
small red-brick Victorian pub,
which is now owned by the community – hence the friendly
atmosphere it exudes. The decor
is simple and homely, and the bar
is warmed by a large wood-burn-
er. There are no music or games
machines, a quiet blessing.
Butts and Hampshire, with
guests such as Greene King,
Hook Norton and Ringwood.
❀ ◑ ❤ ✁ ⛌ ▶ Kennet & Avon
Canal, and a lock

Lockeridge

The Who'd A Thought It
(01672 861255). *About 2½ miles*
west of Marlborough, south of the
A4. An intriguing name and yes,
there is a little story behind it. At
one time this was the village
shop, until Edmund Rebbeck
decided to establish it as a pub.
The landlord of the existing village pub told Edmund he would
never get a licence, and should
forget the whole idea. But
Edmund was successful, and

chose this name as a constant reminder. Now it is a friendly family pub, serving fine home-cooked food along with the ale. The garden has a slide and a climbing frame.

Wadworth, with guests such as Boddingtons, Brakspear, Hook Norton, Marston's and Morland.
❀ 🏥 ◑ ☙

Malmesbury

The Smoking Dog

62 High Street (01666 825823). Standing not far from this ancient town's Norman abbey, this is a friendly and traditional pub and a worthwhile stop if you are visiting the area. Jenga, chess and Trivial Pursuit can be played here, and there are some toys.

Archers, Marston's and Wadworth, with Fuller's, Jennings and Sharp's as typical guests.
♣ ❀ ◑ ☙

Pewsey

Coopers Arms

Ball Road (01672 562495). Tucked away down a side street, this is a thatched pub of great character, with low ceilings and bare boards. Agricultural artifacts are featured. Light snack meals

are served, with curry on Tuesday evenings.

Oakhill and Wadworth, with guests from Bunce, Cottage and Hop Back – usually the stronger ales.
🐴 ❀ ⊁

The French Horn

Marlborough Road (01672 562443). *Just north of Pewsey Wharf, on the A345.* This is a friendly pub and restaurant close to the Kennet & Avon Canal.

Wadworth, with Bass as a guest.
❀ ◑ ☙ ⊁ ▶ Kennet & Avon Canal

The Greyhound

25 North Street (01672 562439). Pool and shove ha'penny are played in this lively, welcoming village pub, which has a restaurant. There is a tree house, slide and swings in the garden.

Flowers and Wadworth, with Ringwood and Tisbury as guests.
♣ ❀ 🏥 ◑ ☙

The Royal Oak

35 North Street 901672 563426). A family pub with a warm welcome, handily situated in the town centre. There are skittles in the function room, and there is a large play area in the garden.

Wadworth.
🐴 ♣ ❀ 🏥 ◑ ☙ ⊁ 🛏

Seend Cleeve

The Barge Inn

(01580 828230). Occupying the former wharf house, which included a bakery and tap room, this extensive pub, with its conservatory overlooking the canal, dates from 1805. At that time it was owned by the Duke of Somerset's family. In 1916 it became home to Fred Kempster, brother-in-law of the landlord, Jim Rayner. Fred, known as the Wiltshire Giant, reached the head-banging height of at least 8 feet 2 inches (some sources quote 8 feet 4 inches – you may need to convert both to metres for the benefit of your children! Good luck!). This extreme stature was not without disadvantages: for example two bedsteads had to be joined together for his benefit, and fitted into one of the bedrooms. But Fred took it all in good part, and often sat in the bar chatting about his altitude problems. The pub is now justly very popular, and handsomely decorated with a fine assortment of canalware and ephemera. The canalside garden is splendid, *but do keep a close eye on young children if they venture close to the water.*

Badger, Hall & Woodhouse and Wadworth, with guests such as Adnams, Morland and Charles Wells.

❀ ◑ ↝ ⅄ ▶ The Kennet & Avon Canal

Sherston

Rattlebone Inn

Church Street (01666 840871). *On the B4040 west of Malmesbury.* This stone-walled 16thC pub is thought to take its unusual name from John Rattlebone, a local hero who fought at the Battle of Sherston in 1016, when Edmund Ironside defeated Canute. Mortally wounded, it is thought that John Rattlebone died on the spot where the pub was later built. Skittles, pool, table football and cribbage can be played here, and there is a boules pitch in the garden. Children are welcome in the restaurant.

Greene King, Smiles, Wadworth and their own Rattlebone, with guests from Bateman's, Fuller's and Titanic. Also bottle conditioned Smiles.

🎄 ♣ ❀ 🏠 ◑ ↝ ⅄

Wanborough

Shepherds Rest

Foxhill (01793 790266). *About 2 miles due east of junction 15 on the M4. Turn north onto the A419, then right at the round-about onto the B4192. Cross over the motorway and take the first left.* Situated on the Ridgeway Path, this is a friendly, traditional rural pub with plenty of beams and brass in the lounge. Children are welcome in the restaurant, and the garden has swings, a slide and climbing frame. Camping in the garden.

Boddingtons, Flowers, Fuller's and Wadworth, with guests such as Adnams and Marston's.

Westbury

The Kicking Donkey
Brokerswood (01373 823250).
Turn off the A36 at Standerwick, north-east of Frome. Turn right in Rudge. You will find plenty of beams and brass in this fine rustic 17thC country pub. There is a very large garden, with a bouncy castle, swings and a climbing frame.

Bunces, Butcombe's, Ushers and Wadworth, with guests from the likes of Fuller's, Marston's, Smiles, Oakhill and others. Also Thatcher's real cider.

Wylye

The Bell Inn
High Street (01985 248338). A very fine old coaching inn next to the church, built in 1373, and with a large and handsome inglenook fireplace and plenty of beams. Alongside their real ales they also offer 21 varieties of fruit and country wines.

Badger and Smiles, with guests such as Exmoor.
21.30
▶ Stonehenge is just 4 miles away

WORCESTERSHIRE

Astley

The Hampstall Inn
Ferry Lane, Astley Burf (01299 822600). *Between the B4194 and the River Severn, south of Stourport-on-Severn.* This friendly riverside pub was once known as the Old Cider House. Pool is played inside, with swings, a see-saw and climbing stuff in the garden.
Banks's and Tetley.
🐴 ♣ ❀ 🏠 ◑ ➳ ▶ River Severn

Bewdley

The Little Pack Horse
31 High Street (01299 403762). *Up from the bridge, and turn left at the church.* The first of The Little Pub Company's pubs, its demeanour is not always totally serious, if the house newsletter is anything to go by! The town is a wonderful place, especially down by the River Severn, which at one time functioned as an inland port.
Burton, Lumphammer and Morland, with guests from Holts and Marston's.
🐴 ◑ ➳ ▶ Bewdley is a fine riverside town, always worth a visit

Bretforton

The Fleece Inn
The Cross (01386 831173). The Fleece is a splendid building with a fascinating history, as well as being a friendly and welcoming inn. It was originally a medieval farmhouse, with animals living at one end, and the family living at the other. At the end of the 15thC the living quarters were rebuilt to make an open hall and solarium (which was the upper chamber in a medieval house at that time). A large fireplace was added in the 17thC, when a rear kitchen was also built. The whole building would have been thatched at that time. In 1848 the farm land was sold by Henry Byrd after his family had occupied it for some 400 years, and he obtained a licence to sell beer & cider from the house. The great grand-daughter of the Byrds, Lola Taplin, ran the house with a rod of iron until she died in 1977 at the age of 83. She left it to the National Trust on the understanding that it would be maintained and run as a country pub. You can see The Brewhouse, rich with artifacts, The Dugout, once a pantry, and The Pewter Room, which contains an outstanding collection of pewter, some of

which is said to have been left by Oliver Cromwell in return for gold and silver plate taken to pay for the Parliamentary army. You can also see ancient cooking implements, such as roasting spits. Careful examination in the Brewhouse and Pewter rooms will reveal 'witchmarks', indentations made by the constant marking of the flagstones. In the garden you will see a fine restored barn and stone mushrooms, where sacks of grain were stored – the overhangs deterred mice and rats. The Fleece is a living museum, giving visitors the chance to enjoy the original atmosphere and to warm themselves at the open fires and contemplate life in times long since past, while enjoying a pint of beer. Good food, prepared in the kitchen of The Fleece, is also served. Shove ha'penny can be played, and the garden has a play area, with swings and a slide.
Gribble or Uley, with Brandy Cask, Fox's Nob, Highgate, Hobsons, M&B and Uley as guests, along with Westons real cider.
♣ ❀ ◑ *not Mon evening, or Sun evening Jan-Mar* ▶ The pub itself

Broadway

Crown & Trumpet Inn

Church Street (01386 853202).
Just behind the village green. There are plenty of oak beams, and warming log fires when the weather is cold, in this handsome 17thC golden Cotswold-stone inn, which is close to the church. Bar billiards, 'ring the bell' and Evesham quoits are played here.
Morland, Stanway and Wadworth, with Boddingtons and Flowers as guests, plus Bulmers real cider.
♣ ❀ ◑ ▶ Pretty village, handsome buildings and fine church

Claines

The Mug House

Claines Lane (01905 456649).
Find the church, and look in the churchyard. You will find this fine old country pub in a rare situation – actually in the churchyard! Plenty of beams create a cosy atmosphere inside. There are three gardens, where you will find a climbing frame and slide. Children are welcome in the snug. Barbecues are held on summer weekends, if the weather is fine.
Banks's, with Morrells as a

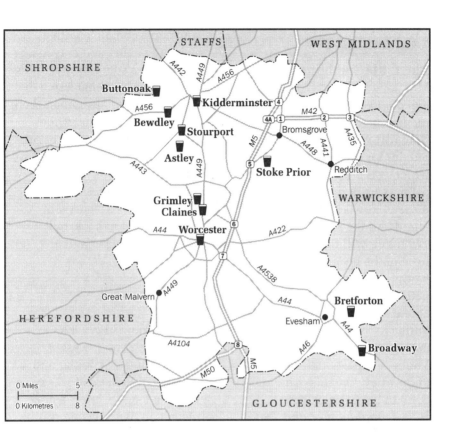

guest.
🐎 ❀ ⚗ ◖ *not Suns* ♥ ⏱ *20.30*

Grimley

Camp House Inn
(01905 640288). *From Grimley village turn into Camp Lane.* The drinking water at this isolated riverside pub is still pumped up from a well. There are moorings at the end of the garden, so it is naturally quite popular with boaters from the River Severn. Cribbage and dominoes are played, and there are swings outside. Touring caravan park, and some fishing. The village church is unusual in having a curious outside staircase by the door. ***Boddingtons and Flowers, with guests such as Enville, Shepherd Neame, Wadworth and Wood, along with Thatcher's real cider.*** ♣ ❀ ⚗ ◐ ▶ River Severn

Kidderminster

The Little Tumbling Sailor
Mill Lane (01562 747527). *When you are looking for the pub, find the lighthouse(!), off Proud Cross Ringway.* A lovely atmospheric pub in this West Midlands town, which was once dedicated to carpet making. It was also the birthplace of Rowland Hill, the founder of the Penny Post, in 1793. You will find his statue in front of the head post office, celebrating his 'creative mind and patient energy'. The town is also at one end of the splendid Severn Valley Railway, which makes an excellent ride along the Severn Valley to the wonderful old port of Bewdley. Outside drinking is done in the Trawler Yard.
Holt, Lumphammer and Tetley.
❀ ◑ ☞ ♉ *21.00*▶ Staffordshire & Worcestershire Canal, Severn Valley Railway

Offenham

The Fish & Anchor
Fish & Anchor Crossing (01386 41094). *North-east of Offenham, by the river on the B4510.* This fine 16thC black-and-white timbered coaching inn is in a fine setting overlooking the River Avon. Children's portions on the menu come complete with a colouring picture and crayons, and there is a soft play area, plus swings and a climbing frame in the large garden. In summer there is also a bouncy castle. Wide range of well priced choices on the menu.
Banks's, Camerons and Marston's, plus guests.
♣ ❀ 🏠 ◑ ☞ ▶ River Avon, George Billington Lock and unusual lock-keeper's hut

Pensax

Bell Inn
Near Abberley (01299 896677). *On the B4202 south-west of Kidderminster.* A popular and handsome pub in what was once a hunting lodge. Children are welcome in the snug and dining room.
Hobsons, with a constantly changing and varied selection of guests, such as Archers, Enville, Isle of Skye and Skinner's.
🖼 ❀ ◑ ☞

Pound Green

The New Inn
Near Buttonoak (01299 401271). *Take the B4194 north-west of Bewdley, and turn right after 2 miles, at Buttonoak. The pub is a*

mile along on the right. Children
are welcome away from the main
bar in this popular country pub
and restaurant, which has entertainment every Fri & Sat evening.
Al Boden and Friends entertain
on the first Wed each month. The
landlord plays keyboards, and
welcomes other musicians for
folk or jam sessions during mid-
week. Log fires in winter, and
pool and various family games
can be played, plus skittles by
appointment. A wide range of
meals, including excellent steaks,
available.
***Banks's and Bass, with a differ-
ent guest each week, such as
Enville, Hobsons and Wood,
along with Westons real cider.***
🐕 ♣ ❀ ◑ *not lunchtimes Sept-
June* ⌣ ⅍ 🛏

Stoke Prior

Navigation
Hanbury Road (01527 870194).
*Behind Stoke Wharf, on the
Worcester & Birmingham Canal.*
A fine spacious pub, situated by
Stoke Bottom Lock, which marks
the start of the canal's breathtaking climb to Tardebigge through
36 narrow locks. If you have the
time and energy, it is well worth
a walk beside the canal to have a
look at this awesome sight, which

provided a considerable obstacle
during the days when the canals
were used commercially, and
time was counted as money. To
speed things up, some boat crews
would urge on their horse (the
boats were horse drawn then)
while their boat was in the lock,
partially opening the top gates. A
block of wood was then wedged
in the gap and extra water would
pour in, filling the lock more
quickly. Such a practice would
not even be contemplated these
days! The Navigation pub was
used by the 'navigators', who
would stable their horses here.
No meals on Sundays, but hot
pork baps are available.
***Davenport's, Greenalls and
Tetley.***
❀ ◑ *not Sun* ⌣ ⅍ ▶ Worcester &
Birmingham Canal, locks

Stourport

Tontine Hotel
(01299 822048). *Between the
canal basin and the river.*
Stourport was once the hamlet of
Lower Milton, until the great
canal engineer James Brindley
decided that his waterway would
leave the River Severn here,
rather than four miles upstream
at Bewdley. This large and handsome pub was built in 1788 by

the Staffordshire & Worcestershire Canal Company as part of their development. Wedged between the basins and the River Severn, it is a splendid base from which to explore the locks, admire the clock tower and warehouses, and have a look at Mart Lane, a fine terrace of 18thC workers' cottages. Pool and dominoes are played here, and the garden often has a bouncy castle. ***Banks's***.

🐎 ♣ ❀ ▦ ◐ *evening meals are usually restricted in winter* ☞ ▶ River Severn, Staffordshire & Worcestershire Canal

Worcester

The Anchor Inn
54 Diglis Road (01905 351094). *To the south of the Cathedral.* Diglis Basin, where the Worcester & Birmingham Canal leaves the River Severn, is a fascinating place – not as smart as Stourport, further up-river, its position closer to the sea gives it a more maritime feel, and there are always plenty of boats to see. It is also worth visiting this 'canal' pub, well situated right by the Basin. It is a comfortable and traditional place, with some canal ephemera, and dominoes, cribbage and a skittle alley for your amusement. ***Banks's, with Marston's and Morrells as guests***.
♣ ❀ ◖ ☞ ▶ Diglis Basin, River Severn, locks and plenty of boats

Acaster Malbis

The Ship Inn

(01904 705609). Once used by Cromwell's soldiers, who commandeered the house opposite as an armoury, this is a 17thC coaching house, both smart and friendly. Its position offers a fine outlook over the river, and recalls a time when it was much used by the bargees. The comfortable and cosy bar has a log fire, and there is a climbing frame in the garden. Good food. Trip boats from York stop here.
Tetley and Timothy Taylor.
※ 🏠 ◑ ⇝ ⅍ 🛏 ▶ River Ouse

Allerthorpe

Plough Inn

Main Street (01759 302349). A fine and popular country pub, with cosy bars and an open fire when the weather is cold. There are some bar games.
Tetley and Theakston.
※ 🏠 ◑ ⇝ ⅍

Appletreewick

The Craven Arms

(01756 720270). A traditional old-world Dales pub, with low beams, wooden settles and warm fires. Dominoes and cribbage can be played here.
Black Sheep and Theakston.
♣ ※ ◑ ⇝

Beverley

The White Horse Inn

22 Hengate (01482 861973). Earliest records of a building here, which belonged to the church, date from 1585. It was certainly in use as an inn in 1666, since an emissary of Charles II used it as an office during that year, while on official business. During the mid-19thC farmers and traders visiting Norwood Cattle Market stayed here, as it once had stabling for 70 horses. It was bought from the church in 1927 by Francis Collinson, a saddler by trade, and was run by his many offspring. Until it was sold to the brewery in 1976 five sisters and two brothers of the Collinson family were on the staff, with Miss Nellie being the licensee. Hence it became known as 'Nellies'. Children are welcome away from the bar, and there is a pool table and pin-ball machine.
Samuel Smith.
♣ ※ ◖ *not Mon* ⇝ ⅍

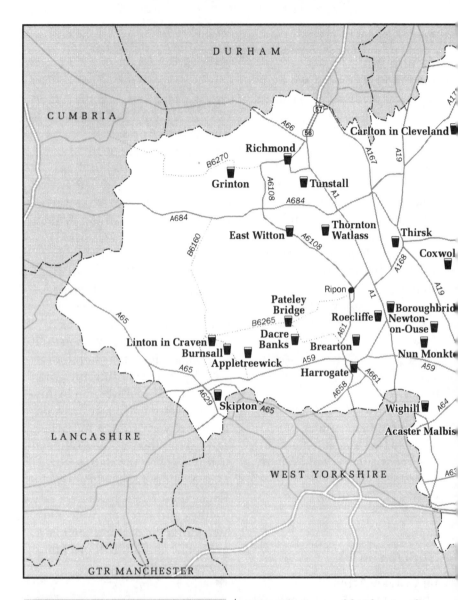

DURHAM

CUMBRIA

57

A66

56

Carlton in Cleveland

Richmond

B6270

Grinton

Tunstall

A684

A6108

A684

A1

Thornton
Watlass

Thirsk

East Witton

A6108

Coxwol

A168

Ripon

A1

A19

Pateley
Bridge

Boroughbrid

B6265

Roecliffe

Newton-
on-Ouse

Dacre
Banks

Linton in Craven

A65

A61

Brearton

Nun Monkt

Burnsall

A59

Appletreewick

Harrogate

A661

A629

A658

A65

Skipton

A65

Wighill

A64

LANCASHIRE

Acaster Malbis

WEST YORKSHIRE

A63

GTR MANCHESTER

Boroughbridge

Black Bull Inn
6 St James Square (01423

322413). *Boroughbridge is adjacent to the A1(M).* Fine old 13thC inn, Grade II listed, with small, cosy rooms and an inglenook.

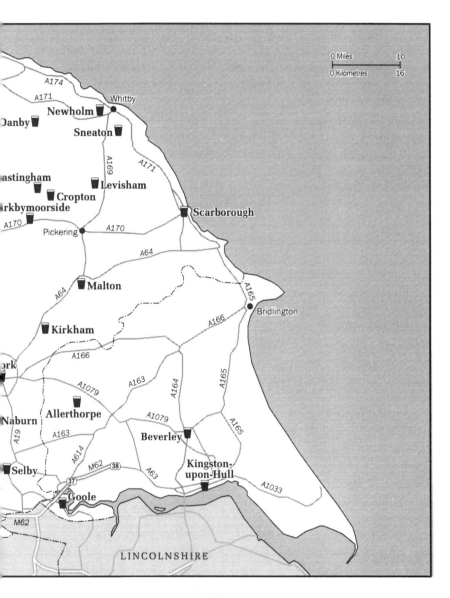

Children's meals can be selected from a special menu, and are all freshly prepared.
Black Sheep and John Smith's, ***with guests such as Clark's, Courage and Theakston.*** ✿ ◐ ☕ ⏱ *21.00*

Three Horse Shoes Hotel

Bridge Street (01423 322314). *Boroughbridge is adjacent to the A1(M)*. Having been in the same family since 1900, this small town hotel, with unchanged 1930s decor, offers a friendly welcome. Dominoes is played here. ***Black Sheep and Vaux.***
🐎 ♣ ◑ 🌥 🛏🕘 *21.00*

The Musketeer

Horsefair (01423 322511). *Boroughbridge is adjacent to the A1(M)*. Boroughbridge was the 44th of about 400 settlements established by the Normans between 1066 and 1348 to unite their new kingdom. It lies on the southern bank the River Ure, and this pub makes a fine stop if you are in the area. There is a pool table and pin-ball. ***Marston's, John Smith's, Tetley and Theakston, with various guests***.
🐎 ♣ ❀ ◑ *not Fri, Sat or Sun evenings* 🌥 🛏🕘 *21.00* ▶ River Ure, and Aldborough Roman Town less than a mile away

Brearton

Malt Shovel Inn

(01423 862929). There are plenty of beams and stonework in this fine 16thC pub. The landlord said 'we have no special facilities for children but we do make them welcome in the same way we welcome adults – they are all our guests'. That sounds absolutely fine to us. ***Black Sheep, Daleside and Theakston, with guests such as Cropton's, Daleside, Durham and Moorhouse's. Pipkin real cider is dispensed during the summer months***.
❀ ◑ 🌥

Burnsall

Red Lion Hotel

(01756 720204). *By the bridge*. This is an old 16thC ferryman's inn standing on the bank of the River Wharfe, with a fine outlook over Burnsall Fell from the front. Baby changing facilities are provided, with a quiet room for breast-feeding. ***John Smith's and Theakston***.
🐎 ♣ ❀ ◑ 🌥 ✄ 🛏 ▽

Carlton in Cleveland

The Blackwell Ox

(01642 712287). *Just off the A172, 3 miles south of Stokesley*. Tastefully refurbished, this village pub stands in an attractive village set at the foot of the Cleveland Hills, and is popular with walkers and campers. Good

food, with Thai dishes a speciality. Children are welcome away from the main bar. There is an adventure play area in one of the two gardens.
Ruddles, John Smith's and Theakston, with guests such as Black Sheep, Hambleton and Village Brewer, and bottle conditioned Black Sheep.
🐕🌼🏥◑🍺⚔🕙 *21.00*

Coxwold

The Abbey Inn
(01347 868204). A welcoming pub opposite the Byland Abbey, quite used to catering for the many visitors. Attractively decorated with plenty of old furniture and bygones, and warmed by open fires when the weather is chilly. It is well placed for visiting the many sights in this area, including Newburgh Priory, built on the remains of a 12thC Augustinian Priory, and where it is said Oliver Cromwell's body lies interred in a bricked-up vault, never opened.
Tetley, with Hambleton as a guest.
🌼◑🍺▶ The Abbey

Cropton

The New Inn
(01751 417330). There is an open fire in the friendly beamed bar in this very fine and traditional village inn. Records reveal that ale was brewed in Cropton in 1613, and this splendid tradition was revived in 1984 in the cellar of this pub with the opening of a micro-brewery. This proved to be very successful and has grown so that guided tours of their new brewery, now next door, are offered (although you must be over 12 years old to join them). The beers brewed here have won many awards, as has the pub itself. Children are welcome in the conservatory and pool room, and there are baby-changing facilities in the Visitor Centre.
Cropton's (brewed here).
🐕♣◑🍺⚔🛏🔽▶ Brewery tours March-November 10.00-16.00

Dacre Banks

Royal Oak Inn
(01423 780200). An oak-panelled 18thC coaching inn, with plenty of beams, and some interesting quotes printed on the walls. Excellent views over Nidderdale. Pool and board games are played

here. Children are welcome in the dining and games rooms.
Black Sheep and Theakston.
🖾 ♣ ✿ ◐ *not Sun evening* ♡ ⏱ *21.00*

Danby

Duke of Wellington
(01287 660351). Built in 1732, when it was used as a staging post and recruiting centre, this is now a warm, friendly and homely country inn. There is a very fine traditional bar, with a log fire. Also excellent walks from the pub – they provide their own leaflet detailing four of them.
Camerons, Ruddles, John Smith's and Theakston.
✿ ◐ ♡ ✄ 🛏 ▶ Danby Lodge, Danby Castle

East Witton

The Blue Lion
(01969 624273). *On the Leyburn to Masham road.* Overlooking Witton Fell, this accommodating pub has a characterful bar and a cheerful log fire on cold days. Children are welcome in the 'new' back bar. Babies can be changed in the large disabled/ ladies toilet.
Black Sheep, John Smith's and Theakston, and bottle condi-

tioned Black Sheep as well.
🖾 ✿ ◐ ♡ 🛏 ▽

Goole

The Old George
Market Square (01405 763147). This friendly town-centre pub was once the 'Vermuyden Hotel' (Sir Cornelius Vermuyden was a Dutch engineer who was responsible for many drainage schemes, and thus the creation of waterways hereabouts, during the 17thC), and has many early pictures of Goole on display. Pool and dominoes are played here. Children are welcome in the rear room.
John Smith's and Stones.
♣ ✿ ◖ ♡ ✄ ▶ Canal, docks, ships and the River Ouse

Grinton

The Bridge Inn
(01748 884224). *10 miles from Richmond on the A6108.* In a peaceful setting beside the River Swale, and with spectacular views over the hills and moors, this is a friendly and hospitable pub catering for those of all ages. Pool is played, and there is a large-screen TV. Babies can be changed in the ladies toilet.
John Smith's, Tetley and

Theakston, with guests such as Hambleton.

🐎 ♣ ❀ ◑ ⌣ ✄ 🛏

Harrogate

Prince of Wales
High Street, Knaresborough Road, Starbeck (01423 884235). *Starbeck is on the A59, towards Knaresborough.* This community orientated pub welcomes children in the lounge and function room. Slides, swings and climbing frames are to be found in the garden.
John Smith's.
🖼 ❀ 🎦 ◖ ⌣ ▽ ⏱ *19.00*

Kingston-upon-Hull

St Johns Hotel
10 Queens Road (01482 343669). Known locally as 'Johnnies', this is the epitome of an English street-corner local – Victorian, multi-roomed, loved by its regulars and welcoming to visitors. Children are welcome in the music or family rooms. No food is served, but you can bring your fish and chips, or whatever, with you and eat it here.
Mansfield.
🐎 ❀ ⏱ *21.00*

Kirkbymoorside

The Lion Inn
Blakey Ridge (01751 417320). *Between Hutton-le-Hole and Castleton.* At the highest point of the North Yorkshire Moors this fine 16thC pub offers breathtaking views. With open fires day and night, and low-beamed ceilings, it offers warmth, shelter and a friendly atmosphere.
John Smith's, Tetley and Theakston.
🐎 ◑ ⌣ ✄ 🛏

Kirkham

Stone Trough Inn
(01653 618713). *1½ miles off the A64 between York and Malton.* A friendly atmosphere awaits visitors to this cosy pub, with its bars warmed by log fires. Pool, shove ha'penny and dominoes are played here. There is a patio and terrace for sunny days.
Jennings, Timothy Taylor, Tetley and Theakston.
🐎 ♣ ❀ ◑ ⌣ ✄ ▶ Kirkham Abbey

Lastingham

Blacksmiths Arms
(01751 417247). This fine traditional inn has a cooking range

and open fires when the weather is cool. Games are played in the pool and darts room.
Black Sheep, Hambleton and Theakston.
🐴 ♣ ✿ ◐ ☕ ⚲ 🛏

Levisham

Horseshoe Inn
Main Street (01751 460240). The Horseshoe is in a village which is a stop on the North York Moors Railway, so you can, if you wish, arrive by steam train. It exemplifies the cosy rural pub, standing snug and secure by the village green. Bar billiards.
Theakstons, with Tetley as a guest.
♣ ✿ ◐ ☕ ⚲ 🛏 ⏰ 21.30

Linton in Craven

Fountaine Inn
(01756 752210). *From Skipton take the B6265 for 8 miles, then turn right at the Tilcon plant.* This friendly inn stands beside a stream, overlooking the village green, where Morris dancers and travelling minstrels sometimes perform. The ancient game of bull ring can be played here.
Black Sheep, Black Bull, and Theakston.
♣ ✿ ◐ ☕ ⚲ ♀

Malton

Crown Hotel (Suddaby's)
12 Wheelgate (01653 692038). *Right in the town centre.* The Suddaby family have run this friendly small Georgian hotel for over 100 years now. It has strong horse racing connections, with the 1925 Grand National winner, Double Chance, once stabled here. Indeed a beer has been named in the horse's honour, and this was once brewed by The Malton Brewery Company in the stable block at the back. Children are welcome in the children's room and the conservatory at the back, which has been created by incorporating the old courtyard walls, covered with bushy climbing plants.
Bateman's and Malton, with guests such as Barnsley, Daleside and Hambleton, plus bottled Daleside ales, including Morocco.
🐴 ♣ ◖ *not Sun, and sandwiches only on Tue* ☕ 🛏 ▶ Castle Howard is just 4½ miles away

Naburn

The Blacksmiths Arms
Main Street (01904 623464). There is a lovely collection of teapots, brasses, plates and prints

in this fine black and white pub. Warmed by an open fire, the building was, for 300 or so years, run as the village smithy. It is friendly and welcoming, and offers excellent food. The River Ouse is just a short walk away with Naburn Locks, which mark the tidal limit on the river, just a little further. They also rent out a holiday cottage, which is in the adjoining stable block.
Mansfield.
🍀 ◑ ⌣ ⏃ *21.30*

Newholm

Ye Olde Beehive Inn
(01947 602703). Fashionable, notable and hospitable, this ancient family-run village inn has plenty of old oak beams, and a pub sign written in verse. Only real ales are served.
John Smith's and Theakston.
🐚 🍀 ◑ *no food on Tue* ⌣ ⏃ 🍺
▽

Newton-on-Ouse

The Dawnay Arms
(01347 848345). The River Ouse flows by the bottom of the garden of this charming 18thC inn, which is a very pleasant place to be when the weather is fine. However, the inside is equally

charming, with plenty of beams, leather chairs and warming open fires. Good food, with an extensive vegetarian menu.
Boddingtons and Tetley, with Morland as a guest.
🍀 🍀 ◑ ⌣ ▶ River Ouse

Nun Monkton

The Alice Hawthorn
(01423 330303). A stylish and comfortable pub on the green, named after a racehorse, and perfectly at home in this spacious and attractive village of brick cottages and houses, laid out around a large triangular green, complete with a maypole and duckpond. At the end of the green, close to the river amongst trees and approachable only on foot, is the Church of St Mary. This traditionally occupies the site of a hermit's chapel destroyed by the Danes in AD867 and is the only building of a Benedictine Priory which survives. Built 1153-1180 in Early English style, the church has a late Norman porch and some handsome arcading above the lower windows, to which access is gained up a staircase in the north-west angle. In between the windows there are niches, which probably once contained effigies of the twelve apostles. Set

into the floor by the altar is the pre-Reformation stone altar, with five crosses cut into it, representing the wounds of Christ. It really is well worth a visit, as is the pub, which has good food in the bar, dining room or restaurant, and a garden. Camping by arrangement.

Boddingtons, Camerons, Tetley and Whitbread, with a guest ale changing each week.
❀ ◑ ➢ ✕ ▶ St Mary's Church, the village green, duck pond and maypole

Pateley Bridge

Half Moon Inn
Fell Beck (01423 711560). Close to Brimham Rocks, this friendly pub has a fine sunny lounge.
Theakston and Younger.
🐎 ♣ ❀ ◑ ➢ 🛏 ▶ Brimham Rocks

Richmond

Black Lion Hotel
Finkle Street (01748 823121). The castle attracts many visitors to this popular town, and the Black Lion makes a fine base for exploration. It is a 400-year-old coaching inn, which offers good family accommodation, including cots. Highchairs are provided in the

restaurant, and there is a private area upstairs for nappy-changing.
Camerons, Flowers and Tetley, with various guests
🐎 ♣ ❀ ◑ ➢ ✕ 🛏 ▽ ▶
Richmond Castle

Roecliffe

The Crown Inn
(01423 322578). *Just over a mile south-west of Boroughbridge.* An exceptionally pretty end of terrace pub, with a fine fire inside, and picnic benches outside for the summer. Children are welcome in the snug.
Black Sheep, John Smith's and Tetley.
🖾 ❀ ◑ ➢ 🛏

Scarborough

The Cask Inn
Cambridge Terrace (01723 500570). *Cross Valley Bridge and it is the first turning on the right.* Owned by the same family for 20 years now, the Cask is a multi-roomed free house, with a fine family room (open all day), and makes a worthwhile stop if you are exploring the town's many delights, which include a spa and the beach. Self-catering apartments above.
Tetley, Theakston and Younger,

with Black Sheep and Ruddles as guests.

☂❀◑⬸⌂▶ The seaside **Scalby Mills Old Hotel** Scalby Mills Road (01723 500449). *Near the Sea-Life Centre, next to the sea and on the Cleveland Way walk.* This fine traditional and historic pub is in what was originally a water-powered corn mill, with fine sea views. The outside drinking area adjoins a beck and pebble beach. The children's room is no-smoking.

Daleside, Highwood, with guests such as Barnsley and North Yorkshire, plus associated bottled real ales.

▣❀◑⬸✄⏰ *18.00* ▶ The seaside, Sea-Life Centre

Selby

Anchor Inn

Doncaster Road, Burn Bridge (01757 270255). *On the A19, 2 miles south of Selby.* Canalside, this pub has an extensive collection of animals in the garden, including lop-eared rabbits and chipmunks. They also have some well-kept aquariums, plus swings and a climbing frame.

John Smith's.

❀▣◑⬸✄▶ Selby Canal, animals in the garden

Skipton

The Royal Shepherd

Canal Street (01756 793178). Another excellent canalside pub overlooking the Springs Branch of the Leeds & Liverpool, and which was named in recognition of King George III's support for the introduction of Merino sheep from Spain into the local stock. The Springs Branch is a particularly interesting stretch of canal, well worthy of exploration. Having left the main line, it soon enters what is virtually a ravine, overlooked by Skipton Castle. It was the Earl of Thanet, the owner of the castle, who built the branch in order to carry limestone from his quarry nearby, where rock was transferred to the boats via 120-foot-long chutes. The quarry still functions, but the stone is now transported by trains and lorries, and the canal has switched to recreational use. The Royal Shepherd is lovely and old-fashioned, with no jukebox or fruit machines. The bars of the pub feature some fine old photographs of Skipton, and the canal, plus some cricketing pictures, depicting the Yorkshire and England teams during their glory days (guess how old they are!). Stained glass panels also show the canal, and there are paintings and poetry for sale. ***Boddingtons, Cains, Marston's and Whitbread***.

❀ ◖ ☛ ▶ The Leeds & Liverpool Canal, The Springs Branch, Skipton Castle and indeed the fine town of Skipton itself

Sneaton

Wilson Arms

(01947 602552). You can walk from this pub into Whitby along an ancient flagstoned Monks' Path, once used by monks to reach the cliff-top abbey, but you will certainly want to have spent some time here first, to enjoy both the pub, its food, and the splendid view. The building dates from the 18thC, and is Grade II listed. Inside it is warm and friendly, with plenty of oak beams and, of course, cosy fires to warm you when the wind whips in off the North Sea. Meals are excellent. Tuesday is quiz night, and there is a pool table. ***John Smith's and Theakston, with the addition of Barnsley and Black Sheep during the summer months***.

🐎 ♣ ❀ ◖ *not Mon-Fri or Sun evening during the winter* ☛ ✂ 🦴 *no accommodation for children under 14 years old*

▶ Whitby, Sneaton Beacon, Falling Foss waterfall

Thirsk

Ye Olde Three Tuns

Finkle Street (01845 523291). This is Thirsk's original coaching inn, built in the 13thC. They often have a bouncy castle in the garden during the summer. ***Tetley, with guests such as Eldridge Pope and Greene King***. 🐎 ❀ ◖ ☛

Thornton Watlass

Buck Inn

(01677 422461). *Just off the B6268 between Masham and Bedale*. Quietly attractive brick-built inn which stands beside the village cricket pitch. The small bar has an open fire. There is a climbing frame, a swing, a slide and a bouncy motorbike in the garden, and quoits are played. Children are welcome, but not in the Function Room at weekends, when there are music nights. Jazz is played every third Sunday in the month. ***Black Sheep, John Smith's, Tetley and Theakston. Guest are taken from local independents, such as Cropton's, Durham and Hambleton. Bottle conditioned*** *ales from Butterknowle and Cropton's.*

❀ ⌘ ◐ ⇌ ⚲ 🛏 ♮ ▶ Fly fishing, golf and horse racing (10 miles)

Tunstall

Bay Horse Inn

(01748 818564). Built around 1736, this fine village coaching house still serves the local community, as well as catering for the many visitors who holiday in this beautiful area of Yorkshire. Pool and dominoes are played here, and there is a pleasant garden, and a caravan park.

Samuel Smith.

♣ ❀ ◐ ⇌ 🕙 *21.00*

Wighill

White Swan Inn

Main Street (01937 832217). *Off the A64 at Tadcaster, south-west of York.* This traditional pub

stands in a pleasant rural village, and the front bar is well used by the locals.

Tetley and Theakston.

🐎 ❀ ◐ *not Tue evenings* ⇌

York

Ye Olde Starre Inne

40 Stonegate (01904 623063). Fragments of this building are over 1000 years old: during the Civil War it was used as a hospital, but it obtained its licence around 1644, making it York's oldest licensed pub. Just 100 yards from York Minster, it is naturally popular with visitors. It has an all-weather heated garden.

Theakston and Younger, with Ruddles as a typical guest.

🐎 ❀ ◐ *not Fri or Sat evenings* ⇌
⚲ 🕙 *20.00* ▶ The City of York, with its many attractions

Doncaster

Wheatley Hotel

Thorne Road, Wheatley (01302 364092). *On the western side of Doncaster.* The comfortable lounge of this large friendly hotel can be divided by fine wood and leaded-glass doors. A slide, swings and a climbing frame will be found in the garden.
John Smith's.
🐎 ❀ ▦ ◑ ❤ 🛏 ⏰ *21.00*

Dunford Bridge

Stanhope Arms

Windle Edge Road (01226 763104). *On a sharp bend off the A628.* Situated in the Peak District National Park, the Stanhope Arms was originally a shooting lodge, and stands amidst dramatic scenery next to a former railway station. Nearby at Dunford Bridge is the entrance to what was the longest rail tunnel in Britain: it is now disused. There is a family room, where children are made welcome. The garden has a large play area with swings and a climbing frame, and pool and cards are played.
Marston's and Theakston, with Timothy Taylor as a guest.
🐎 ♣ ❀ ▦ ◑ *not Mon lunch* ❤
⚲ 🛏

Dungworth

Royal Hotel

Main Road (0114 285 1213). *West of Stannington on the B6076, to the west of Sheffield.* This typically friendly village local is popular with walkers during the summer. During the early winter, in the eight Sundays leading up to Christmas, carols are sung here. Visitors come from all over the country to either listen or join in. It is thought to be the only pub where this takes place, and it is immensely popular. The pub gets *very* crowded at this time, and a great deal of beer is consumed – a firkin in twenty minutes in 1996! Children use the games room, or 'dungeon'.
John Smith's, Stones and Tetley, together with an ever-changing range of guests.
🎿 ♣ ◖ *not Mon lunch* ⚲ 🎤
▶ Country walks

Ingbirchworth

Fountain Inn

Wellthorne Lane (01226 763125). Warm and cosy with open fires, this pub has a large garden overlooking the reservoir.
Mansfield, with Theakston as a guest.
❀ ◑ ❤ ⚲ 🛏

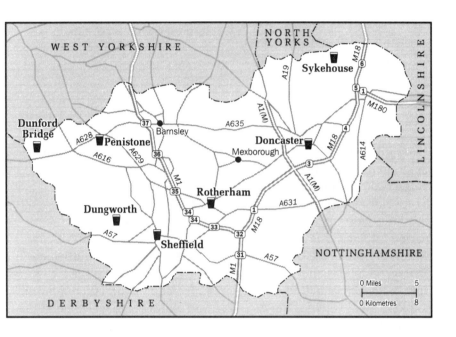

Penistone

Cubley Hall

Mortimer Road (01226 766086). Originally a moorland farm on a Pennine pack-horse trail, this handsome building was a gentleman's residence during Victorian times. Converted into a children's home after the Second World War, it became a pub in 1983, with the restaurant being added in 1990 in the massive stone and oak-beamed barn. The pub was extended to include a hotel in 1996. The spacious interior is both charming and smart, and includes two family rooms. With four acres of grounds incorporating a children's play area, with climbing frames, slides and swings, there are plenty of opportunities for youngsters to run off steam. And look out for 'Flo', the resident ghost – Florence Lockley held her wedding reception here in 1904. Wide range of good food, and baby-changing facilities in the ladies toilet.

Burton, Greene King, and Tetley, with guests from the likes of Marston's and Young's.

▶ A ghost!

Rotherham

The Florence

Moorgate Road, Moorgate (01709 360606). *To the south of Rotherham, not far from junction 33 on the M1.* Built from warm-coloured stone, with a terrace at the front and a sheltered garden to the rear, The Florence is a handsome and roomy pub, with two large bars and a display of period artifacts. The large garden, which overlooks the Dearne Valley, has slides and a climbing area, with some small toys for toddlers. Pool is played here. *Stones and Tetley.*
♣ ❀ ⌧ ◑ ⌒ ⏰ *20.30*

The Moulders Rest Hotel

110-112 Masborough Street (01709 560095). Millmoor football ground is nearby, and this pub has its own team. It is a comfy corner pub, with a pool table and bench seating outside. *Bateman's, Greene King and Ruddles, with these breweries' 'beers of the month' as guests.*
♣ ❀ ◑ *no food Fri evening or at weekends* ⌒ 🛏 ⏰ *21.00*

Sheffield

Carbrook Hall

537 Attercliffe Common, Carbrook (0114 244 0117).

Reputedly haunted, this large three-roomed pub retains many original features. It is decorated with a Civil War theme, due to links with a local Parliamentarian. Pool is played, and there is video and giant screen TV. *Bass, John Smith's and Stones, with Everards and Morland amongst their guests.*
🎠 ◖ ⌒ ⚡

New Barrack Tavern

601 Penistone Road (0114 234 9148). This nicely refurbished pub is popular with the locals. Cards and dominoes are played, and children are welcome in the back room. *Barnsley, John Smith's and Stones, with an ever-changing repertoire of five guests, plus a real cider.*
🎠 ♣ ❀ ◑ *not Sat or Sun evenings* ⌒ ⚡ ⏰ *20.00*

Sykehouse

The Old George Inn

Broad Lane (01405 785635). Very much a family oriented pub, with a heated swimming pool in their 5 acres of grounds, which were once used by the local cricket team, but now contain a large adventure playground, making it very popular with folk from the surrounding area. The pub has been built in what was once a terrace of cottages, used over the years as a farriers, a 'dame's' school, a shop, a butchers and a slaughterhouse. Indeed, if you look in the dining room, you will still see the hook used for hoisting up the animals for slaughter.

In another room the ceiling is covered with old coins – the adhesive being beer froth! *The whole pub is closed Nov-Mar.* **Tetley**.
♣ ❀ ⊞ ◑ ⌣ ⚔ ▶ The swimming pool and playground

Elland

Barge & Barrel

Park Road, Elland Bridge (01422 373623). A fine Victorian-style pub on the banks of the Calder & Hebble Navigation, so it is popular with navigators during the summer months. There is plenty of polished wood and leaded glass in the bar, and the riverside garden is pleasant but, if you have young children with you, keep an eye on them if they are near the water. Pool and pin-ball can be played here, and live bands perform every other Wednesday – rock, blues and covers (of current hits). *Barnsley, Black Sheep, Old Mill, Phoenix and Timothy Taylor, with guests from Cains, Fuller's, Mitchell's and Rudgate's.* ♣ ❀ ◖ ↩ ♟ ⏰ *20.00*▶ Calder & Hebble Navigation

Colliers Arms

Park Road (01422 372007). Standing halfway between Elland and Park Nook Locks on the Calder & Hebble Navigation, this is a smart and friendly cottage pub, with an open fire, stained glass windows and lots of old pictures of the nearby navigation. At the back of the pub is a conservatory, and this is where you are welcome to accompany your chil-

dren. There are no swings or slides in the garden – you will find these handily placed some 30 yards away on the playing field. *Samuel Smith, with bottles of Old Brewery Pale.* 🗙 ♣ ❀ ◖ ▶ *Fri & Sat only* ↩ ✂ ▶ Aire & Calder Navigation, with two locks nearby

Haworth

The Royal Oak Inn

2 Mill Hey (01535 643257). *Opposite the Keighley & Worth Valley Railway station.* It is not often you get the opportunity to enjoy the convivial atmosphere of a former mortuary and court-house, and arrive by steam train to boot! The pub's family room is nicely decorated with railway memorabilia, and the bars are festooned with copper and brass. The splendid Keighley & Worth Valley private railway runs for 5 miles from the station at Keighley, and was re-opened in 1968 after it was closed by British Rail in 1961. In the mornings the service is operated by diesel rail-buses, but in the afternoon the magnificent spectacle of steam trains will be seen on the line. There is a fine collection of steam engines and ancient carriages in

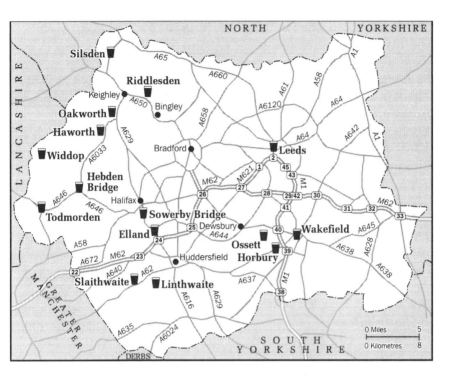

the yard at Haworth. The line achieved great fame when the film *The Railway Children* was made here (timetable: 01535 647777).
John Smith's and Webster's, with Black Sheep as the guest. Keighley & Worth Valley Light Railway

Hebden Bridge

The White Lion Hotel
Bridge Gate (01422 842197). This handsome, stylish and welcoming family-run coaching inn is in a building dating from 1657, and which was added to during the 18th and 19thC, as it became of increasing importance to travellers between Yorkshire and Lancashire. With the building of the turnpike road from Halifax and Rochdale its significance increased, and it was eventually recognised as a Grade II listed building. With open fires in the bars, and a large informal dining area, it makes an ideal stop for refreshment if you are visiting Eureka, the fascinating 'hands-on' museum for children nearby.

Children are welcomed in the family room and no-smoking room. There is also a garden. *Boddingtons, Flowers and Timothy Taylor, with guests from Fuller's, Jennings and Kitchen.*
🐃 ❀ ◑ ↩ 🏠 ⏰ *21.00* ▶ Eureka Children's Museum

Horbury

The Old Halfway House
141 Westfield Road (01924 262090). *Leave the M1 at junction 40 and turn right at the Post House Hotel. Turn left at the end of Queen's Drive and the pub is on the right, after the bends.* A 'Big Steak Pub' in a late 19thC building close to open fields. *Marston's, Morland and Tetley.*
❀ ◑ ↩ 🍴

Leeds

Whitelocks
Turks Head Yard (0113 245 3950). In one of the first buildings in Leeds to have electricity, this is an unspoilt Edwardian pub. There are no electronic machines, but skittles are played. Children are welcome in the Top Bar. *Marston's and Morland, with Selby and Theakston as typical guests.*

🖼 ♣ ❀ ◑ *not Sun evening* ↻ ⏰ *19.00*

Linthwaite

Sair Inn
139 Lane Top, Hoyle Ing (01484 842370). *Just off the A62, south-west of Huddersfield.* As CAMRA's 1997 National Pub of the Year the Sair Inn is clearly something special, and its small rooms, flagged floors and real fires do not disappoint. Historical connections are commemorated with a replica of Enoch's Hammer, as used by the Luddites. Brewing was revived in the 19thC brew-house here in 1982. For entertainment you can play dominoes, draughts, chess, shove ha'penny and Jenga. Children are welcome in any of the three rooms away from the bar area. Brewery tours can be arranged. Fine views over the Colne Valley. No food. *The full range of Linfit beers, from mild to stout, via ginger beer and bitter.*
♣ ▶ Brewery tours (by arrangement)

Oakworth

Turkey Inn
Goose Eye (01535 681339).
Oakworth is on the B6143 south-west of Keighley. If you continue through the village and turn right up the lane at Lane End, you will find Goose Eye. Not to be confused with the Goose Inn at Turkey Eye, this is a friendly country pub, with plenty of cosy places to sit. Goose Eye beer is brewed in Keighley. There is a pool table, and swings in the garden.
Burton, Goose Eye, Greene King and Tetley.
♣ ✿ ⌘ ◑ *not Mon* ↫ ✗

Ossett

The Mill
194 Dewsbury Road (01924 277 851). *Just west of junction 40 on the M1.* Converted from an old mill complex and cottages in a suburban area, this pub has a large and fully equipped outside play area, and a separate baby changing room. Pool is played here, and there are children's parties at Bank Holidays, Guy Fawkes night and Christmas.
Tetley.
🐎 ✿ ⌘ ◖ ↫ ✗ 🛏 ▽ 🎤

Riddlesden

Marquis of Granby
1 Hospital Road (01535 607164). There is a swing bridge (Granby, number 197A) on the canal right by this welcoming waterways pub, which has moorings for passing boaters. Pool can be played, and there are swings in the garden.
Black Sheep and Webster's.
♣ ✿ ⌘ ◑ *not Sat* ↫ ▶ Leeds & Liverpool Canal

Silsden

The Bridge Inn
Keighley Road (01535 653144). Attractive warehouses adorn the waterfront in Silsden, but this pub pre-dates them, and was known originally as the Boot & Slipper. Later it became The Thanet Arms, as the earl of the same name owned much land hereabouts. When the canal was opened here in 1777 an extra floor level was added to the pub to raise it to canal height. Its name was also changed to that most original of canalside pub titles, The Bridge. Friendly and welcoming, there are several cosy rooms, and a garden by the water. Pool and dominoes are played.
Black Sheep and John Smith's,

with Theakston as a guest.
🐎 ♣ ❀ ❤ 🚐 ▶ Leeds &
Liverpool Canal, and an aqueduct

Slaithwaite

The White House

Holthead (01484 842245). *Leave Slaithwaite on the B6109 – the pub is on the B6107 Marsden to Meltham road, which it joins.* Set upon high moorland, this welcoming inn has a cosy bar with a log fire. There is no garden, but a couple of tables are usually set to the front. Good food.
Marston's and Theakston, with Tetley as a guest.
◑ ❤ 🚐

Sowerby Bridge

The Moorings

No. 1 Warehouse, Canal Basin (01422 833940). An ideal venue from which to explore the fascinating canal basins and the newly built Tuel Lane Tunnel, Tuel Deep Lock and the first section of the Rochdale Canal. The Moorings is situated in a fine conversion of a warehouse which dates from 1790: from its spacious interior you can enjoy excellent views over the basin, and watch the boats coming and going.

Black Sheep, Timothy Taylor and Theakston, along with guests such as Charles Wells and Wychwood.
🐎 ❀ ◑ ❤ ✂ ▶ Calder & Hebble Navigation, Rochdale Canal, basins, tunnel and locks

Todmorden

Rose & Crown

355 Halifax Road (01706 812428). Not far from the Rochdale Canal, this fine traditional pub occupies what were once three stone cottages, built in the late 18thC. The bar is approached through fine stained-glass doors.
Boddingtons and Whitbread, with Chester's, Timothy Taylor and Wadworth as typical guests.
❀ ◑ ❤ ▶ Rochdale Canal

Wakefield

The Kings Arms

Heath Common, Heath (01924 377527). *Take the A638 southeast out of Wakefield, and turn left onto the A655. Heath Common is on the left.* Heath village is beautifully preserved, with 18thC merchants' houses scattered amongst other buildings. John Carr built Heath Hall here in 1753, and it is a particularly fine Georgian building. The Kings

Arms is equally exceptional, with a wood-panelled and gas-lit bar, packed full with antiques and atmosphere and warmed, as you would expect, by an open fire. Built as houses in the 18thC, it became a pub in 1841, and enjoys an expansive outlook over the common.
Clark's, Timothy Taylor and Tetley.
❀ ◑ ⌛ ▶ Heath village

Widdop

Pack Horse Inn
(01422 842803). *Widdop is clearly too small to be mentioned on my road atlas. It is about five miles north-west of Hebden Bridge, on the minor road through Slack and on towards Nelson and Colne.* As you will have already gathered, this is a very remote moorland pub, a sturdy stone-built place with open fires, popular with walkers.
Theakston, Thwaites and Younger, with guests from the likes of Morland.
❀ ◑ *Oct-Easter no food Mon and lunchtime Tue-Fri* 🛏🕙 *20.00*
▶ Fine walks

SCOTLAND

HIGHLANDS
&
ISLANDS

EASTERN
SCOTLAND

SOUTH-WEST
SCOTLAND

EDINBURGH & GLASGOW

BORDERS

ENGLAND

Allanton

Allanton Inn
(01890 818260). *South of the A6105, west of Berwick-upon-Tweed.* Outside this historic old coaching house you can still see the hitching rings for horses: inside, the bar is stone-flagged and comfortable. Children are well catered for with a toy box and a variety of games, and there is also a garden. Good food.
Border, with guests such as Brains, Fuller's and Mitchell's, and Westons real cider.
❀ ◑ ☞ ⅄ ⇔

Auchencrow

The Craw Inn
(01890 761253). A friendly and light-hearted country inn, which extends an especially warm welcome to 'well-behaved children with attractive mums'!
Two guest beers.
❀ ◑ ☞ ⅄ ⇔

Denholm

Auld Cross Keys Inn
Main Street (01450 870305). *On the A698 north-east of Hawick.* Could be the only pub in the book famous for cheesy eggs, served at the bar, but well worth visiting anyway for its blazing fires and cosy lounge. And the building is quite picturesque, being built in the 17thC overlooking the green. Excellent high teas in the restaurant. Colouring pads and crayons for young children, who are welcome in the lounge. High chairs available.
Broughton's, with guests, such as Raven and Tomintoul.
❀ ◑ *no food Mon* ⇔

Duns

Whip & Saddle Inn
Market Square (01361 883215). Dating from 1790, this town centre pub is well situated in the town square. Duns was the home of the great Jim Clark, the famous racing driver who was killed in 1968.
Caledonian and Tetley, with Belhaven as a guest.
🐎 ◖ ⅄ ▶ Jim Clark Museum in the Burgh Chambers

Eyemouth

The Ship Hotel
Harbour Road (01890 750224). CAMRA won't mind if we mention that there is a wide selection of rums in this fisherman's hotel, which stands right on the harbour side. Family run and warmed by

a coal fire during cold weather, you are sure of a friendly welcome. On a more sobering note, you could also ponder the sad fate of the fishermen of this town who were subject to one of the worst disasters in Scottish maritime history, when 129 men lost their lives in a storm. Children are welcome in the lounge and dining room. There is plenty of room in the ladies toilets for baby-changing.

Caledonian, with guests from Border and Isle of Skye.
♣ ❀ ◑ ➷ ⅟ 🛏 ▶ The harbour

Innerleithen

Traquair Arms
Traquair Road (01896 830229).
On the B709, south of Inner-lethen and just across the River Tweed. Traquair House has a history stretching back over 1000 years, making it probably the longest continuously inhabited house in Scotland. Over the years it has been visited by Mary Queen of Scots and Prince Charles Edward Stuart amongst others, and every nook and cranny within its walls oozes history. It is also widely known for its similarly named ale, made in an 18thC brew-house in one of the wings. Peter Maxwell Stuart, the

20th Laird, re-discovered the brewery, which had remained unused for over 100 years, in 1965. When Peter died in 1990, production was continued by his daughter Catherine. All the brews are fermented in oak, and about 60% is exported. The Traquair Arms is about 1½ miles away from the house. Warmed by a log fire, the cosy lounge is a welcoming place, and the food served in the adjacent dining room is prepared from fresh local produce.

Traquair and Greenmantle, plus bottle conditioned Traquair and Addlestones real cider.
❀ ◑ ➷ ⅟ 🛏
▶ Traquair House (which is closed during the winter)

Melrose

Kings Arms Hotel
High Street (01896 822143).
Warm and welcoming 18thC coaching inn, with open fires and plenty of beams.

Burton and Tetley, with guests from Border and smaller breweries.
◑ ➷ ⅟ 🛏 🕙 *20.00 in bar areas*

BORDERS

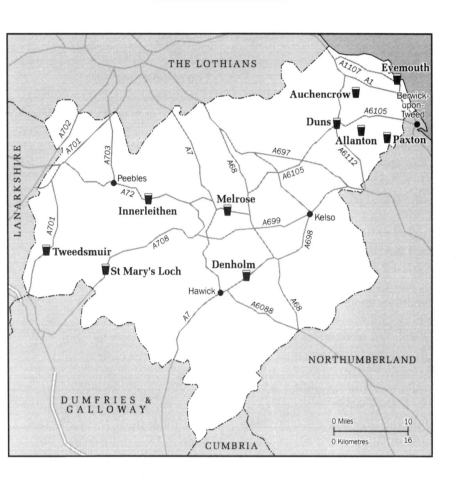

Paxton

Hoolits Nest

(01289 386267). *Just off the B6461 west of Berwick-upon-Tweed.* Hoolits look at you from every nook and cranny in the bar of this friendly village pub. It is a handy place to stop if you are visiting nearby Paxton House, which was designed by Adams and con-tains furnishings by Chippendale – and more importantly the garden has an adventure play-ground. (By the way, for the bene-fit of Sassenachs, a 'hoolit' is an owl).

Caledonian and Orkney, with Alloa and Broughton's as guests.
🕸 🌓 ☙ ⚔ ⏲ *20.45*
▶ Paxton House

St Mary's Loch

Tibbie Shiels' Inn

(01750 42231). *On the A708 half-way between Moffat and Selkirk.* Tibbie Shiels was a lady who looked after the inn for 75 years, until she died at the age of 96 in 1878. Married to a mole-catcher, she was esteemed by the Edinburgh literary set during the Age of Enlightenment. You can find her photo in the charming back bar of this inn, which stands on the shore of what is considered by some to be the most beautiful loch in Scotland. The Grey Mare's tail waterfall is just a couple of miles along the road towards Moffat.

Belhaven and Broughton's.
❀ ◑ ↻ ⚒ 🛏▶ St Mary's Loch, with the Grey Mare's Tail waterfall not far away

Tweedsmuir

The Crook Inn

(01899 880272). *On the A701, 16 miles north of Moffat, 35 miles south of Edinburgh.* Set in rolling hills and forests and claiming to be Scotland's first licensed coaching inn, this fine old building, warmed by log fires on cold days, has a 17thC bar, built in the old kitchen, where Robbie Burns wrote his poem 'Willie Wastles Wife':

'Willie Wastle dwalt on Tweed,
The spot they called it Linkumdoddie;
Willie was a wabster guid,
Cou'd stown a clew wi' ony bodie.'

You can choose a single malt chaser for your ale, and muse upon these lines. In 1891 The Scottish Mountaineering Club held its first official meeting here, and climbed Broad Law, the second highest peak in southern Scotland. Pool and dominoes are played in the inn.

Broughton.
♣ ❀ ◑ ↻ ⚒ 🛏▶ Hill walking

Aberdeen

Carriages at The Brentwood Hotel

101 Crown Street (01224 595440). *Turn left off Union Street opposite the Music Hall. It is halfway down on the left-hand side.* You will get a friendly welcome in this traditional bar with a spacious and comfortable lounge, situated beneath a smart hotel at the heart of 'the granite city'. Children are welcome in the lounge and restaurant.

Boddingtons, Caledonian, Castle Eden, Courage and Flowers, with guests from Black Sheep, Burton, Fuller's, Orkney, Tetley and Tomintoul.

🖾 ◑ ⇆ 🍴(▽planned)

Brig o'Turk

Byre Inn

(01877 376292). *On the A821 between Callander and Aberfoyle.* Log fires will warm you in this atmospheric converted 18thC barn if you have had a day in the hills, walking, cycling or fishing. There is a good selection of Malts to complement their ale. Plenty of festive evenings, such as Hallowe'en, St Andrew's Night and Hogmanay. Nappy changing in the disabled toilet.

Maclay's, with some interesting bottled beers, including Heather Ale.

🌺 ◑ ⇆ ⅍ ▽ ▶ Enjoy the hills

Broughty Ferry

The Fisherman's Tavern

10-14 Fort Street (01382 775941). This 17thC fisherman's terraced-cottage conversion right by the lifeboat station has been in every edition of the CAMRA Good Beer Guide since it began including Scotland in 1975. It has also been CAMRA National Pub of the Year (1994), so it will surely not disappoint. It is busy, low-ceilinged, cosy and friendly. Good food. Secluded walled garden.

Belhaven and Maclay's, with Fuller's and Hoegaarden Wheatbeer as guests.

🌺 ◖ *snacks on Sun* ⇆ ⅍ 🍴 ▽ *by arrangement* ▶ The seaside

Old Anchor Inn

46-48 Gray Street (01382 737899). Traditional ale house with a distinct nautical theme, where partitions provide plenty of cosy nooks. Chess and backgammon are played here, and children are welcome in the snug.

Courage and Theakston, with guests such as Boddingtons, Caledonian, Greene King, Harviestoun and Thwaites.

♣ ◗ *not after 15.00 Mon-Wed, not after 19.00 Thur-Sat, not after 16.00 Sun* ❤ ⅄ ⊘ *19.00*

Carnock

The Old Inn

6 Main Street (01383 850381). This cottage-style pub is right at the heart of this community and is a focus for village life. It has a genuinely friendly atmosphere, and welcomes children in the lounge and restaurant. Dominoes and pool are played here, and there is a garden. *Maclay's, with guests such as Boddingtons and Orkney.*
🐎 ♣ ❀ ◗ ❤

Clova

Clova Hotel

Glen Clova, near Kirriemuir (01575 550222). What is possibly the nation's most remote beer festival is held in this fine outpost each Easter. Walkers and climbers enjoy its hospitality and warming wood-burning stoves. *Caledonian and Orkney, with guests including Caledonian and Morland, and bottle conditioned Alloa and Broughton.*
🐎 ❀ ◗ ❤ ⅄ 🛏 ▶ Walking in the hills

Drymen

Winnock Hotel

The Square (01360 660245). Standing along one side of the village square, this 18thC white-washed inn has a long beamy bar to the front, with a restaurant just off. There are also comfy seats by the entrance. You can enjoy a drink in the garden when the weather is fine, and there are swings for children. Nappy changing area in the disabled toilet. *Broughton's, Burton, Tetley and Wadworth, with Boddingtons as a typical guest.*
❀ 🏯 ◗ ❤ ⅄ 🛏 ▽

Elie

The Ship Inn

The Toft (01333 330246). This is a beautifully situated seaside pub, which has offered its friendly hospitality since 1838, and which has fairly recently, and without detriment, been refurbished. The splendid Elie sands are just across the road, where children can dig, run, play and paddle. Unusually, there are also (slightly) more serious sporting contests on the sands – in the Spring rugby is played against Edinburgh Academicals, and dur-

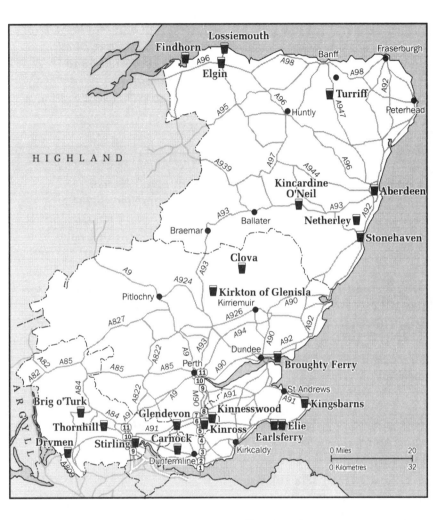

ing the summer there are various cricket matches. What could be nicer than a seat on the harbour wall, a pint of good beer, fine weather and some cheery sport to watch? If you wish to drink inside, the front room is a splendid place, with the bar along one wall, a fireplace opposite, and a few chairs and tables between. The restaurant, which serves fine food, is upstairs. During July and August there is an outside barbecue, overlooking the bay. The bay can also be viewed more closely through the telescope on the

upstairs balcony. Elie makes a wonderful starting point from which to explore the magical Fife coast, with its splendid fishing villages and active harbours. And if anyone in the family likes golf, there are few areas of the country so convincingly dedicated to the sport. Dominoes, cribbage, cards and shut-the-box can be played here. Children are welcomed in the lounge and restaurant. Accommodation can be provided in their guest house, just along the road.
Belhaven and Theakston.
☒ ♣ ⚘ ◐ ↶ 🛏 ▶ Fishing villages, The Secret Bunker, Kellie Castle, Water Sports Centre, harbours, castles, churches and museums

Earlsferry

The Golf Tavern (The 19th Hole)
Links Road (01333 330610). Gas lamps give a wonderfully atmospheric glow in this wood-lined bar, which was built around 1800. Plenty of brass and mirrors give a warm and congenial atmosphere, with a coal fire adding to the mood. Children are welcome in the lounge and Bunker, and dominoes and pool are played here.

Caledonian and Maclay's, with guests such as Bass, Black Sheep, Harviestoun and Inveralmond.
♣ ◐ ⏰ *20.00* ▶ See Elie attractions

Elgin

Thunderton House
Thunderton Place (01343 554921). *Just off the High Street.* With a history which dates from the 11thC, it is not surprising that this pub claims a bevy of ghosts, including that of Bonnie Prince Charlie! Be that as it may, the building has been a church, a Masonic lodge and a factory, and certainly qualifies now as a classic town pub. The family room is nicely decorated with wood and stained glass.
Bass and Caledonian, with Tomintoul as a guest.
🐎 ◐ *not winter Suns* ↶ ⏰ *20.30*

Findhorn

Crown & Anchor Inn
01309 690243). Popular as a seaside resort and a place of pilgrimage and retreat, this is in fact the third Findhorn – the previous two villages having been overcome by natural disasters. The Crown & Anchor is a coaching

inn built in 1739 on the harbour-side of the third village. It has two beamy bars and a dining area. Cribbage and dominoes are played here. Children are welcome in the lounge, and the garden has a climbing frame. There are good beaches just a short stroll away.

Bass and as many as six guest ales, such as Caledonian and Tomintoul, plus some Belgian beers.

🏃 ♣ ❀ 🏠 ◐ ☞ ✄ 🛏 ▽ ▶ The harbour, beaches, nature reserve

Kimberley Inn

94 Findhorn (01309 690492). The front patio of this friendly pub overlooks pretty Findhorn Bay. Very popular, the excellent food is reasonably priced, with chicken tikka recommended.

Black Sheep, Fuller's, Orkney, Tomintoul and Charles Wells.

❀ ◐ ☞ ⏱ 20.00 ▶ As above

Glendevon

Tormaukin Hotel

(01259 781252). *Situated between Kinross and Auchterarder on the A823.* 'Hill of the Mountain Hare' is the translation of the name from Old Scots, and this fine old drovers' inn dates from 1720, when it provided shelter when taking sheep to market. The bars

are both smart and cosy, with beamy ceilings, stone walls and warm open fires. Those who enjoy the open air will welcome the local array of activities – with walking, fishing and shooting nearby, and over 100 golf courses within an hour's drive, you will never be lost for something to do. Good food, and comfortable bedrooms.

Burton and Harviestoun.

🐕 ❀ ◐ ☞ 🛏 ▶ Outdoor activities

Kincardine O'Neil

Gordon Arms Hotel

(01339 884236). This friendly and welcoming Victorian coaching inn, built around 1810, is situated in what is considered to be the oldest village on Royal Deeside, at a point where a ferry crossed once the river. Where Neil Burn Drive joins the main road, you will find the well of St Erchard – he founded a church here in the 5thC. A bridge was built in 1220 by Thomas the Durward, followed by a hospice, erected by his son in 1233. In tradition Macbeth's head was carried to the village on a golden plate. When the railway bypassed the village it declined for a while, but now the trains have long since gone and the village is well established on the tourist trail. Organic wines are kept at the Gordon Arms, the food is good and there is a separate children's menu. Plenty of outdoor activities nearby, and family rooms available for those who wish to stay.

A constantly rotating range of real ales, featuring such names as Boddingtons, Burton, Fuller's, Greene King, Marston's, Timothy Taylor, Tomintoul, Wadworth and so on.

♣ ✿ ◑ ☞ 🍺 ▶ 13thC Kirk of St Mary, Old Smiddy Visitor Centre, outdoor activities

Kingsbarns

Cambo Arms Hotel
5 Main Street (01334 880226). Traditional and cosy pub, with a comfortable sitting room. Board games, cards and dominoes are played here, and there are tables along the front of the hotel for sunny days.

Belhaven, plus guests such as Deuchars, Fuller's and Whitbread.

🐎 ✿ ◑ *no evening meals Dec-Easter* ☞ 🍺 ⏱ *18.00 in the public bar* ▶ Cambo Secret Garden, and the Farm Trail, are nearby

Kinnesswood

Lomond Country Inn
Main Street (01592 840253). A large picture window in the open-plan lounge gives a fine view over Loch Leven. There are slides in the garden, and nappy-changing facilities in the toilets.

Bass and Jennings, with Caledonian and Harviestoun as guests.

✿ ◑ ☞ ✖ 🍺

Kinross

The Muirs Inn
49 Muirs (01577 862270). *Take junction 6 from the M90 and follow the A922 to a 'T' junction. The pub is to the right.*
Traditional Scottish inn which has been refurbished without sacrificing its original feeling, and emphasising its splendid Edwardian fixtures and fittings. Children are welcome in the Wee Still Lounge (which has a wee still) and the restaurant. There is a courtyard.

Belhaven and Orkney, with all the Scottish real ales rotated as guest beers. Also bottle conditioned Belhaven, Broughton's and Caledonian.

🖼 ♣ ✿ ◑ ☞ 🍺

Kirkton of Glenisla

The Glenisla Hotel

(01575 582223). *North-west of Kirriemuir on the B951.*

'Busk, Busk bonny lassie aye, and come awa wi me And I'll take ye tae Glen Isla, near bonnie Glen Shee' You can enjoy this fine hotel as a base from which to explore this splendid glen, which you can follow up to the Monega Pass. The River Isla tumbles spectacularly over the falls at Reekie Linn, changing from a trout stream to a salmon river in the process, while on its banks hide some of the last wild cats to be found in Britain. Built in the 17thC as a coaching inn, its beamy bar is relaxed and friendly, and log fires warm the charming rooms. Kirkton of Glenisla was a centre for the illicit distilling of whisky following the Napoleonic wars, and the excise men would periodically visit the hotel while on their rounds. Seeing them safely ensconced within the bar, the local minister would emerge from the manse opposite, calling 'The Philistines be upon thee Samson', and the local population, and their stills, would make for the hills! Pool and bowls are played here, while outside the opportunities for outdoor pursuits are almost boundless.

Boddingtons, McEwan's and Theakston, with a variety of guests from Inveralmond.
🐕 ♣ ❀ ◑ ☕ ✄ 🛏 ▶ Walking, fishing, pony trekking, clay pigeon shooting and cross country skiing

Lossiemouth

Skerry Brae Hotel

Stotfield Road (01343 812040). An old sandstone hotel with splendid views over the golf course and the sea, with a large bar and a conservatory. Garden and patio, and a nappy-changing unit.

Boddingtons and Theakston, with guests such as Black Bull, Mansfield and Scottish Courage, plus Symond's Old Hazy real cider.
🐕 ♣ ❀ ◑ ☕ ✄ 🛏 ▽
🕐 *21.30* ▶ The seaside

Netherly

Lairhillock Inn

(01569 730001). *South-west of Aberdeen and north of Stonehaven, on the B979.*
Children are welcomed in the conservatory of this hospitable 200-year-old inn, set amidst fine

countryside. An open log fire forms the centre-piece of the bar and lounge, where 50 single malt whiskies are available, and a pianist plays most evenings. Good food.

Boddingtons, Caledonian, Courage, Flowers and McEwan's, with Caledonian, Orkney and Marston's as guests.
🏃 🕸 ◑ ⇌

Stirling

The Birds & The Bees

Easter Cornton Road (01786 473663). *Off Causewayhead Road, near the Wallace Monument.* Friendly, fascinating and award-winning converted farmstead, where you are invited to 'drink sheep-dip, eat a ploughman and kiss a French bull'. So French boules are played, and there is a choice of whiskies. Also a resident magician, plus puzzles to wrestle with. There is a courtyard garden, and a patio to the front. Nappy changing area in the ladies.

Burton, Caledonian and Fuller's, with guests changing twice each week. Also bottle conditioned Alloa.
🐎 ♣ 🕸 ◑ ⇌ ⅄ ▽ ♦ ⓣ *bar area 20.00, restaurant 22.00* ▶ Stirling Castle is always worth a visit

Stonehaven

Marine Hotel

9-10 Shorehead (01567 762155). Standing down beside the attractive harbour, this is an accommodating pub with a traditional, wood-panelled bar and a classic jukebox. Children are welcome in the lounge and dining room, and there is also a pool room. Come to Stonehaven at midnight on Hogmanay and you will witness the fire festival, when the young men of the town march carrying fire-balls, which are made to an ancient recipe. Or come here at any other time to enjoy a breezy seaside town, which has most attractions, apart from a properly sandy beach.

Bass, Caledonian and Timothy Taylor, along with guests such as Harviestoun and Moulin, plus Addlestone's real cider.
🐎 ◑ ⇌ ⅄ 🛏 ▶ The seaside

Thornhill

Lion & Unicorn

(01786 850204). *On the A873 west of Stirling.* Established in 1635, there is a massive fireplace in the original part of the building, which has been extended over the years. The bars are also warmed by an open fire, and stone walls and beamy ceilings maintain the cosy atmosphere. Toys and colouring sheets are thoughtfully provided for children, and there are swings and a slide in the garden.

Broughton, plus a guest, such as Caledonian and Orkney.

Turriff

The Towie Tavern

Auchterless (01888 511201). *About 4 miles south of Turriff on the A947.* Country pub and restaurant, offering a fine selection of single malt whiskies alongside its real ale. Bar skittles and pool are played here, and there is a slide, swings and a climbing frame in the garden. Baby changing area in the ladies toilet.

Theakston, plus a guest.

♣ ❀ ▣ ◑ ➷ ⤨ ▽☺ *20.00*

Balerno

Johnsburn House

Johnsburn Road (0131 449 3847).
Claiming to be Britain's most
awarded pub, it is surely worth a
visit to find out why! The first
buildings here were built in 1760
by Adam Fergusson, who was a
friend of both Robert Burns and
Sir Walter Scott. It is said that
Fergusson arranged the only veri-
fiable meeting between these two
literary giants, which may indeed
have happened here. The upper
floor was added to this baronial
mansion in 1911 by the great
Scottish architect Sir Robert
Lorimer, and the building has
since received architectural
acclaim. *Closed on Mondays.*
Caledonian, with over 200 dif-
ferent guests each year. Also
real cider during the summer,
and the odd bottle conditioned
real ale.

Balloch

Balloch Hotel

Balloch Road (01389 752579).
Call in on the way to Loch
Lomond, and you will find a
friendly welcome in this attractive hotel, where the terrace overlooks the River Leven. Children
are welcome in the lounge and
restaurant.
Burton and Shipstone's, with
guests from the likes of
Caledonian, Orkney and
Maclay's.
20.00
▶ Loch Lomond is nearby

Tullichewan Hotel

Balloch Road (01388 752052).
Friendly and welcoming pub
jointly owned with The
Kilcreggan.
Courage, Marston's, Morland
and Theakston, with
Boddingtons and Flowers as
guests.

Edinburgh

The Abbotsford Bar

3 Rose Street (0131 225 5276). A
Victorian island bar forms the
centrepiece in this welcoming
and traditional bar close to the
city's financial centre. Make
yourself comfortable on the
leather benches amongst fine
wood panelling and beneath a
splendidly moulded high plaster
ceiling, and contemplate time
well spent in this splendid capital city. Children are welcome at
lunchtime and early afternoon.
Always eight real ales, with
brews such as Bateman's,

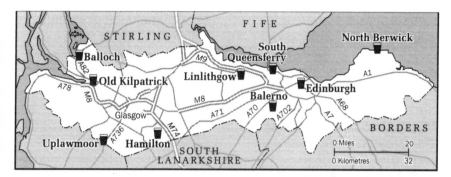

Fuller's and Whim.
◖✆⏱ *16.00* ▶ Edinburgh, too much to mention

Kenilworth

150-152 Rose Street (0131 226 4385). Dating from 1899, the attractive high-ceilinged bar here has an ornately carved wooden island supporting an array of potted plants, elaborately decorated with bank notes.
Marston's, Rose Street and Tetley, with a large selection of guests.
🐎◖✆⏱ *21.00* ▶ Edinburgh, too much to mention

Old Chain Pier

1 Trinity Crescent (0131 552 1233).This welcoming and cosy sea front bar occupies the site of the booking office of the old pier, which was destroyed in 1898. It contains many sailing artefacts and is a great place to watch ships or birds. Children are welcome in the conservatory until 19.00

Black Sheep, Caledonian, Ind Coope and guests.
🏃▶ summer only⏱ *19.00*

The Southsider

3 West Richmond Street (0131 667 2003). Children are welcomed here at lunchtime only, but if you are up in town, doing the shops in Princes Street, it is a handy stop.

Maclays
🏃◖⏱ *after lunch* ▶ Edinburgh, too much to mention

Starbank Inn

64 Laverockbank Road (0131 552 4141). *On the north side of the city, adjacent to Newhaven harbour and village.* With sweeping views over the Forth, and decorated as a virtual museum of brewing, this handsome stone-built pub makes a very worthwhile excursion from the city centre. Restaurant and bar meals, an impressive list of beers and a few single malts for good measure.

Belhaven, Caledonian and Timothy Taylor, with guests such as Adnams, Bass, Border, Broughton, Dent's, Everards, Felinfoel, Greene King, Harviestoun, Jennings, Marston's, Shepherd Neame, Tomintoul, Wadworth, Charles Wells and many others.
◑ ☞ ⅍ ⏰ 20.30 ▶ Newhaven Harbour area

Hamilton

George Bar
18 Campbell Street (01698 424225). *Off Cadzow Street.* This is a traditional pub, with a warm friendly atmosphere, and well worth finding. It has often been voted CAMRA's Lanarkshire Pub of the Year. Children are welcome, except in the seating under the window area.
Maclay's, with guests such as Adnams, Bateman's, Harviestoun and Orkney, plus some interesting bottles.
◖ ☞ ⏰ 18.00

Linlithgow

The Four Marys
67 High Street (01506 842171). Once an apothecary's shop, where David Waldie experiment-ed with chloroform (it was first used medicinally by Sir James Young Simpson), this pub takes its name from Mary Queen of Scots four Maids of Honour. Mary was born in Linlithgow Palace in 1542, and the building remains a wonderful brooding shell over-looking a loch since being gutted by fire when occupied by the Duke of Cumberland during the '45 rebellion. Mementoes of Mary are many in the pub, which has stone walls and a smattering of antiques. Children are welcome in the dining area.
Belhaven and Caledonian, with guests such as Harviestoun, Marston's and Wadworth amongst others.
▨ ◑ ☞ ⅍ ⏰ 20.00 ▶ Linlithgow Palace

North Berwick

Nether Abbey Hotel
20 Dirleton Avenue (01620 892802). *On the A198, ½ mile west of the town centre.* Comfort-able family run hotel in a Vic-torian villa, with a large extended bar/restaurant area. There is a petanque court in the garden. It is ideally situated as a base for exploring the East Lothian coast.
Four guest real ales.
✿ ◑ ☞ 🛏 ▶ The seaside

Old Kilpatrick

Ettrick Bar
159 Dumbarton Road (01389 872821). *Turn off the A82 just beyond the Erskine Bridge.* The Ettrick Shepherd, commemorated in the name, was a close friend of Sir Walter Scott. This traditional village pub is late-Victorian with a fine horseshoe bar and an island gantry, along with a comfortable lounge, where children are welcomed.
Caledonian and Orkney, with Greenmantle as a guest.
🎠 ◑ 👜 ✂ 🍎 *18.45*

South Queensferry

Hawes Inn
Newhalls Road (0131 331 1990). Dwarfed by The Forth Rail Bridge (designed by Sir John Fowler and Sir Benjamin Baker and opened in 1890, and painted with 7000 gallons of paint, when it *is* painted), the Hawes Inn has been mentioned in Sir Walter Scott's 'The Antiquary' (1816) and famously featured in 'Kidnapped' by Robert Louis Stevenson (1886) when David Balfour's abduction is planned here – so it is well worth a visit. Before the adjacent road bridge was opened on 4th September 1964, there had been a ferry here for at least 800 years. The Hawes is a comfortably modernised traditional inn, where dominoes and chess can be played, and there is a climbing frame and slide in the garden. There are also nappy changing facilities.
Arrols and Burton, with Deuchars as a guest.
🎠 ♣ 🕷 🎨 ◑ 👜 ✂ 🛏 ▽ ▶ The Forth bridges, local museum

Uplawmoor

Uplawmoor Hotel
Neilston Road (01505 850565). *Just off the A736 Glasgow to Irvine Road.* Well worth seeking out, this 18thC village coaching inn is very friendly and accommodating. It adjoins the village park, so swings are within easy reach. An old barn has been converted and now contains the restaurant. Pool is played.
Bass and Orkney, with Theakston as a guest.
♣ 🕷 ◑ 👜 🛏 🍎 *20.30*

Cawdor

Cawdor Tavern

(01667 404777). *On the B9090, south of Nairn off the A96.* Oak panelling and a fireplace salvaged from the nearby castle add considerable interest to this traditional country inn, which has just been refurbished. Children are welcome in the lounge and restaurant. Cards, board games and pool, and there is a nappy-changing unit in the toilets. *Alloa and Tetley, with Burton as a guest.*

🏃 ♣ ❀ ◐ 👓 ✄ ▽

Dunvegan, Isle of Skye

Dunvegan Hotel

Main Street (01470 521497). Most of those who visit Skye come to see The Fairy Bridge and Dunvegan Castle, family seat of the Clan MacLeod, who have been in continuous occupation since 1200. It is beautifully situated on the shore of Loch Dunvegan, and contains such icons as the 15thC Dunvegan Cup, Rory Mor's drinking horn and the legendary Fairy Flag, made of yellow silk. Its miraculous powers can only be used three times to save the Clan: there is now only one chance left!

Pregnant ladies should also be warned that they may go into premature labour upon setting eyes on the cloth. Magnificent views on Skye are almost commonplace, but the vista of Macleod's Tables, volcanic peaks across the loch from the hotel, is splendid. *Isle of Skye.*

🐕 ♣ ❀ ◐ 👓 ✄ 🛏 ▽
▶ Dunvegan Castle

Gairloch

The Old Inn

(01445 712006). *On the A832, at the south end of the village near the harbour and golf course.* Friendly and welcoming old coaching inn set amidst stupendous mountains and sea lochs, with a safe sandy beach nearby. It claims to be, at the time of writing, Scotland's top outlet for real ale, with up to 12 guest ales during the season, which reduces to 'only' six in the winter. A micro brewery is planned for 1998. Pool, cards and dominoes are played here. *Up to 12 real ales during the season, with a mixture of Scottish and English brews.*

♣ ❀ ◐ 👓 ✄ 🛏 ▶ Sandy beach (especially at Big Sand, 3 miles north-west), wonderful walking, fishing, bird-watching

Inverness

Clachnaharry Inn

17-19 High Street, Clachnaharry (01463 239806). *On the old A9 north road, on the western outskirts.* The garden here was once part of the old station, and there is a splendid view over the Beauly Firth and the sea lock of the Caledonian Canal from this 300-year-old coaching inn. *Clachnaharry, McEwans, and Tomintoul direct from the wood, with guests such as Courage and Morland, plus some bottle conditioned ales.*

✿ ◑ ❀ ▶ Caledonian Canal

The Pheonix

108-110 Academy Street (01463 245991). 'Jock Tamson's' Scottish theme bar has been created in the lounge bar of this busy and popular town-centre pub. Children are welcome in the family room and lounge. *Bass, Caledonian and Tomintoul, with Orkney and Maclays as guests.*

🐚 ◑ *probably every day, but uncertain as we go to press* ✂ ⏰ 20.00

Sligachan, Isle of Skye

Sligachan Hotel

(01478 650204). At the heart of Skye, this is a friendly and welcoming hotel well situated at the head of a loch, offering superb views of the Cuillins, the stupendous granite mountains which never cease to amaze. It is an excellent base for walking, climbing and cycling, and when you are exhausted you can retire here to enjoy the log fire and good company. There is a large games area with a creche, cartoons and kids' music, and nappy changing in the toilet. Good food. *Isle of Skye, plus guests which include Courage, Marston's and*

Morland.
🐎♣❀◑👓✂🛏▽🎤
▶ Walking the Cuillins

Uig, Isle of Skye

The Uig Hotel
(01470 542205). On the wonderful west coast of Skye, where ferries leave for the Outer Hebrides, the Uig Hotel is an old coaching inn overlooking Uig Bay. Those over six years old can enjoy pony trekking from the hotel's own native pony centre.
Isle of Skye.
♣❀◑👓✂🛏⏱ *20.00*
▶ Pony trekking

Bladnoch

Bladnoch Inn

(01988 402200). *On the A714, 5 miles south of Newton Stewart, just beyond Wigtown.* This traditional stone-built inn is a comfortable and homely rural gem, with hunting-dog drawings featured in the wood-panelled bar. There is room in the ladies to change a nappy.

Courage, Greene King, Morland and Theakston, with Broughton, Fuller's, Marston's and Sulwath as guests.

🐎 ❀ ◑ ☞ 🛏 ▽ ▶ Bladnoch Distillery Museum

Brodick, Isle of Arran

Duncan's Bar

(01770 302531). Just 300 yards from the ferry terminal, so if you haven't had a decent beer since you got onto the boat, it's not far to walk to this comfortable seafront lounge bar with excellent views over to Goat Fell from the patio.

Boddingtons, Marston's and Theakston, with guests such as Broughton, Harviestoun, Orkney and Tomintoul.

♣ ❀ ◑ ☞ 🛏 ▽ ⏱ *20.00*
▶ Seaside, plus the attractions of Brodick and Arran

Ormidale Hotel

(01770 302293). *Head north through Brodick from the pier. Turn left opposite the golf club, and take the first left after Brodick Church.* Another handy stop if you are just off the ferry, and are about to explore this splendid Scottish island. It has a slide, swings and a climbing frame in the garden.

McEwan's.

♣ ❀ ▤ ◑ ☞ 🛏 ▶ Seaside, plus the attractions of Brodick and Arran

Campbeltown

Ardshiel Hotel

Kilkerran Road (01586 552133). *Turn right from the ferry terminal and it is about 20 yards ahead.* Founded under James VI's policy of civilising the natives by establishing villages(!), Cambeltown once had a fleet of 650 herring boats and 30 distilleries. In the bay is Davaar Island, where Archibald MacKinnon painted a crucifixion scene on a cave wall in 1887, and which later caused quite a stir. It is now a rather remote tourist attraction. Illuminated by a shaft of light which shines into the cave, it was touched-up by a local artist in 1956. This can all be contemplat-

SOUTH-WEST SCOTLAND

ed while sipping your beer or enjoying a fine meal in this family-run hotel. There is a swing and a climbing frame in the garden. *Theakston, with Marston's and Morland as guests.*
❀ ▦ ◗ ⬬ ⅍ ⛉ ▸ The seaside

Catacol, Isle of Arran

Catacol Bay Hotel
(01770 830231). *About 1½ miles south of Lochranza, where the ferry calls.* The name of Catacol is taken from Norse, and means 'the ravine of the wild cat'. It is notable for the 'Twelve Apostles', a terrace of twelve identical cottages, which look out over the sound to Kintyre. This small family run hotel makes an excellent stop (or stay) if you are touring this beautiful island. It has a large garden with a slide, swings and a climbing frame. Pool is played. Live music, folk sessions and Ceilidhs are regularly held here. *Black Sheep, Caledonian and Theakston, plus other guests.*
♣ ❀ ▦ ◗ ⬬ ⛉ ⚲ ⌚ 20.00
▸ The beautiful Isle of Arran

Glenluce

Kelvin House Hotel
53 Main Street (01581 300303). *On the A75 between Newton*

Stewart and Stranraer. Family-run, this is a small and friendly hotel in this bypassed village. The family room has a Lego corner, and plenty of books, and babies can be changed in the ladies room. *Orkney, with Allsops as a guest, and bottled Maclays.*
🎠 ♣ ❀ ◗ ⬬ ⅍ ⛉

Gatehouse-of-Fleet

Murray Arms Hotel
(01557 814207). *Off the A75 between Dumfries and Stranraer.* Traditional and friendly Galloway hotel in a building which dates back over 300 years, with a comfortable lounge, and 13 bedrooms. Pool and dominoes are played here. *Theakston.*
♣ ❀ ◗ ⬬ ⅍ ⛉

Gretna

Solway Lodge Hotel
Annan Road (01461 338266). Smart and comfortable, this friendly family-run hotel/motel makes an ideal touring centre for this particularly well-known area of Scotland. *Broughton and Tetley.*
❀ ◗ ⬬ ⛉ ▸ Blacksmith's Shop and Museum

262

Inverary

The George Hotel

Main Street (01499 302111). Log and peat fires warm this historic and beamy pub, owned by five generations of the same family. Old fashioned and comfortable, you will receive a friendly welcome here. Baby changing facilities.

A wide variety of Scottish real ales, including Belhaven, Froach and Orkney.

Irvine

Marina Inn

110 Harbour Street (01294 274079). Very handy for the Magnum Centre and the Scottish

Maritime Museum, this is an attractive harbourside bar with a good reputation for food. Baby changing in the ladies toilet. *Belhaven*.
✿ ◑ ⬮ ▽ ⏰ *20.00* ▶ The seaside, Magnum Centre and Scottish Maritime Museum

Isle of Whithorn

The Steam Packet Hotel
Harbour Row (01988 500334). The remains of St Ninian's Chapel continue to excite much archaeological interest, since this is thought to be one of the earliest landing places of Christian missionaries. A church was built here in AD 397, and an attached monastery was known as Candida Casa, or White House. There is a museum on the road to the priory. Taking its name from a paddle steamer which, during the last century, linked Galloway to the Port of Liverpool, this friendly family-run hotel makes a splendid base from which to explore this fascinating area. Children are welcome, except in the area of the public bar, and the accommodation is reasonably priced. *Caledonian & Theakstons: Boddingtons & Orkney as guests*.
♣ ✿ ◑ ⬮ ⛶ ▽ ▶ St Ninian's Chapel

Kilcreggan

Kilcreggan Hotel
Argyll Road (01436 842243). Welcoming family-run hotel overlooking the Firth of Clyde and just 5 minutes walk from the Gourock ferry. Pool and skittles are played. Eat here and your children's meals are free. *Courage, Marston's, Morland and Theakston, with Boddingtons and Flowers as guests*.
🎱 ♣ ◑ ⬮ ⛷ ⛶

Kildonan, Isle of Arran

Breadalbane Hotel
Isle of Arran (01770 820284). Down at the south-eastern tip of Arran stands this friendly seaside hotel, where you can look out to the island of Pladda and the more distant Ailsa Craig from the lounge or conservatory. Pool and dominoes are played here. *Bass*.
♣ ✿ ◑ ⬮ ⛷ ⛶ ▶ The splendid Island of Arran

Kilmarnock

The Hunting Lodge
14-16 Glencairn Square (01563 522920). A cheery 'olde worlde' pub with lots of bric-a-brac and a

friendly welcome for families. Children's boxed meals, complete with a toy, are available. Pool is played, and there are 2p bagatelle machines. Small patio area for sunny days.
Caledonian and Timothy Taylor's, with Shepherd Neame as a guest, and sometimes real cider from Addlestone's.
🐎 ♣ ❀ ◑ ☕ ⚹ ⦿ *20.00*

Kippford

Anchor Hotel
(01556 620205). *South of Dalbeattie, just off the A710.*
Popular with local yachtspersons, who stroll up from the marina to enjoy this attractive family-run inn, which has a cosy coal fire during the winter. There is a sandy bay just 10 minutes walk away, and a large beach just a short drive away. Rough Island, situated in the bay, is a bird sanctuary owned by the National Trust for Scotland.
Theakston, with a wide selection of summer guest ales, such as Boddingtons and Flowers.
🐎 ♣ ❀ ◑ ☕ ⚹ 🛏 ▶ The seaside

Kirkmichael

Kirkmichael Arms
3 Straiton Road (01655 750375). *On the B7045 east of Maybole.*
Standing in a conservation village, this rural gem of a pub has low beamy ceilings and an open fire in the small bar and lounge. Chess, dominoes, draughts and pool are played here.
Theakston, plus guests from Scottish & Newcastle.
🐎 ♣ ◑ ☕ ⚹

Langholm

The Crown Hotel
(01387 380247). Each week there is a different real ale in this comfortable 18thC inn.
It is different each week.
🐎 ♣ ❀ ◑ ☕ 🛏

Minnigaff

Creebridge House Hotel
(01671 402121). *Just outside Newton Stewart.* Once owned by the Earls of Galloway, this splendid country house hotel stands in 3 acres of idyllic gardens, tended by Bob Farley, close to the River Cree. A magnificent period fireplace provides a focal point in the comfy lounge, and the beamy bar, as well as supplying real ale,

has a good choice of single malt whiskies. Outdoor pursuits feature here, with salmon fishing, golf, pony-trekking and bird-watching readily available. Excellent food, with special theme evenings, such as Thai, Italian and, naturally, Scots. Bar billiards, and croquet in the garden, are played here. *Burton and Orkney, with Hardy and Theakston as guests.*
♣ ❀ 🏠 ◑ ↻ 🛏

Moffat

Black Bull Hotel
Churchgate (01683 220206). Robert Burns is connected with this historic 16thC family-run hotel, which has a comfy lounge and a public bar decorated with railway memorabilia. Moffat was a thriving spa town during the 18thC, following the discovery of chalybeate springs here in 1633, and it is now a sheep-farming centre, a trade celebrated with a large bronze ram atop the Colvin Fountain built in 1875. The town is more recently associated with Lord Dowding, Chief of Fighter Command during World War Two, and celebrated with a fly past of Spitfires on the Sunday preceding Battle of Britain Day in September. The Black Bull has a

courtyard with picnic tables. *McEwans and Theakston, with as many as four constantly changing guests.*
❀ ◑ ↻ ⅙ 🛏

Monkton

Monkton Lodge
Kilmarnock Road (01292 678262). With Prestwick Airport close by, this newly built pub and motel is well situated for travellers, and caters well for families. There is an enclosed play area with a slide, plus a baby-changing unit. *Boddingtons and Flowers, with Caledonian as a guest.*
❀ 🏠 ◑ ↻ ⅙ 🛏 ▽

Saltcoats

The Hip Flask
13 Winton Street (01294 465222). *From the war memorial round-about, take the road towards the beach.* Well situated for both the town and the beach, this small café/bar has a raised seating area which sometimes doubles as a stage for their live music evenings. Newspapers and magazine are available to read. There is a play area in the garden, and baby-changing in the disabled toilet.
Belhaven, with guests changing

each week, but you may find Caledonian, Orkney or Theakston, plus bottle conditioned Belhaven.
❀ ▦ ◗ ↪ ▽ ♟ ⏱ *21.00* ▶ The seaside

Seamill

Waterside Inn

Ardrossan Road (01294 823238). *On the A78 between Ardrossan and Largs.* Your children should enjoy this pub, as it sits right by the beach. It is also a pleasant stop if you are catching a ferry to Arran. There are excellent views over the Clyde, where you will usually see plenty of maritime activity. Outdoor and indoor play areas, and a nappy-changing room.

Boddingtons, plus various guests such as Whitbread, Flowers and Wadworth.
🐂 ♣ ❀ ▦ ◗ ↪ ⚡ ▽
▶ The seaside

WALES

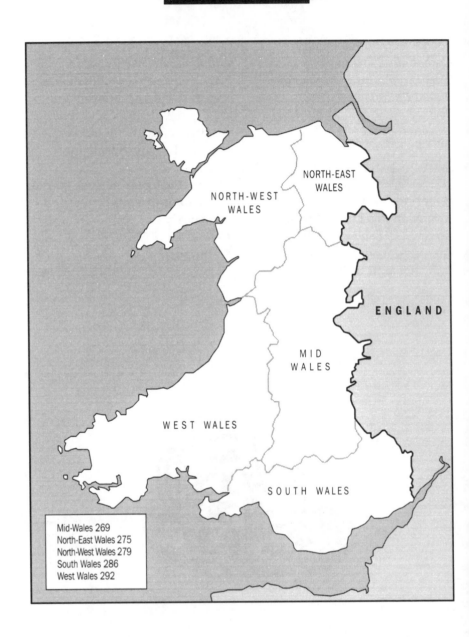

NORTH-EAST WALES

NORTH-WEST WALES

ENGLAND

MID WALES

WEST WALES

SOUTH WALES

MID-WALES

Arddleen

The Horseshoe Inn
(01938 590318). *Between Welshpool and Oswestry on the A483.* Comfortable, friendly and relaxed, this fine old country pub welcomes children in the lounge, and has slides, swings and a climbing frame in the garden. *Marston's and Worthington, with Brains as a guest. Westons real cider is also kept.* 🧗♣🐝🈳◑👞▶ Montgomery Canal

Berriew

The Lion Hotel
(01686 640452). Standing in the centre of a pretty village near to the church, this is a superb 17thC black-and-white hotel, where children are welcome in the bistro or restaurant. *Bass and Worthington, with guests from Greene King, Everards, Shepherd Neame, Ridleys, Wadworth and Young's.* 🧗🐝◑👞🍴🛏🍷🕐 *21.00* ▶ Montgomery Canal and Berriew Aqueduct nearby

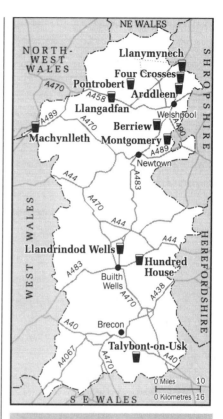

Four Crosses

Four Crosses Inn
(01691 830184). *On the A483 between Oswestry and Welshpool.* A typically friendly village pub, just up the road from Clafton Bridge on the Montgomery Canal. Pool is played here, and there is a play area in the garden. *Boddingtons and Burtonwood.* 🐴♣🐝🈳◑👞▶ Montgomery Canal is just a short walk away

Golden Lion Hotel

(01691 830295). *On the A483 between Oswestry and Welshpool.* This family run hotel is not far from the Montgomery Canal. There is a climbing frame in the garden, and a baby changing area in the ladies toilet. *Worthington, with guests such as Brains, Holdens and Wood to name but a few.*
❀ 🏠 ◑ *not Mon lunch* ⌒ ✄ 🛏
▽ ⏱ *21.30* ▶ The Montgomery Canal is just a short walk away

Glasbury(-on-Wye)

Harp Inn

(01497 8473730). *On the B4350, about 4 miles from Hay, going towards Brecon.* This is a friendly and welcoming village inn, which was once a cider house, situated on the bank of the River Wye. Hay-on-Wye is just 6 miles away, so you could enjoy a browse through the bookshops there (your children will love this!) when visiting the area. The food at The Harp is highly recommended, and can be enjoyed in the riverside garden during the summer. Pool and quoits are played, and there is a slide and see-saw outside.
Boddingtons, Brains and Robinson's, with Adnams, Bateman's and Wadworth as typical guests.
♣ ❀ 🏠 ◑ ⌒ 🛏

Hundred House

Hundred House Inn

(01982 570231). *On the A481 north-east of Builth Wells.* Set amidst fine upland scenery, this old drovers' pub has five separate rooms. There are swings, a slide and a climbing frame in the garden.
Hancock's and Worthington, with a couple of guests.
♣ ❀ 🏠 ◑ ⌒ ✄ 🛏

Llandrindod Wells

Llanerch Inn

Llanerch Lane, off Waterloo Road (01597 822086). *In the town centre, behind the railway station and opposite the police station.* This is a fine 16thC inn set in its own grounds, and featured in Susan Nowak's 'Good Pub Food Guide', which is a sister CAMRA publication. Sue says you will not be disappointed with Llanerch broth Welsh-style, served in a big bowl with a chunk of brown bread, which is just one item on the pub's wholesome and inviting menu. The family room opens onto the garden, and this

contains a children's play park. Having visited the town's renovated spa, a stop at the Llanerch will round off your day nicely. *Hancock's, plus two guest ales, such as Wood or Wadworth, plus local brews.*
🐎♣❀🏤◐ ⌾ ⅝ 🛏▶ The spa

Some early maps mark it a 'Cannon Office', but since a non was a drinking vessel, th amounts to the same thing. *Marston's.*
🐎♣❀◐ *not Oct-Mar* ⌾ ⅝ 🛏
⏱ *21.00*

Llangadfan

Cann Office Hotel
(01938 820202) *On the A458, midway between Welshpool and Dolgellau.* This is a very comfortable and welcoming old coaching inn, with an interesting and unusual (unique?) name. The explanation is this: to the rear of the hotel are the remains of an ancient motte & bailey castle mound. After this castle had fallen into disuse a farmhouse was built in its place. With the coming of the early postal-messenger services in this area in the mid-17thC, a 'post' was established here at 'Tynydomen' (the house on the castle). By this time the building had become an inn, and displayed the requisite sign showing three *cans*, or drinking vessels. So the building was now an inn and a post office (not unusual at the time) and the names were amalgamated into the 'Cann Office' we know today.

Llanymynech

Bradford Arms
(01691 830582). Offa's Dyke and the Anglo-Welsh border both pass through this village, which also stands beside the Montgomery Canal, one of the country's prettiest waterways, and due for complete restoration early in the next century. St Agatha's Church is worth a look: it was built in the 19thC in the rare and unusual French-style Norman, with a lateral bell tower and a large clock face. The Bradford Arms is a friendly and welcoming pub, renowned for excellent food. *Shepherd Neame, with Greene King as a guest.*
◐ *not Mon* ⌾ ⅝ ▶ Montgomery Canal, St Agatha's Church

054 702941).
.. friendly, this
.g inn is one of
..s and pubs in a town
..t one time boasted over
..ity. Well placed at the top of
..ne main street, it is a warm and
friendly place with a comfortable
bar and lounge, which has a
crackling open fire when the
weather is cold. Visitors and
locals mingle in the bar, and
there is a restaurant for more for-
mal meals. Just inside the
entrance hall are photographs
recalling a visit by Lloyd George.
The town is one of Wales' most
handsome, with a tall clock
tower, erected in 1873, marking
the road junction, with The Old
Parliament House along
Maengwyn Street opposite. In
1404, in a moment of brief glory,
Machynlleth was declared the
capital of Wales by Owain
Glyndwr, and the building now
houses an exhibition concerned
with his exploits, with the
Tourist Information Centre next
door. A thriving arts centre has
been established in the
Tabernacl, with a permanent
exhibition, visiting exhibitions,
concerts and an excellent Festival

during August. Celtica, in The
Plas, has various tableaux telling
the story of the Celts. Just north
of the town is the Centre for
Alternative Technology (C-A-T,
or 'The Quarry'), a long established exhibition and centre for
exploring methods of sustainable
living in the home, at work and
in the garden. Stimulating and
thought provoking, it is well
worth a visit. Together with interesting shops, a bustling
Wednesday market, bicycle hire
at Greenstiles Cycles, splendid
countryside and friendly people,
these attractions make
Machynlleth a very worthwhile
holiday venue.

*Flannery's, Flowers and
Morland, with guests from the
likes of Castle Eden, and bottled
Princetown.*

❀ ◑ ⌁ 🛏 ▶ Centre for
Alternative Technology, The
Tabernacl Arts Centre & Festival,
Celtica, Wednesday market,
excellent local walks

Montgomery

The Dragon Hotel

(01686 668359). Montgomery is a
splendidly modest Marches town,
with much to attract visitors,
from the craggy castle ruins,
which were sorted out by Oliver

Cromwell, to the Old Bell exhibition Centre, which contains nine rooms packed with fascinating local history. You will also want to see the handsome town hall, built in 1748, with its clock and tower added in 1921, and visit the church of St Nicholas. Look in the grounds for the Robber's Grave, where John Newton Davies lies buried after being wrongly hanged in 1821 for the theft of a watch valued at £1 10s 0d. Davies continually protested his innocence, and swore that no grass would grow on his grave following execution. And, just as he predicted, for many years there was no grass. The Dragon Hotel is situated at the top of the square. It is an elaborate black-and-white building, a coaching inn dating from the 1600s. It has a charming and unusual enclosed patio leading to the bars, which contain timbers and stonework said to have been taken from the castle following its destruction by Cromwell. It has a small garden, a toy box, and an indoor swimming pool which can be used by *prior* arrangement. Offa's Dyke Path passes the town. Good food. *Wood.*
🐕 🌣 🌓 ↩ ⅍ 🛏 ▽ ⌚ *21.00*
▶ The splendid town of Montgomery

Pontrobert

Royal Oak Inn
(01938 500243). Situated in an unspoilt village, this friendly family-run pub has a large adventure playground along with small swings for babies. Pool, dominoes and cards are played inside. *Tetley and Worthington, with guests such as Bass, Marston's and Morland.*
🐕 ♣ ❀ 🏫 ◑ ↩ ⅍ 🛏

Talybont-on-Usk

Star Inn
(01874 676635). *Half a mile off the A40 between Abergavenny and Brecon.* Right by the aqueduct and not far from the electric lift bridge on the Monmouthshire and Brecon Canal, this black-and-white pub suffered disastrous flooding in 1994, a catastrophe from which it has now thankfully completely recovered. There is a pleasing choice of small bars, with furnishings that have remained unchanged for years. A stunning array of real ales are always on offer: if you are at all confused just take your time, or ask for advice from the bar staff. Children are welcome in the pool room. The gardens are lovely. *Twelve constantly changing real*

ales, which may include
Bullmastiff, Felinfoel, Timothy
Taylor or Wye Valley to name
just a few. Westons real cider is
also offered.

🏃 ♣ ❀ ◐ ➸ 🛏 ⏰ *21.00*

▶ Monmouthshire & Brecon
Canal

The Travellers Rest

(01874 676233). *East of the village.* By Craiglas Bridge on the
Monmouthshire & Brecon Canal,
this bar and restaurant, set below
the canal embankment, specialises in seafood and local game,
from salmon and sole to wood-
pigeon, mallard and rabbit. The
fine large garden is right by the
water. They care about their beer,
and I quote: 'we change our selection of real ales on a weekly
basis. In the summer months we
have five ales which we then
drop to three in the winter
months so as to keep them in
excellent condition'.

This is an example of a typical
selection: Brain's, Buckley,
Felinfoel, Freeminer, Watkin's
and Wye Valley, but you may
find all, some or none of these –
any alternatives should be
equally commendable.

❀ ◐ ➸ ▶ Monmouthshire &
Brecon Canal

White Hart Inn

(01874 676227). *Off the A40
between Brecon and
Abergavenny.* Standing beside
White Hart Bridge on the
Monmouthshire & Brecon Canal,
this is a fine 17thC coaching inn,
complete with an open fire and a
flag stone floor. Children are welcome in the lounge and dining
room.

Bass, Brains and Hancock's with
guests such as Marston's,
Morland and Wadworth.

♣ ♣ ❀ ◐ ➸ 🛏 ⏰ *19.30*

▶ Monmouthshire & Brecon
Canal

Bodfari

Dinorben Arms

(01745 710309). *About 200 yards off the A541 Denbigh to Mold road.* Deifar's Well was uncovered during rebuilding work at the pub, and it is thought that the water from it has the magical property of calming fractious children who refuse to sleep at night. Deifar was a Christian hermit who settled by the well, and had a reputation for great wisdom but, perhaps, not much experience with children. There are splendid panoramic views from the terrace, and a comprehensive play area in the garden. Children are welcome in the restaurants, and there is a nappy-changing area in the ladies toilet. *Aylesbury and Tetley*.
♣❀◑☛✄▽

Chirk

The Bridge Inn

Chirk Bank (01691 773213). 'The last pub in England', which rather assumes you are going into Wales, which is not a bad idea. Standing by the canal, this is a pleasant country pub. Dominoes and cards can be played here. *Banks's, with Marston's as a guest.*

♣❀◑☛☼ *21.30* ▶ Llangollen Canal, with Chirk Aqueduct and Chirk Tunnel a short walk to the west

The Poacher's Pocket

Gledrid (01691 773250). Very nicely positioned by the canal to the south of Chirk, this is a happy and friendly pub which welcomes children in any area at any time of the day. There is a play park outside, and a chummy artificial horse in the stables. *Banks's*.
❀◫◑☛✄▶ Llangollen Canal

Froncysyllte

Aqueduct Inn

Holyhead Road (01691 772481). The aqueduct in question is the Pontcysyllte, on the nearby Llangollen Canal. It is a stunning structure, perhaps the finest on the whole network, and all superlatives used to describe it have been exhausted. Thought to have been wholly designed by Thomas Telford (some knowledgeable folk dispute this) it consists of a cast-iron trough just one boat-width wide, supported on hollow stone pillars which carry the waterway 126 feet above the River Dee. It is 1007 feet long, and to journey across by boat is a stunning experience, and walking

across, if you've a head for heights, runs this a close second. The original concept was initially greeted with derision, but was finally accepted. It took 10 years to build at a cost of £47,018, and opened in 1805 to the amazement of the world, since nothing like it had been seen since Roman times. It has remained in prime condition, a tribute to its design and the craftsmen who built it. So why not incorporate a stroll across before your visit to the pub, although young children *must* be closely supervised! *Marston's, plus a different guest every two weeks.*
♣ ❀ ◑ ☞ ▶ Llangollen Canal, a lift bridge and the magnificent aqueduct

Halkyn

Britannia Inn
Pentre Road (01352 780272). *Take the Halkyn turn off the A55 expressway.* This building started its life as a farm during the 15thC, but it has been added to quite a bit since then. There are fine views over the Dee. Pool, dominoes and cards are played here. *Lees.*
♣ ❀ ◑ ☞ ▽

Hanmer

Hanmer Arms
(01948 830532). *Off the A539 Overton to Llangollen road, about 1½ miles from its junction with the A525.* This friendly pub has for many years extended a warm welcome to families. It is set in attractive undulating countryside close to Hanmer Mere, which is a popular venue for fishermen. *Tetley.*
♣ ❀ ◑ ☞ ✗ 🛏

Llanarmon Dyffryn Ceiriog

West Arms Hotel
(01691 600665). *South of Llangollen, west of Chirk, on the B4500.* Built in the 16thC, this smart and historic inn offers all you might expect: warm fires in vast inglenooks, heavily beamed ceilings, slate-flagged floors, period furniture, good food and a friendly welcome. A visit here in 1854 was recalled by George Borrow in his book 'Wild Wales': "I went to an inn, sat down and called for ale. A waggoner was seated at a large table with a newspaper before him, on which he was intently staring. 'What news' said I. 'I wish I could tell you', he said in very broken

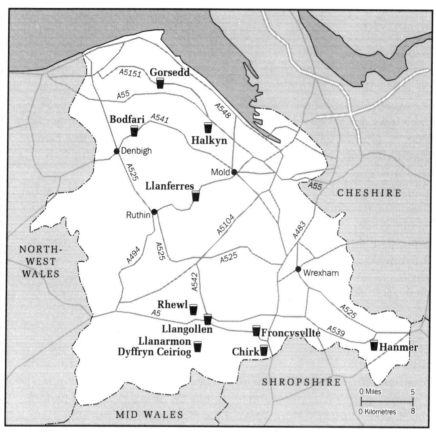

English, 'but I cannot read". Fine gardens beside the Afon Ceiriog. This is an ideal centre for exploring the beautiful countryside hereabouts.

Flowers.

🛏 ❀ ◗ ☕ ⚔ 🛏

Gorsedd

The Druid Inn
The Village (01352 710944).

Standing opposite the church, this is a smart country pub which dates from the 12thC, so you can expect a fine beamy interior and warming open fires. No garden, but there is a patio.

Boddingtons and Timothy Taylor, with guests from Coach House and Moorhouse's.
❀ ◗ *not Sun or Mon evenings* ☕
⚔ ⏰ *20.30*

Llanferres

The Druid Inn

Ruthin Road (01352 810225). *On the A494 Mold to Ruthin road.* Standing by the church, there are fine views down the valley from here. Inside you will find a friendly beamed bar, with wooden settles and a roaring log fire when the weather is cool. Bagatelle, dominoes and pool can be played, and there is a pleasant south-facing patio.
Burtonwood, with Gale's as a guest.
♣ ❀ ◑ ↩ 🛏

Llangollen

Sun Trevor

Sun Bank (01978 860651). *About 1½ miles east of Llangollen, on the A539 towards Ruabon.* Very well known to boaters on the Llangollen Canal, this is a beautifully situated pub overlooking this waterway and the valley of the River Dee beyond. With its origins in the 14thC it is not sur-prising that the interior is beamy, with a warm inglenook enclosed by a curved settle, the whole being decorated with plenty of brass. From this point you can walk along the canal towpath either west to Llangollen or east to Pontcysyllte Aqueduct (see above – about 1½-2 miles in either direction)
Courage and Theakston, and Morland and Matthew Brown's as guests.
♣ ❀ ◑ ↩ ▶ Llangollen Canal

Rhewl

The Sun Inn

Near Llangollen (01978 861043). Not to be missed, this 14thC drovers' inn is a rural gem, with low ceilings and stone floors. It has become a centre for fishing, walking and fell running. Children are welcome, except in the public bar. Pool and bar billiards are played here.
Worthington, with a couple of guests.
🐴 ♣ ◑ ↩

Aberdyfi

Penhelig Arms Hotel
Penhelig (01654 767215). At the eastern end of this exceptionally pretty seaside village, The Penhelig overlooks the estuary, popular with sailing types and windsurfers during the summer. Some say that Penhelig was in fact the true port of Aberdyfi, with strong ship-building connections. If you follow the water's edge inland not far from here, you will find a road carved from the rock, a relic of times when the sea level was lower than now. Perhaps it connected with the Roman fort at Pennal, upstream towards Machynlleth. Indeed the famous legend of Aberdyfi relates to a time when the land extended further west, the sea being kept out by dykes – perhaps the sarnau, or shallow reefs which still stretch out into Cardigan Bay. Leaving all of this speculation aside, the legend of 'The Bells of Aberdovey' lives on in a song composed for the opera 'Liberty Hall' in 1785, and fossilised tree stumps *can* be seen on the beach during low spring tides. When the sun shines, you can enjoy your beer while sitting on the sea wall. Good food.
Bass and Tetley, plus
Bateman's, Brains and Marston's amongst a range of guests.
 21.30 ▶ The seaside, water-sports, walking

Abergele

Bull Hotel
Chapel Street (01745 832115). A typical rural hostelry with two rooms, just outside the town centre. The lounge is large and homely, and transport theme charts adorn the walls. Children are welcome in the dining room, and a party is held for their benefit at Christmas.
Lees.

Bontnewydd

Newborough Arms
(01286 673126). A busy and popular village pub, with swings in the garden.
Bass, Burton, Marston's and Tetley.

Chwilog

Madryn Arms
(01766 810250). Butlins Holiday Camp at Pwllheli is just a mile away from this small and friendly

country pub, so it's handy if you wish to leave the joys of the camp for a while, or if you are just exploring the quietly attractive Lleyn Peninsula. The garden has swings and climbing frames. *Burtonwood.*
❀ ▣ ◑ ☞

Capel Curig

Cobdens Hotel
(01690 720243). *On the A5 in Capel Curig.* 'This is us: no starchiness, no frills, just warm hospitality'. So says their publicity, and that sounds just fine. Standing at the foot of Moel Siabod, this friendly climbers' and walkers' hotel features a natural rock face in the Climber's Bar. Good food on the 'brasserie' principle, plus board games and pool.
Greenalls and Tetley, with Cambrian as a guest.
♣ ◑ ☞ ⚔ 🛏 ▶ Snowdonia for walks

Clynnog Fawr

The Coach Inn
(01286 660212). *On the main A499 coast road.* In a building which dates from the 16thC, this country coaching inn overlooking the sea is full of character, and

lively during the summer months. Entertainments include kite and balloon festivals, motor rallies and Guy Fawkes celebrations. Skittles and shove ha'penny are played here. The garden has a stream with ducks and geese – you can buy food for them at the bar. Family discos during the summer.
Marston's, plus guests: 'lots: too many to list'.
🪀 ♣ ❀ ◑ ☞ 🛏 ⚱

Colwyn Bay

Taylors
Pen-y-Bryn Road (01492 533360). *At the top of King's Road and Drive turn right. It is a mile from the town centre.* There are sweeping views over the town and the bay from this modern pub, built with old bricks. The pleasant interior has lots of natural wood. There are swings and a walkway in the garden, and a baby-changing area in the ladies toilet.
Marston's, John Smith's and Theakston.
♣ ❀ ▣ ◑ ☞ ⚔ ▽

Deganwy

Deganwy Castle Hotel
Station Road (01492 583555). Just 100 yards from the beach, this is

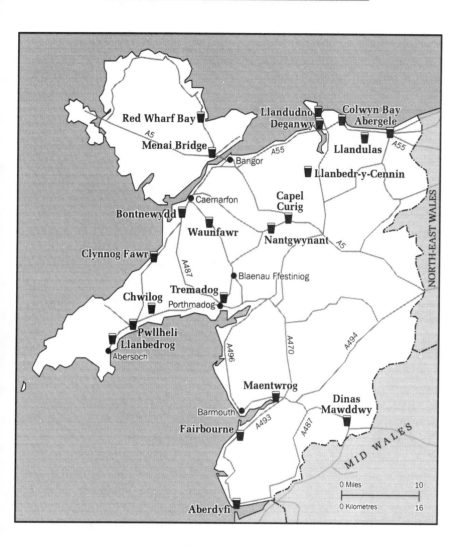

a large residential hotel with lots of separate rooms – children are welcome in the lounge.
Courage, John Smith's and Tetley.
🏃 ❀ ◗ ➷ ✄ 🛏 ▶ The seaside

Dinas Mawddwy

Red Lion

(01650 531247). *Just off the A470 between Cemmaes Road and Dolgellau.* This is a fine and very old village inn. Pool, video games and table football are played here. *Bass and Worthington, with Brains and Felinfoel as guests.*

🐴 ❀ ◑ ⇌

Fairbourne

The Fairbourne Hotel

(01341 250203). This bright and breezy resort on Cardigan Bay boasts fine beaches, a Butterfly Farm and a splendid narrow-gauge railway amongst its attractions. There are plenty of camp-sites around, and windsurfing is a major activity here – it is exhilarating to watch participants when the breeze is fresh. The Fairbourne Hotel is a friendly seaside pub, with a long darkish bar, and a children's room. Table football and pool are played here. *McEwan's and Younger.*

🐴 ♣ ❀ ◑ ⇌ ✄ 🍴

▶ Fairbourne Railway, Butterfly Farm

Llanbedrog

Glyn-y-Weddw Arms (Ty Du)

(01758 740212). *Between Pwllheli and Abersoch, close to the beach.* This is a very nice old-fashioned family pub, close to the beach, so it's popular with both children and sun-seekers. Children are welcome in the snug and family

room, and there is a slide, swing and climbing area in the garden. Sunday lunch carveries, and winter food theme nights: Chinese, Indian, Mexican and fish. *Robinson's.*

🐴 ❀ ▦ ◑ ⇌ ✄ ▶ The seaside

Llanbedr-y-Cennin

Ye Olde Bull Inn

(01492 660508). Built, it is said, using timbers from a Spanish Armada shipwreck, this attractive old drovers' pub enjoys excellent mountain views. It has a large and interesting garden, and there are camping facilities. *Lees.*

❀ ◑ ⇌ ✄

Llandudno

London Hotel

131 Upper Mostyn Street (01492 876740). This pub, as well as having an unusual name and a sign showing Dick Whittington, also has an old red telephone box inside. It is close to the pier and promenade, so it is a handy port of call when you are enjoying the delights of the seaside. Bryn Chamberlin sings here each Friday evening. *Burtonwood.*

◑ ⇌ 🍺 🕐 *19.00* ▶ The seaside

Links Hotel

Conwy Road (01492 879180). Its name revealing its proximity to two golf courses, this spacious and friendly pub is popular with both locals and visitors. Children are welcome in the conservatory and dining area. They modestly stated that they have a 'medium sized' children's play area. Babies can be changed in a separate room which is combined with the disabled toilet.

Lees.

🐂 ❀ 🏢 ◑ ↩ ⚒ 🛏 ▽ ▶ The seaside

Llandulas

Dulas Arms

Abergele Road (01492 515747). *On the old A55 between Llandulas and Old Colwyn.* Once called 'The Railway Hotel' (there is no station now), this six-roomed pub has a lounge, a snug, a games room, a restaurant and fine family rooms. It also has a large garden, with a play area and swings and slides, overlooking the sea. They often have live folk music and a family sing-a-long, accompanied by an organist. Baby-changing tables will be found in the toilets.

Lees.

🐂 ♣ ❀ 🏢 ◑ ↩ ⚒ 🛏 ▽ 🍷
⏱ *21.00*

Maentwrog

The Grapes Hotel

(01766 590365). *Near the junction of the A470 and A496.* Two ghosts are said to haunt this very pretty 19thC stone-built hotel. One is a little old Victorian lady who appears below stairs, the second plays a piano on the residents' landing. Built above a 13thC cellar, The Grapes was visited by George Borrow, who wrote in his book 'Wild Wales' that he entered 'a magnificent parlour and partook of brandy and water'. Other famous patrons have included Lloyd George, Prime Minister during the Great War of 1914-18, and Lily Langtry. The bars are a beautiful mixture of warm timber and stone, warmed by log fires in cold weather. The covered verandah overlooks a walled and fountained garden and on towards the Vale of Ffestiniog, where you may see a distant steam train wending its way to or from Blaenau Ffestiniog. Maentwrog (mine-toor-rog) means 'the stone of the giant Twrog', who is said to have thrown it from the top of

nearby Moelwyn mountain, to land in the church yard behind the pub. Built into the main doorway is another famous stone – a centurial marker taken from the Roman fort near Trawsfynydd, and which signified the completion of a section of wall by 100 soldiers. Children are welcome in the dining room and verandah. *Bass and Dyffryn Clwyd, with guests from a choice of 40 rotating ales, such as Greene King, Theakston and Young's.*
🐎 ❀ ◑ ↶ ⅙ 🛏 ▽

Menai Bridge

The Gazelle Hotel
Glyn Garth (01248 713364). Overlooking the Menai Strait, the pub offers absolutely splendid views of the Snowdon range, standing beyond the Menai bridges. Children are welcome in the comfortable and attractive rooms, as long as they keep away from the bars. Pool is played here, and there is a garden. *Robinson's.*
♣ ❀ ◑ ↶ 🛏 ⏱ 21.00

Ship Inn
(01758 740270). As well as a traditional lounge, you will find a two-tier lounge and eating area plus an unusual 'prow'-shaped extension for the no smoking family room. It is a very pretty roadside pub, with a nice sunny terrace. *Burtonwood.*
🐎 ❀ ◑ ↶ ⅙ ▶ The seaside

Victoria Hotel
(01248 712309). *Just 200 yards from the Menai Suspension Bridge.* With a splendid garden overlooking the Menai Straits, the Victoria is a popular two-bar residential hotel. Children are welcome away from the bar. *Bass, with Fuller's and Marston's as guests.*
🐎 ❀ ◑ ↶ ⅙ 🛏

Nantgwynant

Pen-y-Gwryd Hotel
(01286 870211). *4 miles from Capel Curig, on the A498 between Capel Curig and Beddgelert.* A welcoming climbers' inn, where John Hunt and his team trained for their successful assault on Everest in 1953. Plenty of climbing mementoes, including a selection of boots. *Bass.*
◖ *bar meals* ◗ *in the dining room*
↶ ⅙ 🛏 ▶ Lake and mountains

Pwllheli

Penlan Fawr
Penlan Street (01758 614205).

This is 17thC pub is quite possibly the oldest building in the town. Alterations were being made as this book went to print, so this description is necessarily economical. Children are welcome until 18.00, and there is a garden. *Tetley plus a selection of guests, such as Worthington.* ♣ ❀ ◑ *not confirmed due to alterations* ⏰ *18.00* ▶ The seaside

Red Wharf Bay

Ship Inn
(01248 852568). *Off the A5025 north-west of Menai Bridge.* Beautifully situated right by the beach, this is a fine place to be in any season. In cold weather it is warmed by cosy open fires. *Burton, Marston's and Tetley, with Benskins as a guest.* 🐎 ❀ ◑ 🍴 ▶ The seaside

Tremadog

Golden Fleece Inn
(01766 512421). With plenty of beams, this old stone inn is always warm and welcoming. It has log fires in winter. No garden, but there is a covered courtyard. *Bass and Theakston, with Dyffryn Clwyd and Marston's as guests.* 🐎 ♣ ❀ ◑ ⌣ 🍴 🛏 ⏰ *21.00*

Waunfawr

Snowdonia Parc Hotel
(01286 650409). *About 3 miles south of Caernarfon, on the A4085 Beddgelert Road.* In 11 acres of unspoilt valley in a charming mountain setting, this former Victorian station-master's house is now a large well-furnished family-friendly pub, with an oak-panelled lounge. It also has a 22 x 24 foot carpeted family room, with plenty of big toys for small children, and this stays open while the pub is open. There are also swings, rockers and slides in the garden, and baby-changing facilities in the ladies toilet. Good home-prepared food (including proper puddings), and regular entertainment, from local culture to rock & roll. Accommodation includes a family room, and a camp site. *Marston's, with guests such as Cains, Dyffryn Clwyd and Exmoor. Also the splendid bottled Marston's Oyster Stout.* 🐎 ♣ ❀ 🏠 ◑ ⌣ 🍴 🛏 ▽ 🎤
▶ Snowdonia

SOUTH WALES

Bassaleg

Tredegar Arms
4 Caerphilly Road (01633
893247). *From junction 28 on the
M4, follow signs for Caerphilly.*
Claiming to be 'the biggest stock-
ist of cask ale in Wales', the
Tredegar Arms has a cosy lounge,
and a special area for families.
The decor includes wooden casks
and old brewery-style notices.
The large garden contains a slide,
and a bouncy castle.
*There are always thirteen real
ales at any one time, including
the likes of Badger,
Boddingtons, Brains, Flowers
and Greene King, with ten
guests each week. You should
find something you like.*
🐎 ❀ 🏠 ◑ ↩ 🍴 🕭 22.00

East Aberthaw

Blue Anchor Inn
(01446 750329). Built around
1380, this ancient creeper-clad
inn was reputedly once a haunt
of smugglers, with a long history
connected with piracy and
wrecking. Much of its original
character has survived, with
many intimate rooms set around
a central bar: one of these is
reserved for families. No room for
garden toys, but the sea is not far.

*Boddingtons, Buckley's,
Marston's, Theakston and
Wadworth, with guests from
Cottage.*
🐎 ❀ ◑ ↩ 🕭 20.30

Kenfig

Prince of Wales Inn
(01656 740356). *Leave the M4 at
junction 37 and follow signs to
Kenfig.* This fine pub stands in
what was once the Old Guildhall,
which used to be the seat of gov-
ernment and meeting place of the
Trustees and Parish Council of
Kenfig. The old mace is indeed
still kept here. Yet this is not the
original village of Kenfig, or
Cenfigg, which actually lies
buried beneath the dunes, having
finally succumbed to a great
storm in 1607. Before this it was a
great commercial centre, with
weekly markets and annual fairs,
a great seaport and a military station, guarded by a mighty castle.
But alongside their constant bat-
tles with the sands, the good people of Kenfig were regularly raid-
ed by the Vikings and other
marauders, being 'sacked and
burned' no less than eight times
up to1402. The Prince of Wales is
currently believed to be the only
pub in the UK to hold a weekly
Sunday school: Kenfig Calvinistic

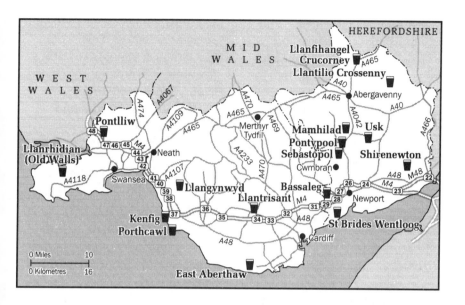

Methodist. It is also adjacent to a Kenfig Pool & Dunes National Nature Reserve, which is well worth exploring. As befits its colourful history, this 13thC pub, a Grade II listed building, is warm and welcoming, with bare stone walls and crackling open fires when the weather is cold. Good food, especially fish, is served. Dominoes and cards. **Bass, Brains, Marston's, Morland, St Austell and Worthington, with many regularly changing guests, such as Fuller's and Highgate**. ⛺♣🐝◑🥾🕗 *21.00* ▶ Kenfig Pool & Dunes NNR, the seaside

Llanfihangel Crucorney

The Skirrid Mountain Inn

(01873 890258). *About 4½ miles north of Abergavenny, signposted off the A465.* Contender for the title 'oldest pub in Wales' (but see below), flagstone floors and sturdy walls certainly seem to back up this claim. Its unique character is enhanced by massive ship's timbers used within the building, along with ancient windows and a splendid open fire in a stone hearth. And if your children are getting bored, you could show them the beam at the foot of the stairs. This building was for many years a courthouse, and over 200 people were sentenced

to death here, and hanged from this particular piece of wood. Of course the atmosphere today is friendly and welcoming, and you will surely enjoy your visit, although such places can get busy during the tourist season.
Ushers, plus Ushers bottled ale.
🐎♣️🕸️◑👟✄🛏️🕙 *21.00*
▶ The inn itself

Llangynwyd

Old House Inn
(01656 733310). Another of Wales' oldest pubs (but see above), this building dates from 1147, and was a calling place of the legendary Wil Hopkin in the story of 'The Maid of Cefn Ydfa'. Indeed it is said he wrote the famous Welsh song 'Bugeilio'r Gwenith Gwyn' in the building. As you would expect of such an ancient establishment, the walls are 3 feet 6 inches thick, the roof is thatched, and inside there are lots of dark beams and a cosy inglenook fireplace. It is well decorated with an assortment of Welsh memorabilia, including old miners' lamps, and is one of the last places in Wales where the 'Mari Lwyd' tradition is still celebrated each year. The fine restaurant occupies what was the very first Non-Conformist chapel in

the Llynfi Valley, dated 1840, and serves excellent food. The 2½ acre garden contains an exciting adventure playground.
Brains, Wadworth and Worthington, with Bass and Morland as guests.
🕸️🉑◑👟✄ ▶ The inn itself

Llanrhidian

The Greyhound Inn
Oldwalls (01792 391027). *Just under a mile west of Llanrhidian, which is at the point where the B4295 and B4271 meet.* This fine large rural inn has a refreshing expanse of country garden, incorporating a fenced play area. There is also a games room with a pool table.
Bullmastiff and Wadworth, with guests from Marston's and Robinson's.
🐎♣️🕸️🉑◑👟✄

Llantilio Crossenny

Hostry Inn
(01600 780278). *On the B4233 east of Abergavenny.* The manager only welcomes well-behaved and quiet children here, and does not welcome babies, so if your lot fit the brief, read on. This is an ancient village local, which dates from 1459. There is a skittle alley,

plus bar skittles and shove
ha'penny. Good food.
Wye Valley.
♟ ♣ ❀ ◗ ➳ ⚡ ⏰ 21.30

Llantrisant

The Barn at Mwyndy
Cardiff Road (01443 222333).
*Leave the M4 at junction 34, and
turn right at the second set of
traffic lights.* True to its name,
this is a nicely converted barn,
surrounded by woodland and
opposite a lake, and warmed by a
log fire. The interior is well decorated, with exposed beams, stone
walls and plenty of rural paraphernalia. There is play equipment in the garden, and a pull
down table for nappy changes in
the toilet.
*Bass and Wadworth, with
Brains, Greene King, Everards
and Fuller's as guests.*
❀ ⌘ ◗ ➳ ⚡ ▽

Mamhilad

Horse Shoe Inn
Pen Croes Hir (01873 880542).
*From Pontypool follow the A4042
towards Abergavenny. Take the
first left after the Du Pont Fibres
plant (ICI). Pass through
Mamhilad village, cross the
canal, and the pub is on the right.*

You will find a sign outside this
pub which reads 'Relax, take in
the view. God made this place
when he finished his apprentice-
ship'. All of this, and a fine rural
inn as well! Notice the unusual
bar, where the optics are sus-
pended from an old wheel.
Occasional musical evenings.
*Bateman's and Flowers, with
Morland and Wadworth as
guests.*
🐕 ❀ ◗ ➳ ⚡ 🛏

The Star Inn
(01495 785319). *From Pontypool
follow the A4042 towards
Abergavenny. Take the first left
after the Du Pont Fibres plant
(ICI).* The Monmouthshire &
Brecon Canal is just a short walk
from this cosy little pub, which
has offered over 350 different real
ales since December 1995, changing at least two each week.
Children are welcome in the
lounge, and there are swings and
a slide in the garden. The restaurant is non-smoking.
*Bass and Hancock's, plus regu-
larly changing guests.*
♟ ❀ ⌘ ◗ ➳ ⚡ ▶

Monmouthshire & Brecon Canal

Pontypool

The Horseshoe Inn
High Street, Pontnewynydd

(01495 762188). *Off the A4043 north-west of Pontypool.* Popular 300-year-old coaching inn, with horseshoes and sketches of local scenes in the lounge. Skittles and pool are played here. Children are welcome in the lounge bar until 21.00, although there is no time restriction on the Games, Dining and Children's rooms. However, proper supervision is insisted upon. The enclosed garden is accessed only through the bars, so your children will be safely contained while they use the play tower, which has swings, slides and a swing boat. *Founders, John Smith's and Ushers.*
🐴 ♣ ❀ 🏥 ◑ ➷

Porthcawl

The Globe Inn
Bridgend Road, Newton (01656 774001). *Newton is just east of Porthcawl.* Just a short distance from Newton Bay and the sand dunes, so you can enjoy a trip to the beach followed by a pint. The restaurant is popular here, and their Sunday night quiz raised £2500 for local charities in 1997. Children are welcome in the dining area. There are toys in the garden, and a baby-changing table in the toilets.

Bass and Hancock's.
♣ ❀ 🏥 ◑ ➷ ✠ ⏱ *21.45* ▶ The beach

St Brides Wentloog

Church House Inn
Church Road (01633 680807). *On the B4239 coast road between Newport and Cardiff.* In a tiny village looking out over the Severn estuary, this is an old country local which serves the rural community hereabouts. Children are welcome in the lounge window area. There are swings and a play-frame outside. *Brains.*
🏃 ❀ 🏥 ◑ ➷ ✠

Sebastopol

Open Hearth Inn
Wern Road (01435 763752). *At the southern end of Pontypool.* Beside the Monmouthshire & Brecon Canal, which has recently re-opened as far as Cross Keys Bridge, about a mile south of here, through Cwmbran Tunnel. Alongside a fine selection of draught real ales, an extensive collection of bottled beers can be seen in the lounge bar. *Archers, Boddingtons, Brains, Buckley and Hancock's, with Butcombe's, Cains and Jennings*

as typical guests. Also bottle conditioned Morland's Speckled Hen.

🐎 ❀ 🏠 ◑ 🍂 🍴 ⏱ *21.30* ▶ Monmouthshire & Brecon Canal

Shirenewton

The Carpenters Arms

(01291 641231). Absolutely packed with antiques, this fine 400-year-old hostelry has flagstone floors and warming log fires. At one time it was a carpenters shop, blacksmith's and pub all at the same time. Children are welcome in the family room. No garden, but there is a terrace for fine days. Local produce is used, so the meals are good.

Flower's, Fuller's, Marston's and Wadworth, with guests such as Gale's, Ringwood and Timothy Taylor.

🐎 ❀ ◑ 🍂 ⏱ *20.30*

Usk

The Royal Hotel

26 Newmarket Street (01291 672931). Castle ruins stand overlooking the river in this fine market town, a renowned centre for anglers. While you are here, why not visit The Royal, an unspoilt Victorian pub with comfy bars and an open fire.

Bass, Everards and Felinfoel, with guests such as Freeminer and Bullmastiff, and bottle conditioned Morland's Speckled Hen.

◑ 🍂

WEST WALES

Abercych

Nags Head Inn
(01239 841200). *Abercych is off the B4332 west of Newcastle Emlyn.* Old Emrys, their own beer, is often brewed in an on-site micro-brewery beside this pub, situated in a converted and well restored and beamy old smithy. There is a children's playground in the garden, and they have a separate children's menu.
Old Emrys, Flowers and Worthington.
🐴❀🏚◑👒✄

Ammonford

Wernoleu Hotel
31 Pontamman Road (01269 592598). Once a Victorian gentleman's residence, this pleasant conversion stands in its own 6 acres of grounds.
Brains and Buckleys, with guests such as Adnams, Badger, Greene King and Shepherd Neame.
🐴❀◐👒🛏

Amroth

The New Inn
(01834 812368). New at the time it was built, some 400 years ago, this fine old seaside inn is divided into small rooms, with flagstone floors, and an open fire when the weather is cold. Pool and video games.
Burton and Tetley, with Morland as a guest (and they would be interested to hear your suggestions!).
🐴♣❀◑ *summer season for food is 1 Apr-31 Oct* 👒▶ The seaside

Brynhoffnant

Brynhoffnant Inn
Brynhoffnant (01239 654413). *Halfway between Cardigan and New Quay.* This pub is ideally situated if you are planning to visit, or are returning from, one of the splendid beaches on this section of coast: Penbryn, Tresaith, Aberporth and Llangranog. It was built in 1860 and externally it has remained fairly unchanged since then. Inside there is a two-way fireplace in one of the rooms. Pool is played here, and there are tables outside on the lawn. The food area is no-smoking.
Courage, Ruddles and Worthington.
❀◑👒✄▶ Seaside nearby

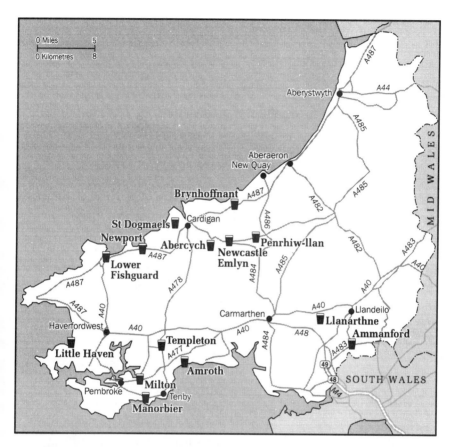

Little Haven

The Castle

(01734 781251). Tucked into the southern corner of St Brides Bay, Little Haven is an attractive seaside village, popular with scuba divers. The Castle is situated right on the front, with a view over the fine sandy beach, much loved by children. Pool and table skittles are played here, and, as you might expect, the fish meals are good. Live entertainment every Friday.

Brains.

♣ ❀ ◑ ⌣ 🛏 ⚑ ▶ The seaside

Llanarthne

Golden Grove Arms

(01558 668551). This family-run country inn has a large play area at the back, with a slide and rope

swings. Pool and video games are played here, and it also has a reputation for good food. They also let a self-catering cottage. *Brains and Buckley's, with guests such as Badger, Greene King and Morrells.*
🐎 ♣ ❀ 🎴 ◐ ➳ 🛏

Lower Fishguard

The Ship
Newport Road (01348 874033). Historic fisherman's pub near the old harbour, with an open fire and plenty of nautical memorabilia and pictures. *Bass and Worthington.*
🐎 🕲 *21.00* ▶ Harbour and seaside

Manorbier

Castle Inn
(01834 871268). *Manorbier is on the B4585, which is just off the A4139 south-west of Tenby.* Giraldus Cambrensis, Welsh ecclesiastic and topographer, was born in the village. He travelled Wales in 1188, along with Archbishop Baldwin, to recruit for the Third Crusade. The first record of the splendid moated ruins of the Norman castle, which overlooks the bay here, were in 1146, and it is thought that the

hall block and the tower might date from that time. Of course the whole thing could have been preceded by an earth and timber construction, but nothing is known for sure. Farm buildings, built within the walls, suggest a later, non-military, use. The pub, the only one in the village, is close by. It makes a comfortable and friendly stop while exploring this fascinating area. Bar skittles, hoopla and pool are played, and there is garden near the beach. *Theakston, with Black Sheep and Wadworth as guests.*
♣ ❀ ◐ ➳ ⚔ 🕲 *21.00* ▶ Castle and beach

Milton

Milton Brewery Inn
(01646 651202). *On the A477 between Kilgetty and Pembroke.* This is now a very old village inn, but alas no longer a brewery. Inside you will find beamy ceilings, stone walls and open fires, although the family room is in a newer part of the building, which leads directly into the garden. This in turn adjoins the village playground, where there are swings and slides close by. It is very handily placed for visits to Carew Castle. Children are welcome in all parts of the pub,

except the saloon bar.
Bass and Worthington, with guests from Pembroke.
🐎 ♣ ✿ ◑ ✇ ▶ Carew Castle

Newcastle Emlyn

The Bunch of Grapes
(01239 711185). Pine floors and furniture fill the single bar area of this friendly 17thC pub. Children are welcome in the dining room, and there is a sandpit in the garden.
Courage and Theakston, with guests including Fullers, Marston's, Ruddles and Wadworth.
🎏 ♣ ✿ 🏥 ◑ *not Mon* ✇ 🕐 20.30

Pelican Inn
Sycamore Street (01239 710606). *In the centre of town, near the High Street.* It was in 1797 that the artist Rowlandson sat in the bar here and sketched a dog working the roasting spit, with the bread oven in the backgound, and this 17thC inn still remains a very hospitable family-run place. Children are welcome in the pool room and restaurant.
Brains.
🎏 ♣ ✿ ◑ ✇ 🛏

Newport

Castle Hotel
Bridge Street (01239 820742). A friendly local, in the centre of town. There is a new play area in the garden, and a disabled toilet.
Morland, Wadworth and Worthington.
🐎 ♣ ✿ 🏥 ◑ ✇ 🛏

Pontlliw

The Glamorgan Arms
Brintirion Road (01792 882409). Originally a farmhouse, this is now a fine place to visit with your children, since they will certainly enjoy the big-screen TV and the board games and play equipment inside, plus the large garden with climbing frames, swings, slides and tractors outside, all illuminated when it gets dark. On Bank Holidays during the summer they organise family karaoke and discos.
John Smith's and Worthington, with Brains and Theakston as guests.
🐎 ♣ ✿ 🏥 ◑ ✇ 🍸

Penrhiw-llan

Penrhiwllan Inn
(01559 370394). Friendly, unspoilt country pub, with a

restaurant. Pool, table football and video games are played, and the garden has a children's play area with swings and a slide, and a new 9-hole pitch-and-putt course.

Bass, with various guests.
🐎 ♣ ❀ ▦ ◑ ☂ ⏰ *21.00*

St Dogmaels

The Ferry Inn

Llandudoch (01239 615172). *You will find this pub on the outskirts of the village, beside the B4546 towards the coast.* On the Teifi estuary near Poppit Sands, this handsome old stone-built inn offers a friendly welcome. The

bars have plenty of character, and there is a large terraced riverside garden.

Brains and Wadworth, with Burton, Felinfoel and Marston's as guests.
❀ ◑ ☂ ✄ ⏰ *21.30* ▶ Poppit Sands nearby

Templeton

Boar's Head Inn

(01834 860286). Fresh hops are used each year to decorate the inside of this traditional pub, which has two bars plus a lounge. Pool is played here.

Bass, Ruddles and Worthington.
🐎 ❀ ◑ ☂ ✄ 🎤

Why not

turn this page

and join

CAMRA?

JOIN CAMRA!

If you like good beer and good pubs you could be helping to fight to preserve, protect and promote them. CAMRA was set up in the early seventies to fight against the mass destruction of a part of Britain's heritage.

The giant brewers are still pushing through takeovers, mergers and closures of their smaller regional rivals. They are still trying to impose national brands of beer and lager on their customers whether they like it or not, and they are still closing down town and village pubs or converting them into grotesque 'theme' pubs.

CAMRA wants to see genuine free competition in the brewing industry, fair prices, and, above all, a top quality product brewed by local breweries in accordance with local tastes, and served in pubs that maintain the best features of a tradition that goes back centuries.

As a CAMRA member you will be able to enjoy generous discounts on CAMRA products and receive the highly rated monthly newspaper *What's Brewing*. You will be given the CAMRA members' handbook and be able to join in local social events and brewery trips.

To join, complete the form opposite and, if you wish, arrange for direct debit payments by filling in the form on the reverse and returning it to CAMRA. To pay by credit card, contact the membership secretary on (01727) 867201.

I/We wish to join the Campaign for Real Ale and agree
to abide by the Rules.

Name(s) ....

Address...

....

....

Postcode..........................

Signature...

Date...............................

I/We enclose the remittance for:

Single:......... £14   Joint:..........£17(at same address)
OAP Single:...£8   OAP Joint:.£11(at same address)
Unemployed/Disabled:...................£8
Under 26:...... £8   Date of birth..............................

For Life and Overseas rates please contact
CAMRA HQ (tel: 01727 867201)

Send your remittance (payable to CAMRA) to:
The Membership Secretary,
CAMRA
230 Hatfield Road, St Albans, Herts., AL1 4LW

Instruction to your Bank or Building Society to pay by Direct Debit

Please fill in the whole form using a ball point pen and send it to:

Campaign for Real Ale Ltd,
230 Hatfield Road,
St. Albans,
Herts
AL1 4LW

Originator's Identification Number

| 9 | 2 | 6 | 1 | 2 | 9 |

Reference Number

| | | | | | | | | | | | | | | | |

Name of Account Holder(s)

FOR CAMRA OFFICIAL USE ONLY
This is not part of the instruction to your Bank or Building Society

Membership Number

Name

Postcode

Bank/Building Society account number

| | | | | | | |

Branch Sort Code

| | | | | |

Instructions to your Bank or Building Society
Please pay CAMRA Direct Debits from the account detailed on this instruction subject to the safeguards assured by the Direct Debit Guarantee. I understand that this instruction may remain with CAMRA and, if so, will be passed electronically to my Bank/Building Society

Name and full postal address of your Bank or Building Society

To The Manager   Bank/Building Society

Address

Postcode

Signature(s)

Date

Banks and Building Societies may not accept Direct Debit instructions for some types of account

- -

This guarantee should be detached and retained by the Payer.

The Direct Debit Guarantee

- This Guarantee is offered by all Banks and Building Societies that take part in the Direct Debit Scheme. The efficiency and security of the Scheme is monited and protected by your own Bank or Building Society.

- If the amounts to be paid or the payment dates change CAMRA will notify you 10 working days in advance of your account being debited or as otherwise agreed.

- If an error is made by CAMRA or your Bank or Building Society, you are guaranteed a full and immediate refund from your branch of the amount paid.

- You can cancel a Direct Debit at any time by writing to your Bank or Building Society. Please also send a copy of your letter to us.

CAMRA BOOKS

The CAMRA Books range of guides helps you search out the best in beer (and cider) and brew it at home too!

Buying in the UK
All our books are available through bookshops in the UK. If you can't find a book, simply order it from your bookshop using the ISBN number, title and author details given below. CAMRA members should refer to their regular monthly newspaper *What's Brewing* for the latest details and member special offers.

CAMRA books are also available by mail-order (postage free) from: **CAMRA Books**, 230 Hatfield Road, St Albans, Herts, AL1 4LW. Cheques made payable to CAMRA Ltd. Telephone your credit card order on 01727 867201.

Buying outside the UK
CAMRA books are also sold in many outlets in the USA and other English-speaking countries. If you have trouble locating a particular book, use the details below to order by mail or fax (+44 1727 867670). Carriage of £3.00 per book (Europe) and £6.00 per book (US, Australia, New Zealand and other overseas) is charged.

UK Booksellers
Call CAMRA Books for distribution details and book list. CAMRA Books are listed on all major CD-ROM book lists and on our Internet site: http://www.camra.org.uk

Overseas Booksellers
Call or fax CAMRA Books for details of local distributors. Distributors are required for some English language territories. Rights enquiries (for non-English language editions) should be addressed to the managing editor.

CAMRA Guides
Painstakingly researched and checked, these guides are the leaders in their field, bringing you pubs which serve real ale and more...

Good Pub Food
by Susan Nowak

448 pages   Price: £9.99

The pubs in these pages serve food as original and exciting as anything available in far more expensive restaurants. And, as well as the exotic and unusual, you will find landlords and landladies serving simple, nourishing pub fare such as a genuine ploughman's lunch or a steak & kidney pudding.

You'll discover cooking from a new wave of young chefs who would prefer to run a pub than a restaurant. Many pubs are producing the traditional dishes of their regions, building smokeries, keeping cattle and goats, growing vegetables and herbs, creating vibrant, modern cuisine from fresh ingredients. Recipes from some of them are dotted about this guide so you can try them at home.

Award-winning food and beer writer Susan Nowak, who has travelled the country to complete this fourth edition of the guide, says that 'eating out' started in British inns and taverns and this guide is a contribution to an appreciation of all that is best in British food...and real cask conditioned ale.

Use the following code to order this book from your bookshop:
ISBN 1-85249-116-7

Room at the Inn
by Jill Adam

242 pages   Price: £8.99

From the first pub claiming to have sold Stilton cheese to travellers in 1720 to old smugglers haunts in Dorset, *Room at the Inn* gives details of pubs up and down the country offering generous hospitality. Travellers and tourists looking for a traditional British alternative to bland impersonal hotels need look no further than this guide.

The guide contains almost 350 inns – plus some hotels and motels – which provide overnight accommodation and a wholesome English breakfast. Some have been welcoming visitors for centuries. You'll also find a good pint of real ale on your arrival. To help you further there are maps, information on pub meals, family facilities, local tourist attractions and much more. *Room at the Inn* is a must for the glove compartment of the family car and vital reading for anyone planning a bed and breakfast break, sports tour or business trip.

Use the following code to order this book from your bookshop:
ISBN 1-85249-119-1

Real Cider Guide
by Ted Bruning

256 pages   Price: £7.99

Cider is making a major comeback and Real Cider is worth seeking out
wherever you are. This guide helps you find one of Britain's oldest,
tastiest and most fascinating drinks. Cider has been made in Britain
since before Roman times. But most cider you find in pubs today has
been pasteurised, with carbon dioxide added, bearing little resem-
blance to the full-flavoured taste of traditional Real Cider.
Reading this guide makes your mouth water as you leaf through details
of more than 2000 pubs selling the real stuff. There are also many
farmhouse producers from all over the country and outlets for Cider's
equally drinkable cousin, Perry – if you bring a container. Some will
even sell you a container! Author Ted Bruning is the editor of the
Cider Press, a quarterly supplement to *What's Brewing*, CAMRA's
national newspaper. He has collated information from all over the UK
to give you a taste of this fine traditional drink. So why not join him
and savour a wealth of different flavours?

Use the following code to order this book from your bookshop:
ISBN 1-85249-121-3

50 Great Pub Crawls
by Barrie Pepper

256 pages   Price: £9.99

Visit the beer trails of the UK, from town centre walks, to hikes and
bikes and a crawl on a train!
Barrie Pepper, with contributions and recommendations from CAMRA
branches, has compiled a 'must do' list of pub crawls, with easy to use
colour maps to guide you, notes on architecture, history and brewing
tradition to entertain you. All you have to do is to move your legs and
arms! A great way to discover the pubs of Britain. Use it well and we'll
make it the first of a series.

Use the following code to order this book from your bookshop:
ISBN 1-85249-142-6

Good Beer Guides

These are comprehensive guides researched by professional beer writers and CAMRA enthusiasts. Use these guides to find the best beer on your travels or to plan your itinerary for the finest drinking. Travel and accommodation information, plus maps, help you on your way and there's plenty to read about the history of brewing, the beer styles and the local cuisine to back up the entries for bars and beverages.

Good Beer Guide to Munich and Bavaria
by Graham Lees

206 pages   Price: £8.99

A fifth of the world's breweries – some 750 – are located in the region covered by this guide. The beers have rich, deep flavours and aromas and are generously hopped. You will find dark lagers, wheat beers, members of the ale family, wonderfully quenching and refreshing beers that have become cult drinks. The guide tells you where to find the best beers and the many splendid bars, beer halls and gardens, and the food to match. You'll also find all the background information for the world's most famous beer extravaganza, the Munich Oktoberfest. Author Graham Lees, a founder member of CAMRA, has lived and worked in Munich for several years and has endlessly toured Bavaria in search of the perfect pint.

Use the following code to order this book from your bookshop:
ISBN 1-85249-114-0

Good Beer Guide to Belgium, Holland and Luxembourg
by Tim Webb

286 pages   Price: £9.99

Discover the stunning range and variety of beers available in the Low Countries, our even nearer neighbours via Le Tunnel. There are such revered styles as Trappist Ales, fruit beers, wheat beers and the lambic and gueuze specialities made by the centuries-old method of spontaneous fermentation.
Channel-hopping Tim Webb's latest edition of the guide offers even

more bars in which an incredible array of beers can be enjoyed. If you are going on holiday to this region then you'll find details of travel, accommodation, food, beer museums, brewery visits and festivals, as well as guides to the cafés, beer shops and warehouses you can visit. There are maps, tasting notes, beer style guide and a beers index to complete the most comprehensive companion to drinking with your Belgian and Dutch hosts.

Use the following code to order this book from your bookshop:
ISBN 1-85249-139-6

Good Beer Guide to Northern France
by Arthur Taylor

256 pages   Price: £7.99

Discover the excitement of the bars and cafes, the tranquility of the village breweries which hold the secrets of generations of traditional brewing. Join the many festivals and cultural events such as the beer-refreshed second-hand market in Lille and the presentation of the Christmas ales. Find out where the best beer meets the best mussels and chips. Cuisine a la bière and more! Arthur Taylor is a leading authority on French beer and a member of Les Amis de la Bière, who have co-operated in the research for this book.

Use the following code to order this book from your bookshop:
ISBN 1-85249-140-X

Good Beer Guide
edited by Jon Preece

546 pages   Price: £10.99

Fancy a pint? Let CAMRA's *Good Beer Guide* lead the way. Revised each year to include around 5,000 great pubs serving excellent ale – country pubs, town pubs and pubs by the sea.
The guide includes information about meals, accommodation, family rooms, no-smoking areas and much more.
Fully and freshly researched by members of the Campaign for Real Ale, real enthusiasts who use the pubs week in, week out. No payment

is ever taken for inclusion. The guide has location maps for each county and you can read full details of all Britain's breweries (big and small) and the ales they produce, including tasting notes.
CAMRA's *Good Beer Guide* is still Britain's best value pub guide – a must for anyone who loves beer and pubs.

Known Gems & Hidden Treasures –
A Pocket Guide to the Pubs of London
by Peter Haydon

224 pages   Price: £7.99

If you live in or visit London, then you need this guide in your top pocket! It will take you to the well-known and historic pubs you must not miss, but also to the pubs which are tucked away and which locals keep to themselves.
The grass roots organisation of CAMRA and beer journalist Peter Haydon have brought London's pubs alive through their descriptions of ale, food, entertainment, history and architecture. These pubs have a story to tell.
The pubs in this pocket, portable, guide are listed by locality with a street address and London postal code districts heading pages so that you can easily match your location with the nearest pub. The guide covers pubs which are near tube and railway stations and gives relevant bus route numbers. It covers central London out to the commuter belts of Bushey and Surbiton.

Use the following code to order this book from your bookshop:
ISBN 1-85249-118-3

Cellarmanship
by Ivor Clissold

144 pages   Price: £6.99

This book explains every aspect of running a good cellar and serving a great pint of real ale which does both pub and brewer proud. It's a must have book for all professionals in the drinks trade, for all those studying at college to join it, and for all those who need to tap a cask of real ale for a party.

The CAMRA *Guide to Cellarmanship* is the only manual dealing with the care of all cask beers. It draws together information previously only known within certain breweries, and adds valuable experience from hundreds of cellar and technical staff.

Farmers, hop growers, maltsters, brewers and drayers all play their part to produce and deliver our great British drink but too often it falls at the last fence: indifferent cellar and bar management – especially in the face of an unknown guest beer – can turn a treat into a tragedy.

Use the following code to order this book from your bookshop:
ISBN 1-85249-126-4

Brew Your Own

Learn the basics of brewing real ales at home from the experts. And then move on to more ambitious recipes which imitate well-loved ales from the UK and Europe.

Brew your own Real Ale at Home
by Graham Wheeler and Roger Protz

194 pages   Price: £8.99

This book is a treasure chest for all real ale fans and home brew enthusiasts. It contains recipes which allow you to replicate some famous cask-conditioned beers at home or to customise brews to your own particular taste. The authors have examined the ingredients and brewing styles of well-known ales and have gleaned important information from brewers, with and without their co-operation. Computer-aided guesswork and an expert palate have filled in the gaps where the brewers would reveal no more.

As well as the recipes, the brewing process is explained along with the equipment required, all of which allows you to brew beer using wholly natural ingredients. Detailed recipes and instructions are given along with tasting notes for each ale. Conversion details are given so that the measurements can be used world-wide.

Use the following code to order this book from your bookshop:
ISBN 1-85249-138-8

Brew Classic European Beers at Home
by Graham Wheeler and Roger Protz

196 pages   Price: £8.99

Keen home brewers can now recreate some of the world's classic beers.
In your own home you can brew superb pale ales, milds, porters,
stouts, Pilsners, Alt, Kolsch, Trappist, wheat beers, sour beers, even
the astonishing fruit lambics of Belgium... and many more.
Graham Wheeler and his computer have teamed up with Roger Protz
and his unrivalled knowledge of brewing and beer styles. Use the
detailed recipes and information about ingredients to imitate the
cream of international beers. Discover the role played by ingredients,
yeasts and brewing equipment and procedure in these well-known
drinks. Measurements are given in UK, US and European units,
emphasising the truly international scope of the beer styles within.

Use the following code to order this book from your bookshop:
ISBN 1-85249-117-5

Home Brewing
by Graham Wheeler

240pages   Price: £8.99

Recently redesigned to make it even easier to use, this is the classic
first book for all home-brewers. While being truly comprehensive,
Home Brewing also manages to be a practical guide which can be followed step by step as you try your first brews. Plenty of recipes for
beginners and hints and tips from the world's most revered home
brewer.

Use the following code to order this book from your bookshop:
ISBN 1-85249-137-X